The Crisis of Liberal Democracy and the Path Ahead

Radical Subjects in International Politics

Series Editor: Ruth Kinna

This series uses the idea of political subjection to promote the discussion and analysis of individual, communal and civic participation and activism. 'Radical subjects' refers both to the character of the topics and issues tackled in the series and to the ethic guiding the research. The series has a radical focus in that it provides a springboard for the discussion of activism that sits outside or on the fringes of institutional politics, yet which, insofar as it reflects a commitment to social change, is far from marginal. It provides a platform for scholarship that interrogates modern political movements, probes the local, regional and global dimensions of activist networking and the principles that drive them, and develops innovative frames to analyze issues of exclusion and empowerment. The scope of the series is defined by engagement with the concept of the radical in contemporary politics but includes research that is multi- or interdisciplinary, working at the boundaries of art and politics, political utopianism, feminism, sociology and radical geography.

Titles in Series:

The Crisis of Liberal Democracy and the Path Ahead

Alternatives to Political Representation and Capitalism

Bernd Reiter

ROWMAN & LITTLEFIELD
INTERNATIONAL
London • New York

Published by Rowman & Littlefield International Ltd.
6 Tinworth Street, London, SE11 5AL, UK
www.rowmaninternational.com

Rowman & Littlefield International Ltd. is an affiliate of Rowman & Littlefield
4501 Forbes Boulevard, Suite 200, Lanham, Maryland 20706, USA
With additional offices in Boulder, New York, Toronto (Canada), and Plymouth (UK)
www.rowman.com

British Library Cataloguing in Publication Data
A catalogue record for this book is available from the British Library

ISBN: HB 978-1-78660-364-7
         PB 978-1-78660-365-4

Library of Congress Cataloging-in-Publication Data Available

Names: Reiter, Bernd, 1968– author.
Title: The crisis of liberal democracy and the path ahead / Bernd Reiter.
Description: London ; New York : Rowman & Littlefield International, 2017. |
Series: Radical subjects in international politics | Includes bibliographical references and
    index.
Identifiers: LCCN 2017008705 (print) | LCCN 2017032204 (ebook) | ISBN
    9781786603661 (electronic) | ISBN 9781786603647 (cloth : alk. paper) | ISBN
    9781786603654 (pbk : alk. paper)
Subjects: LCSH: Direct democracy. | Democracy—Economic aspects. | Capitalism—
    Political aspects. | Social control—Political aspects. | Elite (Social sciences)—Political
    activity.
Classification: LCC JC423 (ebook) | LCC JC423 .R345 2017 (print) | DDC
    321/.07—dc23
LC record available at https://lccn.loc.gov/2017008705

♾™ The paper used in this publication meets the minimum requirements of American
National Standard for Information Sciences—Permanence of Paper for Printed Library
Materials, ANSI/NISO Z39.48-1992.

Printed in the United States of America

Contents

Acknowledgments

Quite a few people were instrumental in moving this book forward, and I am deeply indebted to them. Any intellectual production is a joint effort, and this book is not different. While I would have not been able to achieve what I have without my friends, students, and colleagues; the shortcomings and mistakes are certainly all mine.

Mark Amen read the earliest draft and provided helpful feedback. Thanks Mark! My graduate students not only inspired this work with their commentary, but some of them also read through earlier drafts and provided feedback. I want to particularly recognize and thank Felix Scholz and Cave McCoy for their efforts.

Charles Ragin encouraged and assisted me with the method I applied, which is *his* method. Thanks Charles! Eva Thomann took the time to not only read, but also work through my methods section, suggesting important adjustments and improvements. Thank you Eva! I would have not been able to conduct the systematic qualitative case comparison without the help and input of Deborah Cragun and Ali Bustamante. Thank you so much Deborah and Ali!

Robert Frank, Jacob Hacker, and Anthony Atkinson read through different versions and drafts of the manuscript, offering their insight and experience. Thank you!

I was able to conduct research for this book while on sabbatical from my home institution, the University of South Florida. I want to thank my chair, Steven Tauber, and the university for supporting my research efforts.

In May 2013, I was invited to join the Barcelona-based Institute for International Studies (IBEI) as their Erasmus Mundos Visiting Professor. Thanks to the generosity of Jacint Jordana, IBEI director, as well as the support from my colleagues and friends Matthias vom Hau and Fulya Apaydin, I was able to use my two months in Barcelona to conduct literature research on Spanish Anarchism. Thank you Jacint, Matthias, and Fulya!

From July to December 2013, I conducted literature research on German anarchism. Thanks to a very generous invitation by the University of Kassel, Germany, issued by Hans-Jürgen Burchardt, I was able to spend those months at the university and dedicate some time to the reading of material on the German Räte Republics. Thank you Hans-Jürgen and Stefan!

I spent the last portion of my 2013–2014 sabbatical in Colombia after accepting a visiting professorship at the Universidad del Norte in Barranquilla. Being in Barranquilla for six months allowed me to conduct research among indigenous and black communities of the Colombian Caribbean region. My work on the Wintukua and on Palenque de San Basílio comes closest to the traditional definition of ethnographic field work—even if in a much restricted form. Being in Colombia and having enough free time to conduct research was made possible by Roberto Arana Gonzalez, a historian at UniNorte and the director of their Institute on Latin America and the Caribbean. Thank you Roberto!

Finally, this book would not have become a reality without the support of Ruth Kinna, series editor of Rowman & Littlefield International's Radical Subjects in International Politics series. Thank you Ruth!

This book is for the women in my life: Mali, Miranda, and Karin. I am nothing without them.

Introduction

There are two universal crises today and the two are related. One is the crisis of liberal democracy, which at its core is a crisis of political representation and of politics. Most elected representatives do not really represent us and politics has deteriorated into a spectacle the average citizen merely watches, but no longer controls. The other crisis is economic. There is no end to competition. Taken together, decreasing market returns, resource limits imposed by the global ecosystem, and the nature of relational markets impose a behavioral structure in which average people have to compete harder and harder just to keep up. Under the current capitalist model, the only possible end to this scenario is a less and less attractive world and life for more and more people. While each of these problems is serious in itself, their interaction makes them even more pernicious, as political equality is threatened by extreme economic inequality and political inequality is instrumentalized to advance economic privilege (Frank 2011).

The current state of affairs is made worse by a lack of viable alternatives and coherent visions or utopias—particularly on the left (Albo, Gindin, and Panitch 2010). We are in a poor state of affairs indeed if socialism and communism are the only utopias we can envision. While the left seems not to have a shared vision of a viable and desirable utopia, the vision of the right, while coherent, is even less viable and attractive. Ayn Rand and her followers have a concrete proposal for improving the ethics of our times: less government, free markets, and more competition. Their message is easily understood and, thanks to massive support from the likes of the Koch Brothers, Fox News, Donald Trump, Ron Paul, Ted Cruz, and so many more, it is also broadly disseminated. It has received scientific endorsements by such known scholars as Robert Nozick, Milton Friedman, and Friedrich Hayek. After all, "free markets" sounds very similar to "freedom" in general—even if it is not. While the right's vision is coherent, it is also callous to fellow citizens because its only answer to increased inequality seems to be "it is your own fault." It is also callous to the world because it does not have an answer to the fragility of our shared ecosystem. The right's vision is also poor, as betting on selfish profit motives and hoping for the best is not a vision at all. It is based on poor science and it is morally unacceptable. "More" cannot be our only utopia. Not given the limited resources of this planet (Klein 2014).

The current crisis of democracy and of markets is thus accompanied by a crisis of ideas, which finds expression in a lack of attractive alternatives and viable utopias able to guide our thoughts and actions. To achieve any goal, we first need to know where we are heading (Santos 2014). This also implies a rethinking of what it means to be radical today, as the dogmatic left has captivated this label so that anything not falling within a Marxist framework is deemed bourgeois, liberal, and not truly radical. It is high time to think outside the available socialist-capitalist boxes.

This book shows that it is simply not true that there are no alternatives and that the only alternatives to parliamentarism and capitalism are anarchy and communism. These are lies told by all those who have much to gain from the way the current system works—because it works for them. Our world now has twelve million millionaires, and those twelve million control not just the economies of their countries; they also control politics in most of them and shape the messages that are disseminated to all of us. They rule for us and ultimately they rule us—and they make us believe that there are no alternatives. But they lie. To the over seven billion people living on this planet, these twelve million have been bad and selfish rulers. They have been anything but the enlightened philosopher kings Plato dreamed about. Instead of looking for new rulers, this book argues that with the expansion of education and the communicative capabilities of the twenty-first century, we can all become philosopher queens and rule ourselves. The more we do so, the more we can also rein in our markets and protect them against the abuse by the few.

To prove this point, I present twenty-two empirical cases, historical and contemporary, of societies and groups who have either ruled themselves without relying on political representatives or who have established equitable markets and avoided the formation of great inequalities—or both. I then compare twenty-one cases systematically in order to detect common elements. In doing so, this book seeks to unveil the common and necessary factors that make direct democracy and equitable market organization possible. My main argument and message is: Direct democracy is possible, representative democracy is not the only way to organize even large collectives, and markets can be fair and remain fair over generations if properly institutionalized and regulated.

The evidence collected and analyzed for this book leaves no doubt that there are concrete and viable alternatives to representative democracy and to capitalism—and hence to liberal democracy. This book is written with the explicit intent to showcase these alternatives and to highlight the possible solutions to the problems of elite domination they contain. It is my explicit intent to present a new utopia and a viable alternative to the current scenario of crises—the crisis of political representation and the crisis of capitalism. We *can* create and maintain political and economic systems that allow for more justice, more equality, and more sustainability.

This is, however, not a policy book. Before we can devise policies, we need to find a common goal worth pursuing, which is the contribution this book makes. This is also not a book on how to put new systems in place. It will take political will and social pressure to change the political and economic institutions that currently regulate formal democracies. It will take a strong, pervasive, and consistent global movement.

Some analysts, myself included, believe that such a movement is already under way (Melman 2001; Wolff 2012). Solidarity economies are spreading. A German author presents one hundred empirical examples of alternative ways to organize different parts of our daily lives—from eating to dressing, the way services are provided, living, finance, education, health, communication, mobility, to having "fun" (Habermann 2009). In Austria, a group formed around the idea of an economy for the common good has, as of November 2016, over 7,700 supporters among municipalities, associations, persons, politicians, and companies. (see http://economia-del-bien-comun.org for updated numbers). Gibson-Graham's network of community economics lists thirty-four active academic members, plus an extended research network of several hundred scholars (see http://www.communityeconomies.org/people for updates). In southeastern Turkey and northern Iraq, among the Kurdish minority, a council movement has emerged, practicing self-rule, local autonomy, gender liberation, and agro-ecology (TATORT 2013). In Quebec, Canada, social economy initiatives are sprouting because they receive active governmental support (Bouchard 2013). Fair trade is expanding and has become one of the fastest-growing economic sectors in Europe and the United States, while in the United Kingdom, the Transition Town Movement has not only conquered England, but has spread across the globe, with its message to create more livable and less polluted communities (http://www. transitionnetwork.org/).

Parts of the message this global movement spreads resonate strongly with another worldwide movement—one that found a voice in Tunisia in 2011 and from there traveled all over the Middle East and the world: the movement against corrupt governments that do not represent us (Sitrin and Azzelini 2014). Part of this movement involved uprisings and protests—against

Wall Street, against a Brazilian government more worried about soccer than the well-being of its millions of poor people, against elitist universities in Chile—and in general against "the establishment." In Italy, the Five Star Movement came in second place in the general elections of 2013 with its platform of direct democracy, e-democracy, nonviolence, and de-growth. In Spain, Podemos (Yes, We Can) came in third place in the Spanish general elections of 2015. Similar to Five Star, Podemos has included many policies that aim at reining in the power and influence of multinational corporations and the central state.

The other part of this movement unfortunately found its voice in the support of right-wing and anti-immigrant political parties and movements, all of which are taking advantage of the very pervasive discontent with traditional party politics and traditional politicians by offering yet another nontraditional candidate in hopes to finally side pass the "establishment."

In the United States, this has led to growing support for libertarians who tend to highlight their "against the government" ideology, while downplaying or hiding their oftentimes nasty anti-poor, anti-black, anti-foreigner, and pro-rich policies. The presidency of Donald Trump can only be explained, I think, with this sort of growing discontent with politics as usual and the absence of viable alternatives. In continental Europe, this anti-politics tendency has strengthened the anti-immigrant parties and legitimized the platforms of the Le Pens, Pegida, the Orbans, the Hofers, and their ideological brothers and sisters elsewhere.

For Sandro Mezzadra, "the problem of transition reemerges in each historical moment when the conditions of translation have to be established anew" (Mezzadra 2007, 4). The "conditions of translation" have indeed been lost to many, in many different countries, as nations seem to become more divided and the different camps are increasingly unable to understand the premises and convictions informing the political and cultural choices of other camps.

What unites these phenomena, it appears, is a widely shared and growing skepticism against the way government is practiced today. In the absence of viable alternatives, this discontent finds an outlet in *new* political parties and movements. On the right, they take advantage of this widespread disenchantment and sell it, laced with racism, xenophobia, and pro-business policies. In the absence of concrete and viable alternatives, the left has succumbed to an "against" movement that does not have a concrete, let alone shared, vision for how politics and economics *should* work. Given the hegemonic discourse about what "politics" means and can mean, the only option available is to create another political party. Once social movements become political parties, however, their ability to effectively change politics is lost. They either play along or remain ineffective, as the history of the Green Party in such countries as Germany has long demonstrated.

Without an alternative vision, it is not surprising that there is no left agenda or roadmap of concrete steps that can and must be taken. The left, in short, is in a deep ideological crisis. It is a crisis of ideas and utopias, as well as a crisis of concrete policies connected to a comprehensive vision of a better future. It is a very deep crisis indeed, as there are currently no serious treatments of alternatives to capitalism and representative democracy. Anything outside of this paradigm is presented as lacking seriousness, of being impractical, utopian, or overly radical.

On an even deeper level, the current crisis is rooted in a crisis of the way we organize. The political and economic crises are both "crises of organization," as almost all organizations we currently have, including the biggest and most powerful of all organizations, the state, are organized hierarchically and around the idea of leaders, elites, and rulers. Most societies have erected systems in which the most callous, least scrupulous, and most power-hungry individuals rise to the top of social, political, and economic hierarchies. Once there, most of them find ways to defend their undeserved privileges and entrench their elitism. We need to rethink the way we organize our collective lives—at home and at work, but also in and around our political systems and the state (Laloux 2014).

A NOTE ON METHOD

Theory, the way I understand it, cannot solve social or political problems. Theory is a heuristic tool to order the world and make sense of it by reducing its complexity and by naming and categorizing it. Proposing different causal explanations and models allows us to look at reality a certain way. Nothing guarantees that the world actually conforms to our theories about it. As a result, I do not seek to solve the problems of entrenched political and economic elitism theoretically. Instead, I have spent the past years looking for empirical examples (cases) from which to learn. Each case I found (I have found twenty-two so far) offers a partial solution to the problem of elitism and we can learn from each one. The kinds of solutions I am interested in are institutional solutions; that is, solutions that have become consolidated, repeated, legitimized, produced associated roles for different individuals and groups and predictable behavior that, in a broader sense, contributes to the structuring of a society or group. This interest in institutions is grounded in my conviction that the world is socially constructed and that it is potentially open—even if most institutions, once in place, appear fixed and "natural" to us, even reflecting back at us so that we use them to make sense of our own biographies (Berger and Luckmann 1966).

This book is thus motivated by a search for viable, practiced, and practicable political institutions able to regulate social, political, and economic life better than those we currently have in the Western, "modern" world. Particularly, I set out to find political institutions that have achieved, at one point or another and in one place or another, political and/or economic equity. I found many, and I will describe and list them in what is to come. Knowing these institutions alone, I think, provides a powerful argument against all those who argue that "there are no alternatives" or that we have reached the "end of history." Each single institution described contradicts this claim. Taken together, they provide a formidable political toolbox to address the problem of political and economic elitism and protect fairness and equal opportunity on different markets.

Once listed, the question becomes: How can we compare such a large number of rich cases systematically so that we can learn from all of them, taken together? Traditional analytical tools are of no help here. Fortunately, a relatively new tool, introduced to an English-speaking audience first by the American sociologist Charles Ragin (1987), called Qualitative Comparative Analysis (QCA), promises a solution. Relying on set theory, QCA seeks to identify the common factors or conditions present in all cases examined—and their interaction—in producing an outcome. The assumption is that if some factors are present across all cases with the same outcome, they must be, to some degree, necessary or even sufficient to explain this outcome. Procedurally, this method proceeds by constructing "truth tables" in which values are given to the specific factors present in different cases with the same outcome. Membership in a set at this stage of this still-evolving approach is defined by degrees, ranging from 0 to 1, with different decimal values in between, where 0 stands for "fully out" of a set (that is, a nonmember) and 1 stands for "fully in" (that is, a full member). The 0.5 value represents the "crossover point." What is above the crossover point is more in than out of a set. What is below the crossover point is more out than in. The in between values thus stand for "more in than out," "mostly in," "almost entirely out," etc. Ragin and the growing group of researchers applying this approach have termed partial membership Fuzzy Sets, so that the methods is now called Fuzzy Set Qualitative Comparative Analysis (fsQCA). QCA then relies on the rules of Boolean Algebra for the analysis of causal conditions occurring across different cases.

Ragin has developed a (free) software package so that anyone can now run fsQCA. For the purpose of this book, fsQCA offers a promising, systematic, and rigorous method to compare a larger number of cases and to assess which factors contained in them are of causal relevance for producing and protecting equity in politics and in markets.

THE PLAN OF THIS BOOK

In chapter 1, I will elaborate the conceptual foundations on which the ensuing analysis rests. After highlighting the importance of utopian thinking in the social sciences, I explain and define the way I treat culture, institutions, politics, power, and the state.

Chapters 2 and 3 lay out the theoretical foundations for the analysis to follow. Chapter 2 focuses on democracy and chapter 3 on markets. Without theory, we cannot perceive the world. Theories or theoretical models give us guidance. They inform us what to look for and how to order information in such a way that patterns and meaning emerge. Without theoretical explanations, the world does not make sense to us. Without an *explicit* theoretical framework, we run the risk of adopting theory without knowing it and explaining the world in the terms of someone else's theoretical outlook. To avoid this, I will first spell out the theoretical framework that makes this investigation possible in part I of this book. Part II then presents the empirical findings I have collected over the past years. Part III finally seeks to bring all the empirical cases together for a systematic, qualitative case comparison.

The methodology I have used to analyze my cases is first descriptive. I provide a very short overview of those aspects of a given society or community that are relevant to the purpose of this book. I focus primarily on innovative institutions, regulations, laws, customs, and constitutions. I purposefully brush over the negative aspects or even the (yet) unfulfilled aspects of reality, as I am not concerned with those. This books intends to highlight possibilities and point toward new directions, and I am fully aware that most cases have not achieved the "perfect" state of affairs—or not even the state of affairs written down in their laws, regulations, and constitutions. Any description is theory driven, and in my case, this means that I focus on those aspects of reality, or even of an idealized reality, I find promising and relevant.

The second part of this book thus consists of a description of twenty-two empirical cases that are relevant to the purpose of this book, namely, finding alternatives to liberal democracy. The cases range from ancient Athens to contemporary Zomia in East Asia. In the third part, I compare my cases systematically, using fsQCA with the specific purpose of identifying common and hence necessary factors related to a given outcome across different cases; here direct democracy and equitable markets. The book ends with a summary of my main findings, some conclusions, and some policy recommendations for a better, more sustainable, and more democratic future.

Chapter 1

Preparing the Ground

As anybody working the land knows, before one can plant, one must prepare the ground so that whatever is planted can grow. This chapter prepares the ground into which I will then plant. In it I lay out some of the assumptions I make or take for granted in this exercise. I also define some of the concepts I apply later in hopes to achieve clarity and precision and avoid misinterpretation.

WE NEED NEW UTOPIAS

Given the lack of coherent and encompassing alternative political and economic models at the current time, most public discontent finds an outlet in a frantic search for new leaders, new political parties, and ever newer social and political movements. The political right takes advantage of the widespread disenchantment and sells it, laced with racism, xenophobia, and pro-business policies, in the form of anti-candidates and anti-parties who mostly blame the victims: the poor, minorities, and immigrants. The political left has succumbed to an "against" movement that does not have a concrete, let alone shared, vision for how politics and economics should work. Without a coherent vision, not only are our possible actions deterred, but our analysis of reality also suffers, as we first need "the right" framework so we can ask "the right" questions. Without it, we keep on asking the wrong questions about who the better leader should be or which political party will offer a better solution to our common problems. While relevant, these are the wrong questions when seeking to analyze and understand our current situation. We do not need new or different leaders; we need less of them. Not asking important questions is also the outcome of massive media manipulation and a process of normalization that has elevated representative democracy and capitalism to a status of inevitability.

Scholars have long stood on the sidelines of this dilemma, more concerned with their own advancement and "tenure" than with the social and political problems we all face. As a result, the vanguard for both protest and innovative proposals for change comes from the streets. Christian Felcher, the founder of the Economy of the Common Good, holds no PhD (yet, he is still young and was already invited to teach at some prestigious universities). Rob Hopkins, founder of the Transition Movement, has a similar profile. Innovation these days comes from the Lacandon Mayans before it comes from professors. Today, the Zapatistas have smarter and more inspiring things to say about the economy than Paul Krugman, who holds a Nobel Prize in Economics and charges several thousand dollars for every sentence he says in public.

We need new paradigms, new models, and new utopias—and scholars who systematically elaborate the viability of alternative ways to organize politics and the economy. It is an urgent task that requires some courage as the "discipline" more often than not punishes innovation before it rewards it (Kuhn 1962). Courage, however, is traded shortly among scholars these days, which is why the most promising proposals to reform our societies come not from scholars, but from activists and artists. The Zapatistas of southern Mexico demonstrate, through their praxis, that organizing our societies differently is possible. There *are* alternatives. They are practiced right now. They include alternative ways to organize politics, markets, lawmaking, education, agriculture, and others. While these are practicable and practiced solutions, they also point toward a broader horizon of possibilities. They seem to indicate that much more is in our reach.

Utopian thinking, as Ruth Levitas suggests, "provides a critical tool for exposing the limitations of current policy discourses about economic growth and ecological sustainability. It facilitates genuinely holistic thinking about possible futures, combined with reflexivity, provisionality and democratic engagement with the principles and practices of those futures" (Levitas 2013, xi).

Boaventura de Sousa Santos (2014) refers to this necessity of thinking about concrete possibilities as a "sociology of emergences." He argues, "the sociology of emergences aims to identify and enlarge the signs of possible future experiences, under the guise of tendencies and latencies, that are actively ignored by hegemonic rationality and knowledge" (Santos 2014, 241).

Another author writing in this strain, Ana Cecilia Dinerstein, refers to the whole project of constructing alternative futures as "the Art of Organizing Hope" (Dinerstein 2014, 1). She bases her inquiry into the politics of autonomy in Latin America (the title of her book) on the idea of "prefiguring," which for her "*is* the movements' strategy in Latin America" (17).

Prefiguration refers to probing into possible futures and (yet) unfulfilled possibilities.

Similarly, for J. K. Gibson-Graham, the proper task of social science inquiry is to fill the absences left by "realist" social science with political possibilities (Gibson-Graham 2006, xxxiii).

These authors and I all agree with pioneer H. G. Wells (1906), who argued, "The creation of Utopias—and their exhaustive criticism—is the proper and distinctive method of sociology" (quoted in Levitas 2013, 1).

This book seeks to contribute to the collective effort of finding and assessing the viability of alternative ways to organize ourselves politically and economically. It offers a systematic assessment of selected cases in which such alternatives have been practiced and are currently being practiced in order to identify common elements—necessary and sufficient factors. By doing so, I hope to bring "academia back in"—where "in" is the current worldwide search for alternatives to capitalist market organization and representative democracy. Against the "nasty" positions outlined earlier, I want to present alternatives that are more democratic and fairer for more people. In addition to the gutsy protests from such movements as Occupy Wall Street and the marchers in Brazil, I seek to provide what academia can: systematic assessment.

Inspiration for this task still comes from Ernst Bloch, who wrote:

> Only thinking directed towards changing the world and informing the desire to change it does not confront the future (the unclosed space for new development in front of us) as embarrassment and the past as spell. Hence the crucial point is: only knowledge as conscious theory-practice confronts Becoming and what can be within it. (Bloch 1986, 8)

Utopias, as I understand them, can give us guidance and broaden the horizon of possibilities. The path toward achieving new possibilities must be one of looking for better institutions and better laws, as ultimately, innovation designed and promoted by social movements must consolidate into institutions, laws, and constitutions. New laws and constitutions, to be sure, cannot guarantee new practices and simply enacting new laws is not enough to bring about a new reality. Laws should grow out of praxis and not the other way around. Before the law thus comes culture.

CULTURE

"Culture is a symbolic system which transforms the physical reality, what is *there*, into experienced reality" (Lee 1987, 1). Dorothy Lee thus explains culture. What follows from this understanding of culture, for her as well as for me, is manifold. For her, "the universe as I know it or imagine it in the Western world is different from the universe of the Tikopia, in Polynesia. It follows, also, that I feel different about what I see" (Lee 1987, 1). Culture provides a lens or a way to see and understand the world and to make sense of it. These ways will be different and the worlds we live in will be different accordingly. What to one person is an act of valor, to the other is an act of cowardice, callousness, disrespect, or egotism. We can only attempt to understand others if we attempt to understand their culture and then seek ways to perceive, describe, and explain the world as they do, that is, applying their concepts, not ours. Too much of the nonwhite and non-European world has been described applying European ontological, epistemological, and analytical frameworks. To better understand the world and the diverse groups of people in it, we need to rid ourselves of this legacy and decolonize the social sciences.

Dorothy Lee (1987) offers another valuable insight about the working of culture and its relation to institutional structures. She explains: "Yet actually it is in connection with the highest personal autonomy that we often find the most intricately developed structure; and it is this structure that makes autonomy possible in a group situation" (Lee 1987, 9). It is precisely through this understanding of culture and the structure it provides for community life that the often accused contradiction between individual autonomy and collectivity can be resolved. When cultural structure provides guidance and limitations for individual and group behavior, it also affords freedom to the individual and group. Lee introduces the Navaho Indians of Arizona and New Mexico to illustrate this point. She writes: "In these accounts, we find a tightly knit group, depending on mutual responsibility among all its members, a precisely structured universe, and a great respect for individual autonomy and integrity. We find people who maintain an inviolable privacy while living as a family in a one-room house, sharing work and responsibility to such extent that even a child of six will contribute his share of mutton to the family meal" (Lee 1987, 10).

The same sense of great respect for individual autonomy and community can be found among the Hopi, the Trobrianders, the Lovedu, the Wintu, and many other groups living outside of the Western world and its focus on possessive and competitive individualism. In all of these societies, the typically Western contradiction between individual freedom and equality is resolved through a strong community and a very active participation in it, in which every member, including children, carries responsibilities toward the collective. As Lee explains, this is possible by putting great emphasis and importance to individual autonomy. In the societies she studies, Lee finds true respect for difference and mutual support in the collective effort to live within the structures culture establishes. None of the societies Lee describes rely on institutionalized hierarchies and rule. Whereas in Western societies a dualism between individual freedom and equality exists in which individual freedom has to be restricted to safeguard equal opportunity, Lee finds that "there are societies, however, where dualism is complementary, so that the terms of the duality are not opposed nor measured against each other, nor seem as discrete units" (Lee 1987, 48). Put simply, assuming and accepting that individual freedom and collectivity are opposed to each other is wrong. Collectivism and community can further and support individual agency if it is reliant on a deeply shared culture that provides the rules, restrictions, and guidelines for all. In such a situation, "the authority of the headman or the chief or the leader is in many ways like the authority of the dictionary, or of Einstein. There is no hint of coercion or command here; the people go to the leader with faith, as we go to the reference book, and the leader answers according to his greater knowledge, or clarifies an obscure point, or amplifies according to his greater experience and wisdom" (Lee 1987, 9).

Culture thus provides a framework in which obedience is not driven by individual authority or the authority of a specific group, political party, or the state. Instead it is a broadly shared framework under which all support each other in their effort to act in conformity with its structure and the guidelines and taboos derived from it. As the research of cultural anthropologists shows, there are many societies in which this has been achieved together with safe-guarding individual autonomy and freedom. In fact, as Lee argues, "The concept of equality is irrelevant to this view of man. Here we have instead the full valuing of man in his uniqueness, enabling him to actualize himself, to use opportunity to the fullest, undeterred by the standards of an outside author-ity, not forced to deviate, to meet the expectations of others" (Lee 1987, 46).

Individual autonomy and freedom are thus combinable with equality and equal opportunity if and when strong community ties bring people and fami-lies together in common pursuit, guided by a shared framework or values and guidelines, that is, a shared culture. If that is the case, then, according to Lee,

Here and among the Trobrianders, equality itself is present, I think; that is, we find the fact of equality, as a dimension in relationships, as an aspect of the opportunity to be, to function. But its existence is derivative; it is not a goal, but is incidental to some other basic concept. It derives from the recognition of the right to be different, noncommensurate, unique; from the valuing of sheer being. When it is being itself which is valued, then none can be inferior or superior; would it be nonsense to say this is because all being equally *is*? If absolute fullness of opportunity is afforded, if the culture facilitates and imple-ments freedom, thus making it possible for the individual to avail himself of his opportunity, then equality of opportunity may be said to be present, since all have fullness of opportunity. (Lee 1987, 44)

This is not to say that such a cultural framework exists among all non-Western societies or in all pre-capitalist societies. There are many empirical examples in which the cultural frameworks of non-Western societies produced competition, undermining individual autonomy and with it equality. Careful empirical research has to be conducted in order to determine what the common factors are that allow for the achievement of the double goal of individual freedom and autonomy *and* equality. The empirical examples discussed by Dorothy Lee leave no doubt that achieving both at the same time is a real possibility. The question I seek to address is what the conditions, institutions, and rules are that allow for the achievement of these double goals.

From Lee's account, it becomes clear that community and culture are at the heart of this possibility. It is also clear that when such a cultural framework falls apart, as it has in advanced capitalist societies, the authority of guides who give example and advice gives way to rule. This can be individualistic rule, the rule of the state, the police, of thugs, of religious leaders, or others able to command obedience.

If we accept that some of us live in "post-traditional" societies, in which cultural norms are being challenged, then the question some have asked is: What can replace traditional culture? This is, however, a false problem, as any society and any group relies on some sort of culture to function. It is also not culture per se that allows for the achievement of individual autonomy and equality. It is a specific kind of culture and specific norms, values, and institutions that are able to produce this "win-win" situation, or a "positive-sum" game in the language of games. Many traditional and non-Western societies were and are totalitarian and despotic, as I have mentioned earlier. There is nothing intrinsic about the non-Western world, just as there is nothing about the Western world, that makes it naturally or automatically superior or inferior. It is a matter of identifying those elements that have produced this win-win situation in the past and the present, isolating them through analytical procedure, and detecting possible ways to combine them. Some of the institution so discovered might not be transferable as they rely on a broader cultural context. Culture, however, changes constantly and there is no fixed, predetermined way in which specific groups of humans must organize. At the least, we can all learn from the different solutions found and developed in different places to the universal problem of protecting freedom and equality. Once we know those, we can then proceed with a discussion of where and under what circumstances specific institutional designs fit best, given the particularities of a given community.

INSTITUTIONS AND THE POLITICAL

From the outset, I assume that the economy, as a subsystem of human life, must be subordinated to human needs, which means that it must be politically controlled and hence democratized (Dowbor 2012). Politics, in my vision, thus necessarily trumps economics in that politics must be the realm in which different market interchanges are regulated and controlled. This control must happen through laws and institutions. Ideally, a democratic society collectively decides what kind of economy it would like to have. It does so by collective deliberation and decision making. The outcome of such a collective deliberation and decision-making process becomes a custom protected by law. It becomes institutionalized. Smart institutions are those able to achieve several goals at once, as I have previously argued. Ideally, the laws and institutions regulating land ownership avoid the concentration of property in a few hands, while also ensuring equal opportunity and sustainability.

The basic requirement for this to occur is that a society discusses economic institutions, or better political institutions regulating the economy. In most contemporary capitalist societies, this discussion does not occur. Instead, the economy has taken on a dynamic of its own and, through powerful political alliances, ends up influencing politics. Politics follows the economy, where the most powerful economic actors end up having the power to mold politics to their needs and wants. The first step in any process of democratization toward self-rule thus must consist of asserting the power of primacy over the economy.

This in turn requires that our political life must first be democratically organized in a substantive, not just formal, way, as what is at stake is not merely quantity, but a qualitatively different way of organizing communities and reembedding politics and markets into democratically organized communities. This necessarily also requires a rethinking of political community—its constitution and functioning.

Thus, advancing toward viable alternatives to capitalist market organization requires a rethinking of political community and its connection to political powers and decision making, which automatically requires a rethinking of political representation. Rethinking politics in this way, however, requires a "thinking outside of the box," in which "the box" is increasingly academic discipline. In this, I follow the classic work of Daly and Cobb, who argue, "The change will imply correction and expansion, a more empirical and historical attitude, less pretension to be a 'science,' and the will to subordinate the market to purposes it is not equipped to set forth" (Daly and Cobb 1989, 8). This is precisely what I will try here. In the words of the pioneer Hazel Henderson:

Understanding the real world in which we live requires us to recognize patterns and to abstract reality into mental models. The map is not the territory, as we have been reminded by many epistemologists. The danger is that we routinize our perception through these models, forgetting the need for constant updating and course-correcting as conditions change around us. Thus our mental models are memes that crystallize into habits, dogmas and outdated theories such as those in conventional economics and finance. (Henderson 2011, 61)

We need to rethink our established dogmas and convictions and search for viable alternatives to capitalism and representative democracy so that we can demonstrate that capitalism and representative democracy are not the only options for organizing human interaction. I depart from the conviction that there *are* viable alternatives to both. If successful, this search for viable alternatives or "real utopias" promises to offer solutions to reinvigorate public life, democracy, and the freedom and fairness of markets.

Some institutions, laws, and rules do not grow out of broad public practice. They are instead imposed from above. While it is rare and unlikely that democratic institutions and laws are created from above by elite decree, it is nevertheless possible, as the case of Bhutan, discussed shortly, will show. In Bhutan, a king ended his own absolute grip on power and instituted a constitutional monarchy and a constitution that is very progressive in many aspects. This book, however, is not primarily concerned with the social dynamics bringing about social, political, and economic change. Instead, it focuses on possibilities, visions, and possible utopias able to provide a direction and guidance to all those wanting and working for more democratic democracies and fairer and more sustainable markets. My focus thus stays with institutions, rules, and laws and not with the question of how to enact or enforce them. However, the relationship between institutions, power, and social change is not that straightforward, as institutions, once in place, will impact behavior and, if successful, will spread.

Ideally, then, recurrent behavior creates institutions, but institutions also reflect back and influence behavior. Most institutions can only provide *incentives* for certain behavioral patterns—they cannot enforce them. A given law can impose severe sanctions on some behavior, such as murder, but it cannot rule it out. The effectiveness of *democratic* institutions and laws can thus be measured by the degree to which they induce democratic outcomes and behavior, that is, behavior in line with popular sovereignty and equal opportunity.

To a great extent, the search for alternatives must be a search for "smart" institutions or new institutional arrangements that better achieve the desired outcome. Instead of deriving these institutions from theory or abstract modeling, this book seeks smart institutions in empirical reality and practice.[1] I thus echo the work of Elinor Ostrom, who argues that "new institutional arrangements do not work in the field as they do in abstract models unless the models are well specified and empirically valid and the participants in a field setting understand how to make the new rules work" (Ostrom 2015, 14).

During the past years, I searched—and I continue to search—for fruitful and instructive cases from which we can learn. The project upon which this book is based is thus exploratory. To a great extent, it also is descriptive in that I first seek to describe empirical cases. This description is focused on innovative and promising institutions—institutions that have brought about and protected democratic political practices and egalitarian, as well as sustainable, economic systems. The questions I ask are always: How has this society been able to avoid a concentration of political and economic power? How have they ensured and protected strong civicness, broad participation, or even direct democratic rule? With what laws and institutions? My hope is that by systematically collecting cases of direct democracy or self-rule, as well as cases of economic equity and the protection of equal opportunity, I will be able to identify common factors and conditions. By assembling these common factors into truth tables and by applying Boolean Algebra, I hope to identify not only common factors, but also necessary and sufficient conditions for both direct democracy and egalitarian economies. My main unit of analysis is *political* institutions, that is, institutions that regulate, order, and control social, political, and economic life and thus have the potential to hold elitism at bay.

The discussion about the "right kind of institutions" must move away from 100 percent solutions to the fine tuning of promising institutions—and their mix (Ostrom 2015). How to best protect individual incentives while also ensuring that individualism does not undermine equal opportunity? This is a much more interesting and relevant question than: How to enforce equality?

Ideally, smart political institutions achieve not one aim *against* the other. Instead of zero-sum games, smart political institutions set the stage for positive-sum games in which more than one positive outcome and more than one desirable goal are achieved. Here it is equity *and* individual freedom, agency *and* justice, fairness *and* equal opportunity. My search for viable alternatives to capitalism and political representation is thus a search for smart political institutions that achieve more than one outcome, and particularly institutions that do not achieve one outcome to the detriment of another. For collectives and groups to advance, the individuals that compose them should advance as well and their agency should increase.

Thus when taking a concern for individual agency seriously while still seeking to achieve economic and political equality, the required political institutions must achieve all of these simultaneously:

a. protect freedom and agency;
b. ensure political equality; and
c. provide equal economic opportunity and avoid extreme economic inequality.

Institutions are no guarantee for an outcome and sometimes undesirable outcomes result from unlikely institutional frameworks. This is so because social life is not mechanistic and does not follow a rigid blueprint. Human behavior is to a great extent willful, and it thus takes commitment and effort to bring about social change toward more equity, justice, and fairness. By focusing on institutions, rules, and laws, this book thus commits itself to describing and explaining the conditions under which change toward more democracy and fairer markets *can* be constructed. But constructed they have to be.

POLITICS PROPER

Politics is the realm in which collectives discuss and enact the rules and laws they agree to live by. Politics requires public discussion, ideally involving everyone potentially affected by a collective decision (Habermas 1998; Sen 2009). The more public discussion, the more legitimate and democratic a democracy (Crocker, in Kaufman 2006). How to achieve such a broad public discussion and how to protect and shield it from the undue influences of power, money, charisma, and tradition should be the proper and most central concern of politics. The answers, proposals, and potential solutions to the difficulties resulting from the always present distortions of this process, orchestrated by economic and political elites, demagogues, and by the media they control and manipulate, are practical in nature. Different solutions should constantly be tried; solutions that have protected broad popular participation in the past might not work any longer today and might need to be revisited. How to actively involve large collectives into political processes and collective decisions is certainly not an easy task, but it is the proper task of democratic politics.

Instead we seem to have all given up on even searching for ways to achieve democratic governance. We are told that some people making political and economic decisions for us is the only way to go about politics. This is a lie (Neblo 2017). It is a purposeful lie in that it was invented by political and economic elites in order to justify their elitism. At different times in human history, elites have argued that they know better than the masses or, once this argument lost most of its legitimacy, that large collectives cannot reach collective decisions due to logistics. If that were so, why is there not more research on the upper limit of politically viable collectives? Maybe 435 is too large? The European parliament currently has 735 members—is that the upper limit for collective decision making for others?

Aristotle seemed to have thought that 100,000 people could actively and directly rule themselves in a time without cars, telephones, e-mail, TVs, radios, or the Internet. Is it really true that there are no alternatives to delegating the decisions about our lives—how we should live—to others in hopes they make the right decisions for us? Clearly not. History has shown over and over again and it continues to show us today that political elites do not make good decisions for us. Mostly they make good decisions for themselves.

Just as much as we cannot rely on others to make decisions on core political questions for us, we also cannot rely on traditions. What the founding fathers thought and did is of historical importance and relevant for setting us onto the path we find ourselves on today. They debated, in a fairly public manner, the destinies of the three million people that lived in the United States of their days and they found solutions through broad public debate and compromise—even if this debate was restricted to selected elites. Hoping that the founding fathers somehow have an answer to the problems we face today is not just an illusion—it is again a purposeful lie invoked by those who have to gain from invoking it. Nobody gains from making assault weapons broadly available to everybody—only the weapon industry and those politicians this industry has bought. Justifying a general arms race among the citizenry with reference to the Anti-Federalists, James Madison, and the American Bill of Rights is not honest. Democracy requires that old problems be discussed and debated again and again in the light of new circumstances and insights, as well as changing preferences, needs, and wants. Allowing money to play such a large role in American politics is the furthest from democracy and the democratic spirit of the founding fathers, I venture to say, as possible. Democracy is self-rule. Every day. Over and over again.

POLITICAL POWER AND THE STATE

There is no "around the state" or an autonomy outside of or without the state (Gibson-Graham 2006; Dinerstein 2014). The state as an ontological reality is constituted and reproduced by struggles over political power, dominance, control, and rule. Questions of security and the bureaucracy cannot and should not be avoided when discussing autonomy and self-rule. As an analytical exercise, it might bode well to "think outside of the state" and, as John Holloway (2010) has argued, we might even think about "changing the world without taking (state) power," but when doing so, we should rather try to think of "the state" in different ways instead of avoiding the questions that the conceptual model of "the state" allows us to ask.

As the work of many anarchist scholars, such as James Scott (2009), have shown, free association and "free society" in general is under threat from encroaching states and state power. Almost all historical examples in which anarchism, council democracy, or Soviet rule was practiced show us that these experiments ended because they were created in situations of conflict and (civil) war. From a realist perspective, as movements more concerned with their internal dynamics, they were unable to stand up to the violent onslaught of the Bolsheviks, the Freikorps, the French Army, the fascists, or the socialists. As long as states are controlled by economic elites and corporations, "the state" will serve their interests, against those seeking to establish a more egalitarian order. This is, after all, how states emerged, at least if we follow Elman Service, who explains:

> Here is the economic genesis of the state: From their *material* (economic) beginnings, classes become gradually social, and finally political as well when the rich erect a structure of permanent force to protect their class interests. The political state is thus a special means of repression by the propertied class. (Service 1975, 34)

In fact, according to Pierre Clastres, "Primitive societies are societies without a State" (Clastres 1989, 189). To this day, as James Scott (2009) has shown, many regions of the world have successfully escaped statehood and instead rely on local, administrative bodies to organize their collective lives, selected or elected among community members. The history of the state is, after all, a history of organizing violence and cannot be understood outside of the history of warfare and hostile takeovers of territories. Once created, states tend to become even more powerful and dangerous to their neighbors, thus triggering the emergence of other states in response. European history provides ample examples for this intimate connection of state apparatuses with violence and external threat.

The other face of the state is clearly that of directing violence inward toward the people it seeks to control. States, explains Clastres (1989), serve the purpose of extracting excess from people by forcing them to work more and harder so that profits can be made. According to most accounts, most noncapitalist societies require no more than four hours of work to meet daily needs. Anything beyond that is extra and serves to make profits. According to Clastres, "In primitive society—an essentially egalitarian society—men control their activity, control the circulation of the products of the activity: they act only on their own behalf, even though the law of exchange mediates the direct relation of man to his product" (Clastres 1989, 197f). When states rule over people's lives, egalitarianism and individual or even community control over production all come to an end.

However, given the very real power constellations of today's world, there is no "taking over the state." It is simply not possible and even if it were, it is not desirable, as the many historical experiences of state revolutions have clearly demonstrated. The more recent Arab Spring revolutions once more show that "smashing the state" is not an option, as there is a very real risk for the vacuum created being filled by even worse leaders and their organizations. While very real, "the state" is after all also an analytical construct helping us to talk and think about all of the different institutions and organizations mediated and constituted by the struggle over power and control. The law, money, legislation, courts, and the military apparatus are all complex and highly institutionalized ways of doing and organizing a society. They reflect the power constellations to be and they reproduce them. Given their fetish character, they appear real, fixed, and unchangeable to us, but they are not. Change must thus be social change first and originate in the social realm. It must "travel up" and change those institutions and organizations that administer the power relations to be. There is no other lasting change than "change from below."

Thus, by organizing more democratically and reining in markets so they serve more people and provide more fair opportunities to more, if not all, some people and groups are effectively changing the world through their practice. They also change what statehood is and means, what "money" represents and means, what "the law" stands for, and how we think of courts, legislation, political leadership, politics, markets, etc. The real struggle is about whose representations and whose definitions prevail and are thus given the power and legitimacy to mediate our lives. Today, it is a small minority of rich people, banks, and powerful corporations that are able to disseminate their definitions of political and economic reality, holding the whole world prisoner to it. Similarly, "voting" has become the only legitimate way to think and talk about democratic rule—but this was not always the case. In fact, for the ancient Greeks and for some modern and contemporary thinkers, voting is unrelated to democracy. It is at best one of many ways to channel collective will into policy. The meanings of "political representation," "money," "the law," etc., are similarly widely perceived as given and fixed, when in fact they are historically bound representations of power and highly institutionalized ways of doing things, invented at some point in history in a specific place in order to address a specific problem, such as easing large-scale trade or ordering social life (in some cases) or to control others (in most).

Instead of conquering the state, we thus need to *transform* the state and what it means and stands for. This, I think, can only be done by gradually replacing social and political interactions growing out of controlling the many for the benefit of the few with institutions growing out of truly democratic and egalitarian practice. What matters in this process is not so much what people say or write, but what they do, even though the end result of change must be the replacement of one dominant discourse with another: here the replacing of domination with self-rule and democracy. Once we do things differently, we have already created a different reality and changed the mediating institutions helping us to organize our lives. To some extent, we have already created a different meaning of "the state."

The role of academia, of thinking, talking, and writing about this change, is to point out possibilities and to analyze them more or less systematically. Academics can also, and should, play a role in collecting and disseminating counter-hegemonic practices and related discourses everywhere and, by doing so, enrich current debates. Academics, after all, are the only ones that have the freedom and the time to unveil such nonorthodoxies, discuss them, showcase them, analyze them, and disseminate them. If academics are not doing this, then who else will?

Under conditions of complete democracy, that is, popular sovereignty and self-rule of all citizens, in which 100 percent of political powers rests with all citizens, the state ceases to exit. Or maybe the citizens *are* the state. It is not self-evident how much state we need or even how much state is good for us and, following the general approach advocated here, I suggest that this question is best addressed empirically. All we can say theoretically is that the more democratic and involved a citizenry, the less state is needed, or even the more political power is held and exercised directly by the people, the less need there is for the state to wield it. This analytical model thus suggests that in societies in which the people are very actively engaged in politics, political power will be diluted and controlled directly by people and their local communities. If most political decisions are made locally, not much is left to be decided centrally. How far this devolution of political power can go remains to be seen and analyzed. History suggests that the existence of strong states is closely related to external threats and the need to defend a community, society, or country, and most empirical examples of attempts to do away with states and replace them with local soviets, communes, or councils failed not because of internal problems, but because most of these attempts came under external threat and were defeated.

Hence one of the great ironies of historical attempts to establish egalitarian societies in which political power is held and controlled by local communities and by the people: by doing so, central state apparatuses were weakened and became vulnerable to external threats. The history of these attempts clearly demonstrates that one of the core preconditions for establishing egalitarian societies and politics is peace, particularly the absence of external threats. War and external threats make egalitarianism impossible precisely because true democracy weakens centralized power. The failure of most historical experiments with egalitarianism thus almost always fell victim to external threat to the point where we have not have much opportunity to truly see egalitarianism at work for long.[2]

In a representative democracy, the state has differentiated itself from the people to the point where almost all collective and political power is controlled and exercised by the state—by its government, its representatives, and by its bureaucracy. While this occurs in the name of the people, the perspective advocated here is that no such delegation can exist in a democracy. Political power, the way it is treated here, is held either by you or by me. You cannot hold power over me without me losing power. In a democratic system, there also cannot exist a justification for such a handing over of power. While some might claim that they know better what is good for me and thus seek to justify their power to make decisions for me, exercising power for others is tutelage and thus stands in opposition to democracy, as Immanuel Kant understood when stating: "Nobody can compel me to be happy in his own way. Paternalism is the greatest despotism imaginable" (quoted in Berlin 1998, 208).

Thus, the way to assess the democraticness of any system is simple: How much power rests with the people? Not the intermediate state branches at the state or provincial levels. Also not with the municipal administrations, as all of these are still part of the state apparatus. But with the people. How much can ordinary citizens decide and how much money do they have to carry out their decisions? How much of the 100 percent? Instead of focusing on private versus public or centralization versus decentralization, or even communist versus capitalist, our main questions should be: How much can citizens decide and how much political power and authority do they wield? In a true (while utopian) democracy, the people make all decisions. If they do so, they *are* the state.

In this way of thinking about political power, power functions as a zero-sum resource, that is, if more political power is shifted toward the bottom, then the top loses power. This must be so, as otherwise instead of a shift of political power we are dealing with the emergence of parallel and contentious power, which instead of leading to more democracy is more likely to lead to faction and secession. This way of thinking about political power also implies that there will also not be a power vacuum, as some social force will always fill a power void. We can thus allot a numerical number to political power, say 100, and then depict how it is distributed among the polity. There will be no power-free zone and no adding additional power on top of the 100.

It is thus helpful, I find, to analyze democracy not through the lens of what model it falls into (Held 1987) or how consolidated it is (Huntington 1991), but instead through the lens of power. Along the lines of John Locke (1986 [1689]) and his *Second Treatise on Government*, first published in 1689, political power can be understood as the right to make laws and enforce rules over a polity.

CONCLUSION

The way political power is used, administered, and divided is at the core of democracy, self-rule, and popular sovereignty. Political power, in this realm, is a constant, and a fruitful way to think about it is to take it as given. The main question to ask then is how it is distributed among different actors and how effectively they can use it. Is it strongly concentrated in but a few hands or is it diluted among all citizens? If one person is able make all public, that is collective, decisions, then we have a kingdom. The more political power is distributed among all citizens, the more democratic the governance. If all the people of a polity hold equal power to govern without anyone holding more, then we have a (utopian) 100 percent democracy. What we see in most cases is a mixed form of governance in which the exercise of power is located somewhere in between these two extreme poles. The two main indicators to assess degrees of democraticness are thus the authority to make collective decisions and the ability to carry them out, which is strongly related to control over public money.

Representative democracies have diluted this straightforward assessment by delegating the power to make collective decisions about politics and the budget to elected representatives, who claim to make those decisions in the name of the people and for them. Such a system, rather than representative, is best called one of tutelage.

NOTES

1. Once identified, the next question is how to implement them, which is of course a political question—and well beyond the possibilities of this book.

2. According to Thusydides, the Athenian model of democratic self-rule did not succumb to external threat, but rather to hubris, as Athenians became exceedingly proud and arrogant about their democratic system, leading them to start a war with Sparta. It thus seems as if democracy is under threat from both external as well as internal developments. With the exception of Athens, however, the more known attempts to establish egalitarianism came under external attack, which in turn justified, at least in the eyes of some, the shifting back of political power toward the centralized state. This is the story of the Russian Soviets, as well as the German Räte Republics. Spanish Anarchism was constructed in the midst of civil war and some historians have blamed it for the ultimate victory of the fascists.

Part I

THEORY

Chapter 2

Beyond Political Representation

The crisis of liberal, representative democracy is deep and has many consequences. As ordinary citizens become more and more withdrawn, apathetic, and alienated, they also become more and more manipulated by those who care about nothing but their own interests and bank accounts. Fewer and fewer people actively participate in political affairs. Even when reduced to the parameters of representative democracy—voting—democracy has stopped working in most formal democracies, as participation in voting is extremely low in most countries. While some citizens voluntarily abstain from even the minimal political involvement that is voting, others, particularly minorities, are often forced out of their political rights and actively disenfranchised. In the United States, over six million citizens cannot vote due to having committed a felony. This active disenfranchisement affects African Americans disproportionally, leading some to refer to the current situation in the United States as one of a "New Jim Crow" (Alexander 2012).

When fewer and fewer people participate, we give license to those that rule in our name, even if not on our behalf. We also give license to the extreme voices of those who are strongly invested in achieving certain outcomes, often to the detriment of those who think that they don't have much at stake. The outcomes of such distortions are all too obvious. Elected officials rule over us without much constraint or even consideration for the common good. They do whatever it takes to win the next election. Meanwhile, the extreme voices of the Tea Party, racists, bigots, and false prophets all overpower the voices of the majority. The majority watches the spectacle of politics, sometimes in disbelief, sometimes in disgust. The message this book seeks to spread is that politics cannot be done *for* citizens. Citizens have to do it themselves. The (classical political liberal) view that we can just go about our private lives and leave "politics" to the (elected or selected) few has proven

19

wrong. A people cannot have democracy, which translates as "self-rule," and not participate in it. Self-rule cannot be delegated.

The current state of affairs is not just American. It is global. Nowhere, as far as I know, are people happy with the democracies they once fought for. And for good reason, as nowhere are democracies delivering what they once promised: self-rule, self-determination, control over one's own destiny, and also equal opportunity, a fair chance to succeed, and a system in which effort counts, not your name or who your parents are.

This chapter starts with a critical reevaluation of the idea of democracy, in which I seek to demonstrate that the core of democracy is not voting but self-rule. I then delve further into the argument that political representation is not related to democracy. It might, in fact, be opposed to it. I then provide some empirical evidence in support of my theoretical argument by highlighting some of the realities of the current EU and U.S. legislative bodies, whose members hardly represent their constituents in any meaningful way. I end this section with the rhetorical question: Do we really need professional representatives? From the available literature it becomes clear, at least to me, that the solution to the crisis of political participation must be constructed on much stronger political communities and much more involved public deliberation. This chapter concludes with a list of five points that must be taken into consideration when seeking to overcome the crisis of liberal, representative democracy. The purpose of listing them here is to set the framework for the empirical analysis.

DIRECT DEMOCRACY AND SELF-RULE

The core idea of democracy is that the ruled should also rule. This idea has proven extremely inspiring and continues to mobilize people to stand up against those that rule them. However, in most cases, democracy promises more than it seems able to deliver. Some people have died for democracy and many are still struggling for it, but once they have it, democracy often turns into just another type of elite rule—this time of elected officials and unyielding bureaucracies. In most countries where democracies have long been established, elite rule seems so entrenched that any mention of the will of the people seems naïve. Ordinary people know this and constantly seek a new and fresh type of leader, one that is not corrupted by the political system or "the establishment." This quest is mostly frustrated, as true outsiders cannot make it to the top of most political systems and outsiders, once they are elected, have to "play by the rules" if they want anything to be done.

There are no outsiders in the political systems of contemporary democracies, and looking for new saviors is done in vain because the problem is not one of corrupted political elites. It is one of relying too heavily on elites to begin with. In other words, the whole concept of representation needs rethinking, or as the *Economist* stated in 2004, "At a time when representative democracies everywhere are suffering from disillusionment with politics, it is well worth thinking about alternatives" (*Economist* 2004, 18). This is, I agree, an urgent and very relevant task because in the absence of viable alternatives, the long-prophesized "End of History" might indeed become a self-fulfilling prophecy.

When rethinking representative democracy, we necessarily also need to rethink what a political community is; that is, on what basis democracy must rest and how political community can be practically linked to collective decision making and rule. To successfully tackle this task, one must consult, and if possible integrate, the many different strands of literature that already exist on this topic. There are many books and articles on "deliberative democracy," but they all remain fairly vague in their examination of how to create and sustain deliberative forums (Bohman 1998; Gutman and Thompson 2004; Elster 1998). Most works in this genre instead focus on elaborating the philosophical foundations of public deliberation. The same is true for the works of Hannah Arendt (1973), Jürgen Habermas (1998), Amartya Sen (2009), and Jean Cohen and Andrew Arato (1994), or the work deemed "classic" of such authors as Benjamin Barber (1984) and Carole Pateman (1970).

The body of literature on "participatory democracy" is less abstract and dwells more on the analysis of empirical examples, but it is also limited by shifting participation in the civil society sphere and treating it as complimentary to "normal" representative democracy (Fung 2006; Fagotto and Fung 2006; Williamson and Fung 2004; Cohen and Sabel 1997; Nylen and Dodd 2003; Baiocchi 2005; Avritzer 2009). However, by accepting the separation of state and civil society, even if only for analytical purposes, these authors are only able to analyze a very limited segment of what self-rule has meant and can mean.

There also exists a family of academic books and articles on concrete direct democratic experiences in such countries as Switzerland (Kriesi 2008), as well as on experiences of plebiscites, referendums, and public initiatives in the United States and elsewhere (Arx 2002; Cronin 1989; Ellis 2002), but these also tend to have a very narrow technical focus and they do not elaborate the possibilities and conditions for genuinely different ways to reach collective decisions.

In addition to all of this, there are myriad think tanks, centers, and academic institutes dedicated to democracy, democratic participation, deliberative democracy, and direct democracy. The Swiss Center for Democracy in Aarau, for example, hosts a "Centre for Research on Direct Democracy," which is the home of a vast data collection on referenda and plebiscites worldwide (see http://www.c2d.ch/), but it also does not bridge the gap between technical information on very limited issues and the broader discussions about the need to develop viable alternatives to representation.

Part of this lack of bridging the different knowledge already available to us can be explained by the way contemporary knowledge production is achieved, namely in universities and by professors, who are evaluated based on their contributions to their narrowly-defined academic disciplines. Public policy researchers simply do not engage much with philosophers and anthropologists. On a more fundamental level, however, it appears that a very severe and extremely consistent framing of this issue has produced a very widely shared agreement that representation is the only viable way to organize large collectives. This agreement is perceived as so normal and mainstream that anybody arguing for alternatives to representation is deemed either naïve, utopian, or extremely radical. Such a framing, in other words, has delegitimized any serious efforts to think beyond political representation, and by doing so it has added layers upon layers of legitimacy to representative democracy.

In addition to finding alternatives to the liberal democracy, we also need to find ways to escape the overwhelming discursive hegemony that has presented political representation and capitalism as the only viable options and has foreclosed any serious research on viable alternatives (Laclau and Mouffe 1985; Gibson-Graham 1996, 2006). I intend to demonstrate that the broadly shared assessment depicting representative democracy as the only feasible system of political organization is wrong.

In fact, there are many empirical examples—historical as well as contemporary—of different polities organizing themselves without relying on political representation. The most well-known ones reach back to ancient Athens. Historical examples include several medieval European city states, the short-lived "Räte Republics" established after World War I in Germany, the creation of "colectividades" during the period of Spanish Anarchism in 1936 and 1937, the Paris Commune of 1871, several nineteenth-century Owenite communities, Tolstoyan communities, and other, less well-known examples.

Some of these historical examples of sustaining political community without representation live on, even if their institutional designs have changed. Some cantons of contemporary Switzerland still practice direct democracy (Kriesi 2008). Several towns in Vermont still routinely practice direct democracy (Bryan 2004). Given the Western pedigree of representation, it is also not surprising that many non-Western societies were and continue to be able to rule themselves without relying on political representation. Examples include many tribal societies of South America, Africa, the Pacific, Asia, and the Middle East. James Scott (2009) has described in detail how a whole region of Southeast Asia, known as "Zomia," which comprises some 100 million people of diverse backgrounds living in an area of some 2.5 million square kilometers, has been able to resist formal state rule and hence systems of representative government until today.

Given the ideological hegemony of representative democracy, most of the political, philosophical, institutional, and policy implications of direct democracy have been left unexamined. While elaborating all of them systematically is an impossible task for one person to accomplish, it is clear that direct democracy bears important implications for public administration and federalism, as it must go hand-in-hand with decentralization and devolution. It also has implication for the related fields of education, philosophy, communication, and economics, as a direct democracy would make different demands on its citizens and rely heavily on effective communication. The relationship of decentralized direct democracies to highly-concentrated economic markets has to be explored, as well as the role of economic governance and how to link or hold apart economic from political power. Some of the implications of direct rule have already been elaborated, for example, by Amartya Sen's (1999) work on *capabilities*, whose stress of agency is much in tune with a system of democratic self-rule, or by all those scholars who have explored the institutional requirements for direct rule, reaching back to Cleisthenes (ca. 570–508 BCE). What is still missing from all these disperse bodies of work is to pull them together and formulate a concise description of the theoretical possibilities, as well as the concrete and practical conditions and institutional requirements of direct rule.

THE DIAGNOSIS: DEMOCRACY *AGAINST* REPRESENTATION

Self-interested action does not spontaneously produce common political goods, as Adam Smith (1976 [1776]) has argued for markets. Even markets fail, create distortions, and produce externalities, as Smith readily admitted. Markets rely on such a vast amount of necessary conditions that equilibrium is theoretically impossible and empirically highly unlikely (Schumpeter 1976). In the realm of political community, self-interested action produces nothing but an agglomeration of nasty and narrow-minded selfish actors who do not share a common bond. Theirs is not a society, let alone a community in any meaningful definition of these words. To the contrary, such a group is not even a true group, but consists of discrete individuals whose main aim is to secure their own advantage and survival, against that of all the other players in this brutish game. Democracy cannot survive in such an environment. For Jane Mansbridge, "Adversary democracy is the democracy of a cynical society. It replaces common interest with self-interest, the dignity of equal status with the baser motives of self-protection, and the communal moments of a face-to-face council with the isolation of a voting machine. Such a system invites reaction" (Mansbridge 1980, 18).

How can this be avoided and overcome? Clearly, classical liberalism, with its focus on individual liberties and freedoms, does not provide an answer to this question. Communism and socialism, on the other hand, have consistently fallen back on even worse elite rule and statist control, thus blocking the way of genuine freedom and community. What alternatives do we have? Nationalism is an obvious candidate to foster common interest. If people are sufficiently nationalistic, then the theme of "my country first" could provide a common interest, even if a nasty one. However, given the inherent negative components of nationalism (xenophobia, racism, and exclusion), the question arises if there are any other viable and more desirable ways to foster and maintain political community.

While we have not advanced much toward developing viable solutions to the crisis of political representation, recent work in this field has at least made us more aware of the problem. Hanna Pitkin, probably the most recognized scholar in this field and the author of the 1967 classic *The Concept of Representation*, has had a change of heart and now argues that "representation, at least as a political idea and practice, emerged only in the early modern period and had nothing at all to do with democracy" (Pitkin 2004, 337). Pitkin shows that the rule of the people, demo-kratia, is a different idea, has a different pedigree, and demands a different practice than the idea of representation. Pitkin thus adds her voice to that of Hannah Arendt, who argued earlier that "representative government has in fact become oligarchic government. . . . The age-old distinction between ruler and ruled which the Revolution had set out to abolish through the establishment of a republic has asserted itself again; once more, the people are not admitted to the public realm, once more the business of government has become the privilege of the few" (Arendt 1965, 273, 240). For Pitkin, "The arrangements we call 'representative democracy' have become a substitute for popular self-government, not its enactment" (Pitkin 2004, 340). Indeed, as I have argued earlier (Reiter 2013), political representation was not introduced out of necessity, but as a means by powerful elites to secure power and privileged access to specific goods and rights.

The diagnosis is clear, at least to some observers: "Despite repeated efforts to democratize the representative system, the predominant result has been that representation has supplanted democracy instead of serving it. Our governors have become a self-perpetuating elite that rules—or rather, administers—passive or privatized masses of people. The representatives act not as agents of the people but simply instead of them" (Pitkin 2004, 339). The effect this has on the people is also quite clear: "Their constituents, accordingly, feel powerless and resentful. Having sent experts to tend to their public concerns, they give their own attention and energy to other matters, closer to home. Lacking political experience, they feel ignorant and incapable. ('The President has access to all sorts of classified information we don't have,' I've heard repeatedly in recent months. 'He must know what he is doing.') Not that people idolize their governors and believe all the official pronouncements. On the contrary, they are cynical and sulky, deeply alienated from what is done in their name and from those who do it" (Pitkin 2004, 339). The final result of such a state of affairs is also not difficult to discern: "The arrangements we call 'representative democracy' have become a substitute for popular self-government, not its enactment. Calling them 'democracy' only adds insult to injury" (Pitkin 2004, 340). Indeed, the public approval of the American Congress hovered around 10 percent in 2014, temporarily falling under the 10 percent mark in November of 2014. Coupled with the fact that the majority of citizens do not participate in elections, calling such a system one in which the people rule is indeed a travesty.

Hannah Arendt's verdict is equally devastating, but to her, not all hope is lost: "Genuinely democratic representation is possible, she held, where the centralized, large-scale, necessarily abstract representative system is based in a lively, participatory, concrete direct democracy at the local level" (Pitkin 2004, 340). Pitkin also offers glimpses of potential solutions. To her, the problem lies in the mix of concentration of power and wealth, which has produced an alienation of the average citizen from political decision making, together with the power of large companies that have taken control of important decisions affecting our lives, coupled with a media-instilled passivity. All these problems can be addressed and overcome, even if they require a concerted effort that Pitkin finds beyond her means to achieve.

Michael Saward, another prominent political scientist, has added his voice to this critical canon. His diagnosis is similar to the ones voiced by Arendt and Pitkin: "There can be little doubt that the time is ripe for revisiting the idea of representation. In a number of countries, not least many established Western democracies, and in regional and international bodies, there is a great deal of real concern about its practice. Voters are disaffected and voting rates are in decline. Political leaders and parties face high levels of cynicism and distrust. Many groups do not feel that their views are properly represented, or at least not in mainstream politics. In this context, can representation still be democratic?" (Saward 2008, 1000). Saward dwells on another specialist on this issue, Andrew Rehfeld (2006), who has plausibly demonstrated that democracy and representation are not related. Saward also agrees with Pitkin that the idea and practice of representation are not old. He writes: "It was only with what Dahl (1989) calls the 'second transformation' of democracy that our modern understanding of 'representative democracy'—as a system in which the people choose the rulers at regular intervals in elections, combining elements of democratic choice with political representation—began to take shape" (Saward 2008, 1001).

The critique of representation can also count on an influential and well-respected pedigree of philosophers. The Greek philosopher Cornelius Castoriadis (1922–1997) has certainly contributed much to our understanding that political representation is antithetical to the rule of the people:

> These "elections" themselves constitute an impressive resurrection of the mystery of the Eucharist and the real Presence. Every four or five years, one Sunday (Thursday in Great Britain [Tuesday in the United States], where Sundays are devoted to other mysteries), the collective will is liquefied or fluidified and then gathered, drop by drop, into sacred/profane vases called ballot boxes [*urnes*], and the same evening, by means of a few additional operations, this fluid, condensed one hundred thousand times, is decanted [*transvasé*] into the thenceforth transubstantiated spirit of a few hundred elected officials. There is no philosophy of "representation," though there is an implicit metaphysics; neither is there any sociological analysis. Who represents whom, and how does he represent her? Forgotten without any discussion are the critiques of representative democracy, begun with Rousseau, considerably broadened since then, and unreservedly validated by the most superficial observation of contemporary political facts. Wiped out is the alienation of the sovereignty of those who delegate to the delegates. Such delegation is supposed to be limited in time. But as soon as it is instaurated, everything is over. Rousseau was wrong in this regard: the English are not even "free once every five years." For, throughout those five years, the alleged choices about what the electors will be called upon to pronounce themselves on will have been completely predetermined by what the deputies will have done between the two elections. These five-year terms obviously have cumulative effects, and the "choice" of the elector finds itself reduced to such grandiose dilemmas as François Mitterrand or Jacques Chirac, George Herbert Walker Bush or Michael Dukakis, Margaret Thatcher or Neil Kinnock, and so on. And as soon as a small separate political body exists, it cannot help but look after its own powers and interests and enter into collusion with the other de facto powers that are set up within society, notably economic ones. (Castoriadis 1990, 211ff)

Another classic verdict comes from Jean-Jacques Rousseau (1712–1778). For Rousseau, "the moment a people allows itself to be represented, it is no longer free: it no longer exists" (Rousseau 2003 [1762], 66). Rousseau explains that "the idea of representation is modern; it comes to us from feudal government, from that iniquitous and absurd system which degrades humanity and dishonors the name of man. In ancient republics and even in monarchies, the people never had representatives; the word itself was unknown. It is very singular that in Rome, where the tribunes were so sacrosanct, it was never imagined that they could usurp the functions of the people, and that in the midst of so great a multitude they never attempted to pass on their own authority a single *plebiscitum*" (Rousseau 2003 [1762], 65). The same is true for the legislative process. For Rousseau, "Law being purely the declaration of the general will, it is clear that, in the exercise of the legislative power, the people cannot be represented" (Rousseau 2003 [1762], 65). According to Rousseau, what makes a republic democratic is not the fact that citizens elect representatives, but rather that citizens themselves make the laws they live under. This task, for Rousseau, cannot be delegated.

The idea of political representation only enters the scene through Thomas Hobbes's *Leviathan*.[1] From there, it inspired the architects of both the French and the American Republics—particularly the latter, who had the explicit intent to limit the power of ordinary people. While one can understand the fear of aristocrats and the "educated upper crust" of the likes of Hobbes, Sieyes, Hamilton, and Madison against "mob rule," we must ask ourselves if those fears justify the dominant system of political representation today. The essence of political representation was then and continues to be to hand over the power of the masses to the few who are "better equipped" to decide "for all of us." However, recent history rather indicates that instead of deciding in our best interest, our lawmaking representatives make laws that do not necessarily favor all of us. We are also facing the question of if we are indeed served well with more and more laws and if law making indeed needs to be done by professionals. The time has come to rethink the legislative branch of government.

THE CURRENT STATE OF AFFAIRS: PLUTOCRACY AND ALIENATION

Rousseau's critique of professional legislators who enact laws on behalf of the people can be illustrated by analyzing the situation of different lawmaking bodies in different countries today. In the United States, for example, there are 435 members of the House of Representatives and 100 senators, thus 535 federal legislators. Political scientists have calculated the amount of money it takes to get elected today into the U.S. Senate passes $1 million. To become president, one needs to be able to spend at least $10 million. Where only the rich have a chance to get elected, democracy gives way to plutocracy—the reign of the rich. Where most representatives graduate from the same universities (Harvard, Yale, Princeton, Stanford: the top and most expensive among all American universities), and where attendance to these universities is highly circumscribed by money (the annual costs of attending Harvard as an undergraduate in 2013 were slightly higher than the U.S. median family income for the same year: $59,000 vs. $52,000), democracy and equal opportunity have both become a mockery.

Incumbency is one of the many problems of the current system in the United States and elsewhere. In the U.S. House of Representatives, the reelection rate hovers around 90 percent. In the Senate, those rates have only been very slightly lower over the past fifty years. Incumbency, however, contributes to the consolidation of a political class, each year more distanced from their constituencies. With repeated incumbency we see the emergence of the professional politician—someone who no longer represents anybody but his or her own interests and on whose independent opinion the public relies. Under such conditions, the people have handed over the state to a group of elites who run it among themselves under the guise of "our" best interest. Hardly a shadow of representation remains and "the people" watch what their representatives do or fail to do in relative awe (or disgust). What do they do?

In 2012, the U.S. Congress met on 153 days, for a total of 726 hours (House) and 930 hours (Senate). This is about half of the amount of hours average Americans work per year (1,790 hours in 2012). Considering that in 2012, the median income of Americans was just under $43,000 and that of their representatives $174,000—about three times a much—the whole idea of "representation" stands on weak grounds to begin with.

In 2012, a total of 193 of bills were signed into law. In 2011, the members of the House and Senate met more often (175 days for the House and 170 day for the Senate) for a total of 992 hours (House) and 1,100 hours (Senate). However, that year a total of only ninety bills became law. The numbers are not much different for the preceding years (2011: ninety laws; 2009 and 2010: 383 laws in two years). This makes for less than one law per year for each elected representative in both federal chambers and should raise questions about the true necessity of having and paying for professional lawmakers.[2]

In countries relying on codified laws systems, which they inherited from the Romans, it is even less clear how the elected representatives spend their time, and the situation gets worse when examining supranational legislative bodies, such as the European Parliament, where "Roman conditions" have long been accused.[3] There the average Member of Parliament (MEP) earns $291,000 per year, several times more than the people he or she "represents." It is also impossible to find out what exactly these MEPs do on a daily basis, how many hours they work, how many laws they pass, and what other routine activities they engage in. Of course, professional lawmakers also engage in activities such as budgeting, but as the revolving crisis around federal budgeting in the United States suggests, professional lawmakers seem not the best suited to propose and pass collective budgets to begin with. Budgeting, if politicized and taken out of the hands of local collectives and technical staff, becomes a residue for political dispute—a dispute that should happen elsewhere, namely among citizens and at the local level.[4]

The problem of political representatives is thus not an American problem alone. In Germany, about one-quarter of elected politicians serve on the boards of private and public companies. Some ministers of some German states serve on six different boards (Scheer 2013), not only earning significant amounts of money "on the side," but also unduly representing the interests of these companies in a sort of institutionalized lobbying scheme.[5] Whom do they represent? In whose interest do they act? Who is served by such a crossing of constituents? Certainly not the general public and the supposed "constituents" whose interests these elected officials are supposed to represent. The member of the German federal government Dagmar Wöhrl (CSU) has earned at least 623,000 Euros in 2015, in addition to her parliamentary salary. She earned over 324,000 Euros from serving on the board of the "Nuernberger" Insurance Company and 215,000 Euros from serving on the board of the Swiss Bank Safra Sarasin. As a federal lawmaker, her regular monthly salary is 9,300 Euro. Wöhrl is ranked number six in the list of top earners in the German Parliament. The top earner is Philipp Graf (Lord) Lerchenfeld (CSU), who earned "at least 1,729,500 Euros in addition to his salary" (Holzschuh 2016, front page).

In most formally democratic countries, the "political class," as politicians are often referred to in many Latin American countries, has long decoupled from the citizenry. They have become a class for itself. The citizenry has bestowed on them the power to use reason for them, deliberate for them, and make decisions for them. Politicians thus rule over the citizenry and "democracy" has been reduced to the voting process, even though voting is but a technical side aspect of self-rule. In this process, professional lawmakers have thus secured much more power than any meaningful conceptualization of "self-rule" can allow. As political power shifted away from people to their representatives, democracy became about how to get elected, opening the door to the sorts of media manipulations we routinely witness today.

Do we really need to pay some people so they represent us every day of the year to make laws on our behalf? It is far from obvious and it is possible that we would be better off if our representatives actually worked less and passed fewer laws every year. It also seems that at some point we should have enough laws and would only need to decide on specific problems and issues as they arise, a task that hardly seems to require professional legislators. Indeed, most popular calls for legal reform demand more accessible, simpler, and fewer laws, not more—a call echoing such classic liberals as those voiced by Benjamin Constant (Constant 2003, 65). Ironically, this task is then delegated to professional lawmakers, who become "professional" simply by winning an election and whose main task it is to propose new laws. No special knowledge or training is required. We might be able to do this ourselves, it seems, particularly when we can already dwell on a constitution and a system of laws that we inherited from the past—even more so in countries where the laws have been codified and written down in books.[6]

A FOCUS ON POLITICAL COMMUNITY

The constitution of political community is the very foundation on which democracy rests, as only if a group of people understands itself as a community can they act together. Jane Mansbridge (1980), taking inspiration from Aristotle's *Nicomachean Ethics*, found that sharing a common interest is the core condition for achieving unitary democracy, that is, to overcome adversary democracy, which is characterized by a sort of collective decision making resulting not from mutual agreement and understanding, but by default, by counting the different preferences voiced and then deciding by the majority principle. If people share a common interest, they can come to an agreement on how they want to live and organize themselves, how to spend the money they have as a collective, and what rules and laws they want to enact for themselves that regulate their lives. For Aristotle, himself not a supporter of democracy, mutual friendship was indeed a necessary basis for the state. In Book VIII of the *Nicomachean Ethics*, we read,

> Friendship seems to hold states together, and lawgivers to care more for it than for justice; for unanimity seems to be something like friendship, and this they aim at most of all, and expel faction as their worst enemy; and when men are friends they have no need of justice, while when they are just they need friendship as well, and the truest form of justice is thought to be a friendly quality. (Aristotle 2009, 128)

Aristotle further explains that,

> For in every community there is thought to be some form of justice, and friendship too; at least men address as friends their fellow-voyagers and fellow soldiers, and so too those associated with them in any other kind of community. And the extent of their association is the extent of their friendship, as it is the extent to which justice exists between them. And the proverb "what friends have is common property" expresses the truth; for friendship depends on community. (Aristotle 2009, 137f)

Finally, Aristotle ponders about the relationship between sharing a common aim, building a community, and justice:

> Now all forms of community are like parts of a political community; for men journey together with a view to some particular advantage, and provide

something that they need for the purpose of life; and it is for the sake of advantage that the political community too seems both to have come together originally and to endure, for this is what legislators aim at, and they call just that which is to the common advantage. (Aristotle 2009, 138)

Jane Mansbridge, in turn, writes that "any polity based on friendship must be a democracy, for it is based on a fundamental equality among its members" (Mansbridge 1980, 9). To her, voting fosters division and faction and consensus requires friendship and shared interest. Mansbridge shows that consensual politics, the one that does not assume conflictual interest up front, is indeed common and widely practiced in such institutions as village councils, corporations, and among legislators (Mansbridge 1980, 32). She explains that "the consensual process differs in form from strict unanimity rule in that no vote is taken, and it differs in purpose from strict unanimity rule in that people usually adopt it when they expect to agree, not when they expect to differ" (Mansbridge 1980, 32). For Mansbridge, face-to-face interaction is essential to achieving consensus, as it "increases the perception of likeness, encourages decision making by consensus, and perhaps even enhances equality of status" (Mansbridge 1980, 33). The opposite of consensual democracy for Mansbridge is adversary democracy: "adversary democracy is the democracy of a cynical society. It replaces common interest with self-interest, the dignity of equal status with the baser motives of self-protection, and the communal moments of a face-to-face council with the isolation of a voting machine. Such a system invites reaction" (Mansbridge 1980, 18).

Mansbridge's pioneering work highlights that shared interest is an inherent and necessary condition for democratic rule. Shared interest is also a remedy against elitism. Elite rule, if in the form of monarchy, aristocracy, oligarchy, or plutocracy, is in its very essence opposed to the rule of the people. A shared political interest can prove strong enough to unite common people and keep them motivated and on constant guard, as old elites will most likely dispute the claims of the masses and new elites tend to constantly emerge, seeking to establish and justify hierarchies. The questions this raises are: How can shared interest be fostered and maintained? What constitutes political community?

The classical examples of the Cleisthenian reforms of democratic Athens point to a system in which a shared interest was forced onto diverse groups, as they had to join and "deal with" each other's concerns in the *trittyes* associations that Cleisthenes created in 503 BCE, thus breaking the power of ethnic, regional, and status bonds and replacing them with civic ones (Trail 1975). According to Max Weber, early European free towns constituted themselves in the north of Italy as communities of faith and emerged as homogeneous communities *against* an increased populational heterogeneity. Following Weber,

"To develop into a city-commune, a settlement had to be of the nonagricultural-commercial type, at least to a relative extent, and to be equipped with the following features: 1. A fortification; 2. A market; 3. Its own court or law and, at least in part, autonomous law; 4. An associational structure (*Verbandscharakter*) and, connected therewith, 5. At least partial autonomy and autocephaly, which includes administration by authorities in whose appointment the burghers could in some form participate" (Weber 1968, 1226).

Reinhard Bendix, who follows Weber's analysis when analyzing changing social orders and how they relate to nation building and citizenship, points at the necessity of trust among rulers and ruled. He argues that "ultimately, it is a question of 'good will' whether the laws and regulations of political authority are implemented effectively by the officials and sustained by public compliance and initiative" (Bendix 1969, 23). Both Weber and Bendix also explain how the solidarity fostered by guilds and faith in cities was substituted by nationalism once democracy was extended beyond city limits. Hence if shared interest is indeed a crucial condition for self-rule, then faith, association, and nationalism have been suggested as means to bring it about, where civic associationalism seems the most promising (read: least exclusive) way to foster it.

If civic associationalism is indeed the most promising way to foster political community, then the questions move into the practical realm, namely: How and with what sort of institutions can we foster and maintain a political community that nurtures a shared interest? How far can such an association be extended? It is already clear from the onset that a shared interest can only emerge, be recognized by all, and serve as a guiding principle if all citizens actively participate in public affairs. The practical questions emerging at this juncture are those that motivate this research project, namely: What kinds of institutions are conducive to the creation and maintenance of shared interest and political community? What kind of institutions have proved successful in barring elitism from taking a hold of a political community and thus allowed this community to maintain the political equality of all its members? I hope to present some telling empirical examples shortly that shed some light on these questions and provide some informing examples.

THE CENTRALITY OF DELIBERATION

A deliberative conception of democracy helps us understand why most democracies are weak and why political processes are oftentimes so distorted. For Jürgen Habermas (1998), Bernard Manin (1987), and the many authors they have inspired, individual preferences cannot be understood as given and stable, but as influenced by economic, social, and cultural conditions. Seyla

Benhabib argues that "legitimacy in complex democratic societies must be thought to result from the free and unconstrained public deliberation of all about matters of common concern" (Benhabib 1996, 68). And Bernard Manin writes:

> It is, therefore, necessary to alter radically the perspective common to both liberal theories and democratic thought: the source of legitimacy is not the predetermined will of individuals, but rather the process of its formation, that is, deliberation itself. An individual's liberty consists first of all in being able to arrive at decision by a process of research and comparison among various solutions. As political decisions are characteristically imposed on all, it seems reasonable to seek, as an essential condition for legitimacy, the deliberation of all or, more precisely, the right of all to participate in deliberation. We must, therefore, challenge the fundamental conclusion of Rousseau, Sieyès, and Rawls: a legitimate decision does not represent the will of all, but is one that results from the deliberation of all. (Manin 1987, 351f)

In short, public deliberation must play a central role in all democratic societies and political systems must be designed in such a way as to allow all those potentially affected by a decision to partake in its making. Voting is not the core element of democracy. It is, in fact, peripheral to it. The many critiques of deliberative democracy have not undermined its central claim. They have only allowed us to see how easily deliberation can be distorted and abused.

In fact, direct deliberative democracy is practiced today in several towns in Vermont and Maine (Bryan 2004). Some Swiss cantons meet regularly to decide in public assembly what collective actions they should take and how to allocate their yearly budgets (Kriesi 2008). In Botswana, most villages count on a *kgotla*, or system of village democracy, in which smaller civil cases are settled and agreed upon. Similar systems exist in most African countries. In Afghanistan and some parts of Pakistan, councils of leaders or elders meet regularly in *jirgas* to make collective decisions based on consensus. In the Southeast Asian region of Zomia, some 100 million people organize outside of representative states.

If we believe Elman Service (1975), pre-Neolithic societies were all egalitarian and humankind moved into the construction of social hierarchies only slowly and reluctantly—the rule of some over others never being accepted without contestation. Quoting the anthropologist Lewis H. Morgan (1877), Service argues, "primitive society, Morgan had discovered, was basically communistic, lacking important commerce, private property, economic class, or despotic rulers" (Service 1975, 33).

Murray Bookchin (1996, 1998, 2004) has given us a detailed account, in three volumes, of what might be called a genealogy of self-rule. He writes:

From the largely medieval peasant wars of the sixteenth-century Reformation to the modern uprisings of industrial workers and peasants, oppressed peoples have created their own popular forms of community association—potentially, the popular infrastructure of a new society—to replace the oppressive states that rules over them. Generally these popular associations shared the same goal: the de facto political empowerment of the people. In time, during the course of the revolutions, these associations took the institutional form of local assemblies, much like town meetings, or representative councils of mandated recallable deputies. (Bookchin 1996, 4)

Bookchin's work provides an important source for my own effort to reconstruct this genealogy, even if my aim here is not to provide a complete account of popular movements toward self-rule worldwide. It is nevertheless of great value to demonstrate and highlight, as does Bookchin, that oppressed people tend to converge on similar patterns of self-organization, namely around councils, and that this can be explained from the experience of communal life as it existed and still exists in some villages, towns, and free cities, where the burgers rule themselves. To this end, Bookchin (1996) explains that "in a very real sense, then, movements of oppressed strata or classes were clearly civic movements, rooted in the communal life of villages, towns, cities, and neighborhoods, not only landed estates, small shops, and factories—a fact that has not received the recognition it deserves from historians of the great revolutions" (Bookchin 1996, 5).

Indeed, Bookchin demonstrates that this motive is discernible in the late medieval peasant uprisings, such as the 1381 English Peasant Revolt, the 1420 Bohemian Taborite Commune, the 1350 Jacquerie revolts led by Etienne Marcel, as well as the early fourteenth-century Flemish Town Revolts (Bookchin 1996). Similar organizational patterns were constructed by the revolting peasants of sixteenth-century Germany, known as the German Peasant Wars.

The English Revolution saw the emergence of the "Levellers" and the rise of such leaders as Rainborough, Sexby, Wildman, and Petty, who took inspiration from the Swiss experience of direct, canton democracy (Bookchin 1996). After the defeat of the Levellers in the second civil war, groups such as the Diggers emerged, advancing "communistic ideas" (Bookchin 1996, 133).

The American Revolution also created spaces for communal politics and institutions to take root, for example, in the New England town hall meetings and in the program advanced by Thomas Paine in 1776 in his pamphlet *Common Sense*. In the Philadelphia of 1774, citizens created committees and found ways to wrestle power away from the Philadelphia government. According to Richard Ryerson, "In these twenty-six months more than 180 Philadelphians served on civilian committees; another hundred sat on the city militia's Committee of Privates. In rural Pennsylvania, another thousand persons were committeemen on civilian boards alone" (Ryerson 1978, 4).

What came to be known as Shays' Rebellion actually consisted of several "Committees of the People," all formed in the mid-1780s. According to Bookchin, "Their militias, moreover, were organized along typically libertarian lines, structured around county committees ('Committees of the People')" (Bookchin 1996, 236). Similar to the American Revolution, the French Revolution also provided opportunities for self-organization in the form of clubs and revolutionary societies that, in the city of Paris, mostly operated out of the forty-eight districts or sections. According to Bookchin, "The sixty electoral districts of Paris [later to be reduced to forty-eight] had essentially become permanent neighborhood assemblies of active citizens" (Bookchin 1996, 299). Through the revolutions of 1830 and 1848, France maintained a dense network of clubs and neighborhood-based associations, most of which practiced some degree of local self-government and cultivated radical ideas. This radicalism finally found a vehicle in the 1871 Paris Commune, which controlled the city for two months. Bookchin explains:

> As a substitute for the ministries that existed under the Government of National Defense, the Communal Council created nine commissions, whose operations were supervised and coordinated by an Executive Commission. Although each commission was charged with a specific governmental portfolio, the Communal Council as a whole tended to preempt most of the activities of its commissions, which often meant that many practical details were neglected except in emergencies. Coexisting with the Communal Council was the Central Committee of the National Guard . . . , as well as the Delegation of the Twenty Arrondissements, and the Trade Union Federation. In addition, popular clubs existed in every arrondissement of Paris, which also could be placed, together with the other organizations, under the rubric of "the Commune." (Bookchin 1998, 228)

The program of the Paris Commune did not ask for the abolition of private property, but instead for the liberty of work and for the universalization of power and property. On April 16, the council decreed that abandoned factories and workshops would be transformed into self-managed cooperatives and it sought to promote voluntary producers associations (Bookchin 1998, 233).

The historian John Merriman states that "the Commune was something of a 'permanent feast' of ordinary people who celebrated their freedom by appropriating the streets and squares of Paris" (Merriman 2014, 52). Revolutionary daily newspapers flooded the streets of Paris and artists found new freedoms under it. According to Merriman, the average communard was the average Parisian of the time: young, to a great extent born outside of Paris, and active as craftsman or artisan. "Only 2 percent had secondary education" (Merriman 2014, 61). Women were communards, even if men outnumbered them. According to Merriman, "Indeed, the solidarity and militancy of Parisian women, who had suffered such hardship during the Prussian siege, jumps out as one of the most remarkable aspects of the Paris Commune" (Merriman 2014, 64).

The Russian Revolution provided yet another opportunity for local self-rule and communal organization. In 1905 and again in 1917, local soviets were created, where soviet translates into "community." The Petrograd Soviet formed in February of 1917 against the warnings of Lenin and the Bolsheviks. According to Bookchin,

> In the months that followed the February uprising, soviets were established in the *uezdy* and the provinces of the old empire, while the large cities and towns of the realm formed municipal soviets. Often even a village *skhod* would be renamed a "soviet," although many of them remained direct democracies, in contrast to the representative system used by the urban soviets. By the end of 1917 an estimated 900 soviets existed in Russia. (Bookchin 2004, 168–69)

Inspired by the creation of political and administrative soviets, factory workers in Petrograd formed factory worker committees. Still in 1917, soldiers and peasants followed suit. Facing an allied front of Germans, French, and British, however, council power in Russia gave way to a centralized Bolshevik state, run and controlled by Lenin and his party, putting an end to soviet rule (Bookchin 2004, 212ff).

Attempts to establish local self-rule and councils, however, did not start in Western Europe and did not die at the hands of the Bolsheviks. In medieval Spain, local councils filled the power gap that the fleeing monarchy left behind. Open Cabildos were instituted and also reached the Americas, where they continue to survive among indigenous and black populations to this day (Bayle 1952; Tapia 1965). In 1936, Spanish Anarchists provided a space for the peasants of Aragon and Andalucía to form local cooperatives and take over the means of production previously held by large landowners.

To this day, it appears that whenever communities organize spontaneously during times of crisis or once hierarchical power structures have been smashed, councils are the way to organize, as in contemporary southeastern Turkey, Iraq, and Syria, where the Kurdish minority is seeking to construct a council democracy (TATORT 2013). Many hunter-gatherers, such as the Mbuti Pygmies, organize in egalitarian ways to this day, without relying on pronounced hierarchies (Turnbull 1968). Colin Turnbull indeed shows how the Mbuti people of the Congo live not only in harmony and peace with each other, without the formalized and institutionalized leadership of a king or chief, but also live in peace and harmony with the forest—giving the title to Turnbull's book *The Forest People*. In their lives, there is no space or need for evil spirits and fear of the unknown. Instead they organize in extended family clans and base their social structure on mutual aid and solidarity.

Mutual aid, according to Peter Kropotkin (2014 [1902]), is as much a factor in human evolution as competition and is actually the "natural" tendency of human groups. It is only through abuse and distortion, exerted by the privileged few who seek ways to first construct and then defend their unmerited privileges that hierarchy and rule enters into human affairs. Kropotkin explains:

> But it is not love and even sympathy upon which Society is based in mankind. It is the conscience—be it at the stage of an instinct—of human solidarity. It is the unconscious recognition of the force that is borrowed by each man from the practice of mutual aid; of the close dependency of ever one's happiness upon the happiness of all; and of the sense of justice, or equity, which brings the individual to consider the rights of every other individual as equal to his own. Upon this broad and necessary foundation the still higher moral feelings are developed. (Kropotkin 2014 [1902], 7)

Following Service, "The first stage is that of direct communal property and it underlies all the others, everywhere. It is best seen in historical times in the Orient and in Slavonic communes" (Service 1975, 35).

When given a chance, it appears that most people seek ways to organize in such a way that they maintain control over their lives and their work, thus forming councils of equals and taking over factories or agricultural units so they can protect their work and secure the benefits and rewards of their labor. Theory, not practice, led to the abolishment of private property and abuse, not reason, to the establishment of political hierarchies.

CONCLUSION

Some factors seem clear and as such can guide the empirical search for alternatives: Popular sovereignty is and must be the basis of any democratic system. The lawmaking process must remain with the people for "popular sovereignty" to exist. For "the state" to remain close to society, we cannot hand it over to a group of professionals, elected or not. Where and when we have to choose people to take on administrative tasks that concern us all, their tenure must be limited and incumbency must be severely limited, if not undermined all together. Politics, after all, does not require special knowledge, as Protagoras argued as early as in the fifth century BCE.

Democracy means first and foremost self-rule, and self-rule cannot be done for others. Democracy and representation are opposites. A representative democracy, thus, is not a democracy at all. It is a system in which a group of people makes decisions for others, the majority. Depending on the ways the elites are selected and on their composition, such a system should be more appropriately called an aristocracy, a plutocracy, or simply "elite rule." It does not change the character of the system if these elites were elected or if they took power themselves. They are elites and make decisions for others.

The basic insight, expressed by Immanuel Kant, quoted earlier, remains as true today as it did 200 years ago: *Nobody can compel me to be happy in his own way.* Politics, properly defined, is the realm of reaching collective agreement on how to live, under what laws and regulations. It is by definition based on deliberation and mutual agreement. It does not require special knowledge. This is confirmed by the fact that none of the political elites currently making decisions for us having any special knowledge in most of the fields they control. In many cases, they apply one set of rules and criteria to themselves and another, entirely different, to the "rest" of us. This is not surprising. Leaders will lead and power has to be administered once given to a group of people. The solution to this problem cannot be the selection or election of new leaders. It can only be in a much broader distribution and dilution of political power.

A people without political power will become an individualistic, materialistic, cynical, and self-interested people. Many famous political scientist and philosophers have demonstrated the validity of this dynamic. Without power, there is no responsibility toward the collective. And without responsibility toward the collective, there is no society, let alone community. This is what we experience right now in many of the "advanced" democracies. The consequences of such a state of affairs are dismal. However, there is also hope. Wielding more political power, communities are likely to nurture more responsibility among community members. Politically empowered local communities also promise to enlarge the individual freedom of their members, as individual freedom and agency must be upheld and defended by the community. The road toward more individual freedom and agency is thus one of more powerful local communities.

Empowered local communities that wield political power to make decisions about their own lives and economies are the "normal" way of collective organizing, as the historical examples discussed earlier clearly show. If left to themselves, most people will form councils of equals and they will seek ways to protect their work and the fruits of their labor. The path toward political hierarchy and alienation from labor is one traced by elites, despots, and theorists, who use analytical models not to understand the world, but to mold it.

This discussion indicates several important factors that should be taken into account when conducting an empirical assessment of the possibilities and conditionalities of direct or self-rule. In sum, they are:

1. The many authors who have analyzed participatory mechanisms (Fung 2006; Abers 2000; Baiocchi 2005; Avritzer 2009) all point out one condition for these mechanisms to work: participants must have the power to make relevant and consequential decisions for them to continue to participate. This very basic logic seems to apply to broader political processes as well: if people feel powerless, they are less likely to participate. Or put more simply, if there is nothing to decide, why should anyone participate? The knowledge that one's opinion and actions do not matter to the collective must be seen as one of the core reasons for widespread political apathy and alienation from politics. Political ignorance is not the cause, but the effect of nonparticipation.[7] Citizen involvement, in whatever form, must be real and bear tangible results. This is a sine qua non, or necessary condition, for sustained participation in public or common affairs and politics. It is certainly not sufficient.

2. The theoretical literature discussed earlier clearly highlights the importance of deliberation for democracy. Deliberation, that is, the possibility to discuss public matters broadly, is certainly another necessary condition for sustained participation. For deliberation to produce the desired outcomes, it must be inclusive and free so that all those potentially affected by a decision can have a voice in its making and feel free to say what they think and want.

3. It also seems clear that mutual or shared interests are not a given that can be produced exogenously (Ostrom 2015). While this has been tried, through such mechanisms as fostering nationalism, the negative side effects of nationalism outweigh the benefits it is able to bring. Nationalism is also not a viable or desirable solution for a more and more interconnected world and the shared problems we all face. Instead of seeking exogenous ways to secure shared interest, it rather seems promising to search for a more procedural approach: mutual interest is the by-product of mutual obligation and criss-crossing responsibilities. If people perceive themselves as stakeholders, they are more likely to participate. If they have to interact and reach collective decisions together and if they are connected to each other through mutual obligations and responsibilities, shared interest is very likely to be the immediate side effect or outcome.

4. For self-rule to be meaningful and consequential, it must be local. Administrative decentralization and a significant devolution of power to the local, municipal level must be a central part of any reform or policy aiming at establishing strong and meaningful direct rule and self-determination. This does not mean that states are obsolete or to be overcome all together. It does mean to supplement central government with local, self-ruling government structures in which ordinary citizens can have a voice in the shaping of their own destinies—particularly with regard to the laws they

will be subject to. As such, federalism must be the default institutional design of any larger polity. The more citizens and local communities are invested with decision-making power and the necessary resources to carry them out, the less "state" we need, the utopia being a situation in which the citizens *are* the state. While getting there is certainly a process that requires practice, training, and experience, concrete steps in this direction are being made wherever local communities make decisions on budgets, development plans, or new laws.

5. Lawmaking has to be rethought. Instead of more laws and more compli- cated laws, we should think of ways to increase the stakes of citizens in the lawmaking process, something that should start at the local level, but could also involve innovative ways to give citizens a say in the crafting of those laws they have to live under. While there is no substitute for face-to-face interaction and deliberation, we could easily devise a "legislative duty" and involve ordinary citizens in lawmaking, similar to the ways they are already involved in the judicial system through jury duty. For larger col- lective decisions, mechanisms must be created that allow for meaningful citizen input. Here too alienation and nonparticipation must be seen not as the cause but as the effect of powerlessness. If a TV channel can get thou- sands of people to call in and vote for their favorite American Idol, there is no good reason to believe that we could not use similar mechanisms for making collective political decisions, as long as the consequences of such actions are concrete and tangible, affecting all those who participate.

NOTES

1. See also Carpenter 1996.

2. In 2010, the average annual salary of a member of Congress was $174,000, plus benefits, thus 535 × $174,000 = over $100 million per year. Given that these legisla- tors meet on average for some 160 days per year, we pay them about $1,000 per day of work. Each state, of course, reproduces this model on a smaller scale.

3. http://www.dailymail.co.uk/news/article-2329554/EU-expenses-MEPs- Brussels-earn-740-average-citizen-enjoy-free-haircuts-gallons-petrol.html.

4. The participatory budgeting mechanisms, as originally introduced in Porto Alegre, Brazil, provide a good example of a much more fruitful process.

5. Nils Schmid, Minister of Finance and the Economy in the state of Baden Wuertemberg (SPD) served on six boards (Aufsichtsraeten) in 2013; Heiko Maas (SPD), Minister of the Economy in Saarland, also served on six. The Bavarian Finance Minister Markus Soeder (CSU) served on four in 2013 (Scheer 2013).

6. Most European and Latin American countries have such legal codes. In these countries, one never hears complaints about "not enough laws." However, one can

often hear complaints about "too many laws" and confusing legal systems, requiring highly specialized lawyers to even understand them.

7. A quick look at elected representatives confirms this assessment, already advanced by Rousseau: elected representatives are not trained and do not have specialized knowledge of "politics." They join the ranks of those able to make decisions about public life, and as soon as they do, their alienation and apathy is over. Active participation breeds interest.

Chapter 3

Beyond Capitalism

In this second and last theoretical chapter, I will delve a bit deeper into the economic contradictions growing out of high asset concentration and economic inequality. I do so in order to lay the last piece of groundwork on which the empirical research must rest.

The chapter starts with an analysis of markets and what the concept "market" means and stands for. I seek to show that there are many different types of markets, some of which are highly contributive to fulfilling our needs, wants, and desires, while others, namely capitalist markets, work to the detriment of our collective well-being (Harvey 2014). My central argument here is that markets are not bad per se and that we need to find ways to rein in markets so they fulfill their purpose of allowing for the interchange of goods and services, while also building trust, community, and sociability. Anyone who has ever been in a traditional African market or a Middle Eastern souk has witnessed that markets can be places of encounter, friendship, the renewal of trust, the interchange of news, and as such central to any society. Those are the kinds of markets we need and need to protect or bring back.

After discussing markets, I explore the connection of inequality and democracy and self-rule, relying to a great extent on the recent works by Carles Boix (2015) and Thomas Piketty (2014). Both authors convincingly demonstrate that inequality undermines the very foundations of democratic self-rule. To make this point even stronger, I delve further into the contradictions and disastrous consequences of high asset concentration, identifying it as the main factor undermining both equality and equal opportunity. This section is titled "Irrational Capitalism." It relies heavily on the work of Fred Hirsch (1976). After having provided the theoretical basis for the analysis of inequality and asset concentration, I highlight some of their consequences, particularly a yet undertheorized aspect of high asset concentration: the ability of the superrich to withdraw assets from general accessible markets via high price mechanisms. The easiest and clearest way to demonstrate this phenomenon is through a brief discussion of the real estate market in those cities where millionaires and billionaires abound, such as New York or London. The rich effectively take away space and opportunities from all of us, as the richest 1 percent of wealth holders already own 50 percent of all household wealth (Credit Suisse 2015). Credit Suisse, who produces data on worldwide wealth distribution, also found that "while the bottom half of adults collectively own less than 1 percent of total wealth, the richest decile holds 87.7 percent of assets, and the top percentile alone accounts for half of total household wealth" (Credit Suisse 2015, 11). The main insight growing out of this analysis is that we would all be better off without the top 1 percent.

Education provides another case able to elucidate this phenomenon, as elite education is undermining the chances of all of those unable to afford it. The only way to counteract the pernicious effects of the rich undermining the opportunities and life chances of average people is, in my mind, to institute limits to asset holding and policies that bar the passing on of assets accumulated during a lifetime to the next generation. While this might seem a radical proposal, I dedicate the rest of this chapter to demonstrating that those two proposals (limits to asset holding and blocking the passing on of assets to the next generation) can indeed count on a long and fairly mainstream pedigree, particularly in American political thought. They are central themes in the writings of Thomas Jefferson, James Madison, John Locke, the young John Adams, and even Adam Smith.

After the American founding fathers, this theme was picked up and further developed by the anarchists of the International Workingmen's Association, most notoriously by Pierre-Joseph Proudhon, Mikhail Bakunin, and Peter Kropotkin. However, the proposal to limit asset holding and restrict inheritance to a maximum also finds support in the British Nobel Prize–winning economist James Edward Meade (1965) and is further advanced by the anything but radical liberal philosopher John Rawls (2001) and his equally liberal counterpart the economist Amartya Sen (2009), as I demonstrate in the section on "Property-Owning Democracy and Pre-Distribution" toward the end of this chapter. More recently, such prominent authors as Anthony Atkinson (2015) and Jacob Hacker (2011) have proposed different policies aimed at achieving the same goal: securing equal opportunity by avoiding some pulling away too far from the mainstream and thus enshrining unequal opportunities for themselves.

The chapter concludes by highlighting the importance and urgency of instituting such policies as the only viable and peaceful alternative to the kinds of opportunities that are provided otherwise, under capitalist conditions, by crisis, war, and economic breakdown. We simply cannot hope for the next financial meltdown for average people to be able to afford decent housing, education, or health.

MARKETS

At this stage, the word "market" has lost its ability to capture an ensuing reality, as many market interactions have become decoupled not only from labor, but also from personal face-to-face interactions. They have become highly abstract and alienated. And so have the profits made on those markets. David Ricardo explained in 1817 that "possessing utility, commodities derive their exchangeable value from two sources: from their scarcity, and from the quantity of labour required to obtain them" (Ricardo 1817, 1). According to Karl Marx, "The value of a commodity is determined by the *total quantity of labor* contained in it. . . . The *surplus value*, or that part of the total value of the commodity in which the *surplus labor* or *unpaid labor* of the working man is realized, I call *Profit*" (Marx 2000 [1865], 21; emphasis in original).

With the securitization of markets, that is, the introduction of stock market capitalism, values and profits have decoupled from labor (Dore 2000; Roy 1997). No longer can we assess the value of a commodity by the amount of labor contained in it. Today, a broker or even a private investor can earn millions of dollars in a day simply by clicking a mouse on his or her computer and selling and buying securities. The values associated with some financial products are fictitious to a great extent, based not on the labor contained in them, but on the price for which they are traded.

To make matters worse, banks have designed financial products that only very vaguely relate back to the original commodity upon which its value is constructed. Derivatives and different futures and insurance products offered on commodities become further and further retrieved from the original commodity, making it very easy and morally cheap to buy and sell them without bothering, or even knowing, what the original commodity was. According to David Harvey, "The percentage of total profits in the US attributable to financial services rose from around 15 percent in 1970 to 40 percent by 2005" (Harvey 2011, 51). For Harvey, the increased volatility and the global reach of financial transactions was one of the main factors producing the 2008 global financial crisis.

Trading securities and related financial products such as insurances and derivatives allows for profits that are not sustained in reality and not based on labor or even scarcity. Some stocks can rise based on a mere word uttered by the chair of the Fed, only to drop days, sometimes minutes, later. The values created are not grounded in reality.

The more capital one has to invest, the more profit can be made. Thomas Piketty (2014) has clearly demonstrated this reality by examining the publicly available data on university endowments: "the return increases rapidly with the size of the endowment" (Piketty, 2014, 316). Piketty shows that the average real annual rate of return, after deduction of inflation and all administrative costs and financial fees, for 1980 to 2010 was 10.2 percent for Harvard, Yale, and Princeton, who started with endowments in the magnitude of $20 to $30 billion each. For endowments of less than $100 million, the rate of return was 6.2 percent (Piketty 2014, 316). Thus the more money one has when entering these markets, the more profit one can make. As a result, the large fortunes of the superrich are not based on hard work, or even luck. They are based on returns on capital and real estate, as well as on the salaries of CEOs. As authors such as Thomas Piketty have shown, we are witnessing the return of the turn of the twentieth century rentier societies, when 10 percent of the society controlled 90 percent of the national wealth—the only differences is that today, most rents are made not from land, but from real estate, capital, and by managers. One of Piketty's subheads thus reads "The Rentier—Enemy of Democracy" (Piketty 2014, 297).

The profits made on such markets are ultimately not justifiable. Nobody "deserves" to make a million dollars by simply betting on a security, not knowing, in most cases, what kind of reality this financial product stands on, or if it stands on one at all. The markets on which these sorts of financial products are traded are highly alienating, disconnecting us from the realities associated with the commodities we trade.

Serious academic engagement with markets requires a recapturing of the real-life and everyday dimensions involved in their working. Instead of abstract theorizing, we need more concrete and applied analyses of real-life markets in different places of the world. Markets are places where people interact to interchange goods and services. This is done in myriad different ways depending on the specific set of rules in place, as well as the different backgrounds, interests, and strategies employed by the interacting parties. No two markets are the same, nor is the outcome of a bargain struck. According to Arturo Escobar, we need to anthropologize the economy. He explains that "the Western economy can be anthropologized and shown to be made up of a peculiar set of discourses and practices—very peculiar at that in the history of cultures" (Escobar 2011, 59). This indeed applies to all markets, Western or not. Markets are specific places, if real or virtual, entered by different people with diverging interests and strategies to pursue them—even if self-interest can be assumed to drive most that enter any market. However, beyond self-interested, expressed in "making a good deal," many other factors are always at work. Even what "a good deal" represents will differ depending on circumstance and the specific interests of all involved. Very few universals apply to market interactions, and if they do, they operate at high levels of abstraction, far removed from real-life markets.

Human beings can and have created any kind of market they want. Real markets are richly textured and deeply embedded in local cultures. Making short-term, individual profits in disregard of all long-term results and potential harm to others is but one of many possible motivations to engage in them. To assume that all those entering a market will do so based on vile principle alone is not only shortsighted, but will produce faulty explanations and wrong predictions.

Markets that build trust and community abound in this world—in Africa, Latin America (actually not so much in "Latin," but in Native and Indigenous America), in Asia, and, maybe most famously, in the Middle East. The souks, bazaars, and medinas of Syria, Lebanon, Iraq, Morocco, Tunisia, and many others allow us to see what markets can be today: dense networks, deeply embedded in local cultures, set up to satisfy needs, regulated by local customs and traditions, and institutionalized in such a way as to protect repeated and long-term interactions among people that either already know each other or get to know and trust each other through their repeated market interactions. Most of these markets are indeed so culturally embedded and regulated that no written contracts are needed to ensure compliance. A handshake is traditionally enough. Instead of undermining trust, these markets build trust with every new round of interaction.

Local markets that involve repeated face-to-face interactions certainly function much differently than virtual markets that do not involve any personal contact and do not lead to repeated transactions. The more abstract a market interaction, the more likely participants are to engage in a base and shortsighted manner. After all, as we have learned from psychology, most people are willing to take nasty action as long as the consequences and the victims of such actions remain unknown to them (Milgram 2009 [1974]).

If eye contact, let alone the proverbial handshake, are no longer required to seal a deal, honorable behavior cannot be assumed. The more virtual and abstract the interaction and the more distant the partners, the more incentives for cheating, unsustainable, unethical, and shortsighted behavior. Buying stock online on the New York Stock Exchange from a company promising high yields while polluting a river in a specific village in China will most likely not bother a German stockbroker. In the absence of vigorous and effective rules, which are notoriously difficult to enforce in a global trading environment, nasty, unsustainable, and shortsighted behavior is very likely to ensue. In other words, if everybody tries to make as much money as quickly as possible without having to face the consequences of such interactions, nasty behavior will become the rule and markets will become unsustainable. The latest global financial crisis gave ample testimony to this tendency.

As markets become more global, more virtual, less personal, and more dominated by corporations who only follow a highly instrumental profit motive, competition tends to become more ruthless and consumption more driven by concerns over (global) social positioning and relative advantage. In such a world, nasty behavior tends to become the norm and cheating is to be expected. Long-term goals are at constant risk of being undermined by immediate profits and those who were able to enter markets earlier and/or were endowed with more assets.

This is the reality of capitalist markets, that is, markets that are dominated by the few who use their wealth and power to their own advantage and to further boost their privileges. To call such markets "free" adds insult to error, as the freedom contemporary Western-type capitalist markets offer only applies to the rich. This type of market is characterized by anonymous interaction, virtual connection, monopolies, cartels, corporate fraud, tax evasion, and the creation of a caste of superrich billionaires. It is not a fair or rational market, as it is not growing out of fair or rational market interaction. As I have already argued, fair and rational market interactions build trust, whereas corporate-dominated capitalist market interactions undermine it. Rational market interaction builds community, whereas Western-type capitalist market interaction undermines it. Rational market interaction is sustainable and long term, whereas stock market capitalist market interaction aims at short-term profit, no matter the burden on the environment and future generations. Rational market interaction protects equal opportunity, whereas capitalist market interaction protects the unfair advantages of capitalists. Rational markets are possible and a reality, as are capitalist markets.

Capitalist markets are not universal, not necessary, and not the only way to structure human interactions aimed at barter and interchange. Capitalist markets are Northern- and Western-dominated markets upheld by Northern and Western institutions, laws, and regulations rooted in colonialism, exploitation, destruction, and domination. They are markets for the rich, defended by the rich, to the benefit of the rich. They receive the endorsement of Northern and Western economists. They are not free, not fair, and not sustainable. They undermine trust, community, the environment, and the future of the species—human, animal, and plant alike. That alone should make us refrain from calling them "rational." The freedom they provide is a shallow freedom that threatens to enslave us all. We need to urgently decolonize markets and rescue those political institutions that have for millennia upheld and protected indigenous markets, African markets, medinas, souks, bazaars, and all those other markets where people engage in long-term, repeated, and hence trust- and community-building barter and exchange.

BEYOND SCARCITY: THE CURSE OF
ASSET CONCENTRATION

Carles Boix (2015) has recently demonstrated, relying on game theory, that inequality undermines cooperation. In his analysis of pre-Neolithic as well as historical and contemporary hunter and gatherer societies and small stateless settlement communities, Boix finds that rational, self-interested individuals and groups will cooperate, without needing a state to coerce them to do so, as long as living conditions are broadly equal and technological advance is broadly shared. He finds that "the price of growth is then inequality. And inequality brings about, in turn, the breakdown of cooperation that exists in the 'state of nature'" (Boix 2015, 9).

Given his methodology, Boix is quick to formulate a general rule: "under a condition of anarchy all individuals cooperate among themselves and follow a productive strategy provided there is one key condition in place: that all their resources remain similar or, in other words, that there are no substantial changes in the initial condition of equality that characterizes the state of nature" (Boix 2015, 22). Boix also highlights the importance of open time horizons, of technological innovation and who controls it, and of mobility. His findings are confirmed by all of the anthropological and archeological accounts we have from pre-Neolithic societies, as well as from modern and contemporary stateless societies, which demonstrate that cooperation among individuals and groups is our natural state of affairs (Kropotkin 2014). In fact, long preceding the game theoretical insights produced by Boix (2015), who in turn relies on Robert Axelrod's (2006) earlier work on "tit-for-tat" repeated games, the French anthropologist Marcel Mauss (2000, first published in English in 1954) has affirmed that gift making is in most societies a way to establish reciprocal obligations.

Such a system of reciprocal sharing and cooperation is only disrupted or ended when some individuals or groups start accumulating more assets than everybody else. In such cooperative societies, culture plays a central role in sanctioning such egoistic, accumulative behavior.

Boix's findings are worth quoting in detail:

> human societies with no political hierarchies exhibit relatively homogeneous interpersonal patterns of consumption, high levels of wealth equality, and very limited levels of intergenerational transmission of (nongenetic) assets. Moreover, a multitude of ethnographies reveal that self-enforced or spontaneous cooperation is the result of a long-run tit-for-tat game conducted among strategic, self-interested individuals that try to maximize their income while making sure that no other individual gets more than what they earn. (Boix 2015, 23)

For Boix, "cooperation is only sustainable if there is some fundamental equality of income" (Boix 2015, 28). He also finds that such cooperation is only possible as long as the communities are relatively small as, in the language of game theory, a large number of individuals participating in this tit-for-tat game will "undermine the expectations of future exchange" and "shorten the shadow of the future" (Boix 2015, 29). In other words, both equality and the insurance of reciprocal rewards are hard to control and enforce in large communities. Concretely, his data show that "whereas the probability that foragers live in small settlements (those with less than two hundred individuals) is 0.83, it falls to 0.27 for extensive agricultural societies and to 0.08 for intensive agricultural communities" (Boix 2015, 42).

Another interesting finding produced by Boix's game theoretical analysis, which nevertheless relies on extensive empirical material mostly obtained from the *Ethnographic Atlas*,[1] is that any community relying on cooperation must put in place mechanisms of risk sharing. Risk sharing, and hence cooperative stability, is successful as long as two conditions are met: external shocks must be random and uncorrelated across individuals (Boix 2015, 32). The implications of this finding are far reaching, particularly with regard to race: when external shocks systematically affect one group more than another, equality is undermined and cooperation will break down, as it is not reasonable to cooperate with those that are repeatedly and constantly the ones losing out. Cooperation among ethnic groups that have been given different chances to succeed is thus undermined.

Boix's findings allow us to extrapolate that the extreme inequality of incomes and wealth we witness almost everywhere today undermine the very basis of democracy, as they contradict the core on which democracy must rest: that everybody has an equal opportunity to be successful, that everybody is fundamentally equal, that everybody bears an equal amount of risk, and that nobody should be privileged by birth, race, gender, or creed. While some countries have been able to protect these promises to a larger extent, particularly in northern Europe, where inequalities of income and wealth are the least pronounced in the world, the global tendency seems geared toward more and more inequality, with some countries, such as the United States, on the forefront of the general trend. According to Thomas Piketty,

Global inequality of wealth in the early 2010s appears to be comparable in magnitude to that observed in Europe in 1900–1910. The top thousandth seems to own nearly 20 percent of total global wealth today, the top centile about 50 percent, and the top decile somewhere between 80 and 90 percent. The bottom half of the global wealth distribution undoubtedly owns less than 5 percent of total global wealth. Concretely, the wealthiest 0.1 percent of people on the planet, some 4.5 million out of an adult population of 4.5 billion, apparently possesses fortunes on the order of 10 million euros on average, or nearly 200 times average global wealth of 60,000 euros per adult, amounting in aggregate to nearly

20 percent of total global wealth. The wealthiest 1 percent—45 million people out of 4.5 billion—have about 3 million euros apiece and average (broadly speaking, this group consists of those individuals whose personal fortunes exceeds 1 million euros). This is about 50 times the size of the average global fortune, or 50 percent of the global wealth in aggregate. (Piketty 2014, 309)

In the United States, according to the same author, "the most recent survey by the Federal Reserve, which covers the same years [2010–2011], indicates that the top decile own 72 percent of America's wealth, while the bottom half claim just 2 percent" (Piketty 2014, 184). The superrich make their money not through work. Instead they let their money work for them, a euphemism for making profits while not working at all. According to Piketty, "past a certain threshold, all large fortunes, whether inherited or entrepreneurial in origin, grow at extremely high rates, regardless of whether the owner of the fortune works or not" (Piketty 2014, 309).

IRRATIONAL CAPITALISM

Another insightful author of the dynamics associated with advanced capitalist systems is Fred Hirsch (1976). Hirsch argues that most private consumption bears a social component so that the amount of satisfaction gained from it is reduced when too many people share in:

Advance in society is possible only by moving to a higher place among one's fellows, that is, by improving one's performance in relations to other people's performances. If everyone stands on tiptoe, no one sees better. Where social interaction of this kind is present, individual action is no longer a sure means to fulfill individual choice: the preferred outcome may be attainable only through collective action. (We all agree explicitly or implicitly not to stand on tiptoe). The familiar dichotomy between individual choice and collective provision or regulation then dissolves. Competition among isolated individuals in the free market entails hidden costs for others and ultimately for themselves. (Hirsch 1976, 5)

In other words, supposedly "free" capitalist markets force us into a rat race without end in which we all compete against each other, using every little bit of advantage to carve out a better relative position for ourselves. Given the limited amount of space and resources of our planet, this fight of all against all gets harder and harder as more people compete against each other over limited or scarce resources and no happy end is in sight. Instead of having machines and computers do our work for us so we can have more free time and relaxation, we are forced to use every new technical invention to become even more efficient, productive, and competitive. Technical innovation has become a curse. We have never worked so hard and we have never been as efficient as we are today. And we have never been as neurotic, sick, and psychologically ill.

Classical and neoclassical theorizing about the workings of markets all assume the rational behavior of all market-participating agents both in production and in consumption. Thorstein Veblen (1857–1929) was probably the first economist to assume irrational spending patterns among the affluent. Their "conspicuous consumption" is aimed at increasing their social standing vis-à-vis other market participants. Once basic needs are covered, economic behavior tends to become less and less rational and more and more influenced by cultural and social dynamics, as such economists as Robert Frank (1999, 2011), Avner Offer (2007), Fred Hirsch (1976), Joseph Schumpeter (1976), Herbert Simon (1990), and Thorstein Veblen (2009) have clearly demonstrated. While general equilibrium and marginal utility theories could still be saved with reference to the "rationality" of seeking status advantage, Fred Hirsch (1976) dealt a final blow to the idea that market participants, once they have met their basic needs, act rationally and based on economic motivation alone.

Hirsch argues that once basic needs are met, the social components of economic behavior increase and competition moves into the arena of positional or relational goods. The satisfaction from consuming such goods is not derived from their absolute value or utility, but depends on the behavior of all the other market participants in a given market. The more people compete over limited goods, the more connected these goods become to the behavior of all the other market participants. These goods only deliver the expected satisfaction as long as not everybody else has them. Educational degrees are a case in point. If everybody has a college degree, having a college degree no longer guarantees access to good jobs, and educational requirements will rise. At the same time, the costs in terms of investment required to have the same outcome also rise, in a process Hirsch calls "screening" (Hirsch 1976, 41).

Hirsch also demonstrates that in competitive markets over limited goods, the maintenance of privilege relies on the better starting position. When applying this insight to the relational good of "scenic property," Hirsch explains that "what matters in the acquisition of scenic property is less one's own present income than the present and past incomes of other people. To secure the objects in the auction catalogue, it is relative rather than absolute income and wealth that count. A head start in this competition for relative ascendancy accrues to those who acquired such assets in earlier, less expensive auctions" (Hirsch 1976, 36). After all, there are only so many properties available on the beaches of this world. Furthermore, once the beach gets crowded, the beach house loses its ability to satisfy, as it can no longer deliver the values of quietness and solitude.

Hirsch's logic is powerful. If left unregulated, markets will deliver less and less satisfaction while demanding more and more input from us. Because most private consumption has an inherent social dimension in which what one person consumes is influenced by others, all participants will be worse off at the end if no rules are in place that oblige all (Frank 2011).

The consequences of these dynamics are all too obvious: under unrestrained conditions, competition steadily rises. There is no catching up with those who entered markets earlier or with more assets. Instead, demands and requirements will keep on rising without delivering increasing returns. Market participants are required to invest more to obtain the same, and competition will steadily rise. If finding a job in yesterday's market required a high school diploma, today it requires a university degree. Even though the required investment (time and money) have risen, the returns have not, as earnings have remained the same. Marginal returns have decreased. Today's youth will not be able to increase their standard of living compared to their parents, at least in advanced markets. Hirsch calls the private goods that have a public component "positional goods" because the satisfaction that can be derived from their consumption is determined by the consumption of other participants in the same market. Add resource scarcity and the resulting scenario is one of a never-ending rat race in which the main factor determining the chances of being on top is the amount of assets with which one enters the competition:

> What the wealthy have today can no longer be delivered to the rest of us tomorrow; yet as we individually grow richer, that is what we expect. The dynamic interaction between material and positional sectors becomes malign. Instead of alleviating the unmet demands on the economic system, material growth at this point exacerbates them. The locus of instability is the divergence between what is possible for the individual and what is possible for all individuals. Increased material resources enlarge the demand for positional goods, a demand that can be satisfied for some only by frustrating demand by others. The intensified positional competition involves an increase in needs for the individual, in the sense that additional resources are required to achieve a given level of welfare. In the positional sector, individuals chase each others' tails. The race gets longer for the same price. (Hirsch 1976, 67)

This situation is worse in all those markets in which the main factor responsible for creating value is no longer labor but capital. In markets in which value is mostly based on financial transactions and millions can be made with the click of a mouse, the amount of time and effort spent to produce a product no longer matters. What matters is how many assets one can allocate—and how quickly. The proverbial twenty-two-year-old broker dealing in derivatives and hedge funds can "earn" millions in a few seconds—and lose them again the next. As the unrestrained financial system creates volatility for all of us, it also changes the way that value is created and how profits are made. In such a thoroughly financialized world, the amount of financial assets one holds when entering a market almost exclusively determines the outcomes.

To a great extent, this is so because of the nature of compound interest. The consequences of compound interest are far reaching and easily underestimated. People with capital, that is, people who have money to invest, can more than double their initial principal every twelve years if their average return stays above 6 percent annually. If they add some money to the pot every month, their earnings increase exponentially. Donald Trump, who said he "only" received the meager sum of $1 million from his dad when he started out as a businessman (1973), could have earned over $4 million had he simply put all his money in the American bond market, assuming an average annual yield of 7 percent. In contrast, someone saving $500 every year during the same twenty-five years and also earning 7 percent on his or her investment would have been able to accumulate $380,000. The lesson from compound interest is clear: the earlier one starts investing, the greater the earnings, and the more one has to invest initially, the more the earnings are later on. This also means that there is no catching up to people who have entered capital markets early on and with more money. You can save and invest $1,000 every month and end up with some $400,000 after twenty years of investing at an average return of 5 percent. If, however, you started out with $1 million, you will end up with $2.7 million after twenty years (assuming the same 5 percent return) without any additional monthly payments— over six times as much. This also means that once someone has accumulated large amounts of capital, he or she can just live off the generated interest and dividends. The popular saying that "the first million is the hardest to earn" can easily be translated into "the first million is the *only* one you need to earn," as $1 million, assuming a quite reasonable 5 percent interest rate, produces $50,000 interest every year, which is about the median income of American families. If only part of the earned interest is reinvested, the interest-earning capital as well as the monthly earnings increase exponentially every year.[2] In 2014, according to Glassdoor, an economic research blog that relies on official SEC data, the average American CEO pay across 441 of the 500 S&P 500 American companies was $13.8 million per year (https://www.glassdoor.com/research/ceo-pay-ratio/#_ftn1).

In a world in which what matters most is not how hard one is willing to work but how much money or how many assets one can bring to the game, the dream of making it from dishwasher to millionaire is no longer realistic (if it ever was). You can work three jobs all your life and not even come close to the amount of money a broker can make in one day by simply investing large amounts of money, or the annual interest earned by someone investing millions.

In such a world, work will not make you rich. Capital will, and those with capital will become even richer, while those relying on their work will be stuck. This is the world a lot of us have been living in since the 1980s. Wealth and assets have become more concentrated and decoupled from average incomes and, as a consequence, opportunities for the average income earners have diminished.

Nowhere are the consequences of relational markets clearer than in race relations, as here, one racial group, whites, benefit today from a 300-year head start on competitive markets and blacks are asked in most post-slavery societies to "let go" of the past and compete with whites "on equal terms." However, considering the advantages that past accumulation can produce, nothing is further from "equal terms" than a competition of former slaveholders and former slaves—even if they both enjoy equal rights and protections today. It should come as no surprise that in 2016, the United States counted 2 total of some 10.4 million millionaires, but only 35,000 black millionaires among them.

According to the PEW Research Center, "From 2010 to 2013, the median wealth of non-Hispanic white households increased from $138,600 to $141,900, or by 2.4%. Meanwhile, the median wealth of non-Hispanic black households fell 33.7%, from $16,600 in 2010 to $11,000 in 2013. Among Hispanics, median wealth decreased by 14.3%, from $16,000 to $13,700" (http://www.pewresearch.org/fact-tank/2014/12/12/racial-wealth-gaps -great-recession/).

Today, asset holding and wealth in the United States is more unequal along racial lines than it was under South African apartheid (in the United States in 2014, white households held eighteen times more wealth than blacks, whereas in apartheid South Africa whites held fifteen times the wealth of blacks). Inequality, in other words, has never been as high as it is now and it has clear racial dimensions. According to Asante-Muhammad and colleagues,

Over the past 30 years, the average wealth of White families has grown by 84%—1.2 times the rate of growth for the Latino population and three times the rate of growth for the Black population. If the past 30 years were to repeat, the next three decades would see the average wealth of White households increase by over $18,000 per year, while Latino and Black households would see their respective wealth increase by about $2,250 and $750 per year. Over the past 30 years, the wealth of the *Forbes 400* richest Americans has grown by an average of 736%—10 times the rate of growth for the Latino population and 27 times the rate of growth for the Black population. Today, the wealthiest *100* members of the *Forbes* list alone own about as much wealth as the entire African-American population combined, while the wealthiest 186 members of the *Forbes 400* own as much wealth as the entire Latino population combined. If average Black households had enjoyed the same growth rate as the *Forbes 400* over the past 30 years, they would have an extra $475,000 in wealth today. Latino households would have an extra $386,000. (Asante-Muhammed et al. 2016, 5)

The same authors explain that "the lingering effects of generations of discriminatory and wealth-stripping practices have left Latino and Black households owning an average of six and seven times less wealth ($98,000 and $85,000, respectively) than White households ($656,000). Even more unfortunate, the extreme rise in overall wealth inequality over the past three decades has only served to further compound and exacerbate this racial wealth divide. Over that time, the wealthiest 20% of Americans have taken 99.4% of all gains in wealth while the bottom 80% have been left to split just 0.6% among themselves (Wolff 2014). As shocking as this disparity in wealth concentration is, it's even more startling when we realize that today, America's richest 400 individuals—with a collective net worth of $2.34 trillion—now own more wealth than the entire Black population, plus one-third of the Latino population, combined" (Collins and Hoxie 2015, 17).

It is virtually impossible to win a competitive game played on a relational market when one player or group benefits from a past of exclusive access—to wealth, education, professional career jobs, and even decent health care. However, it also appears that even those who tend to win in these competitive games suffer from the ever-increasing pressure created by rising stakes and crowding out, as the tendency of relational markets is to demand more and more effort and investment from the participants to achieve the same benefit.

A 2013 OECD study found that the use of anti-depressant medicine is on the rise in rich countries, where in some countries one in ten now takes them regularly.[3] More competition over limited resources under conditions of social scarcity leads not only to decreasing returns, but also to a faster rat race, exerting greater stress on all market participants. Furthermore, irrational market interactions, as argued earlier, undermine trust and community so that more and more market participants suffer the consequences of having to engage in such interactions. Neurosis and other psychological illness are thus intrinsically connected to capitalism, as is the loss of trust and community.

We are, in short, all trapped by relational markets, even if some of us, namely all those who were not allowed to accumulate intergenerational assets and were held back from entering competitive relational markets over hundreds of years, do not have even a theoretical chance to ever catch up with the intergenerational asset holders and early starters. It is this aspect of capital versus labor that Thomas Piketty (2014) was not able to include in his analysis. Had he done so, he would have found that even if economic growth provides opportunities for wage earners to eventually catch up with capital holders, racism—past and present—undermines his formula. To be sure, black and indigenous groups not only suffer from past exclusions, but also continue to be targeted by those seeking to defend their privileged access today, leading some to label the current times in the United States "the New Jim Crow" (Alexander 2012). In most former colonial or colonized countries, the former colonizers dominate politics and most markets to this day. Native people and the descendants of African slaves everywhere experience the long-lasting effects of slavery and different degrees of new and old Jim Crows today.

MARKET WITHDRAWAL OF THE SUPERRICH: EATING HALF THE PIE

What happens when a significant amount of rich people withdraws their assets from markets, shielding them from others through the mechanism of unattainable prices or simply by effective market withdrawal?

While it is by now undisputed that fighting social exclusion is one of the main ways to create bigger, more inclusive markets and through them overall economic growth, not much attention has been paid to the other population segment that does not effectively participate in markets because it has withdrawn its assets from mainstream competition, thus effectively reducing the amount of tradable goods and services: the rich. Following Fred Hirsch's logic outlined earlier, it becomes clear that affluent people and groups have long understood that some goods are only good as long as they are not equally shared. They have thus long shielded their beach houses, vacation homes, luxury apartments, etc. from the common market, making them inaccessible to the average consumer and by doing so diminishing the overall size of marketable goods.

The New York City real estate market provides a good example: once the affluent have secured all the desirable apartments in Manhattan, the "rest" of us must look for apartments elsewhere. This rest, which is the majority of income-earning people, are thus not only crowded out of the Manhattan real estate market, but also forced to compete with more and more people over smaller and less attractive markets—in Queens, Brooklyn, Staten Island, the Bronx, and New Jersey. The very same logic applies to the real estate markets of almost all larger cities on the planet. It is also applicable to understanding other markets, as most goods and assets in today's world are worth more when fewer people have access to them. This is true for educational degrees, jobs, and even citizenship.

Affluence leads to market withdrawal as the "upper crust" tends to shield its assets from open market competition and passes on assets to the next generation. The houses, lands, and assets bought by the early Rockefellers, Fords, Kennedys, and Carnegies, to name but a few, are not for sale. They are inherited. The more Rockefellers and Fords we have, the more assets are withdrawn from open market competition. It comes as no surprise that the cities with the most millionaires (London, New York, Tokyo, Hamburg, Munich) are also the ones with the highest real estate prices, making it unaffordable for middle-class families to find decent housing there. In 2013, 389,000 millionaires and 70 billionaires lived in New York City (Boseley, Chalabi, and Rice-Oxley 2013). How big might their average living space be, that is, how much space do they occupy? How many of them actually live there? It is impossible to know. It is, however, fairly safe to assume that the nonmillionaires of New York would have a better chance on the housing market without them.

Imagine a New York in which all the apartments on the Upper East and West Sides would be still available for potential renters with average incomes (some $40,000 for individuals and $50,000 for families). It would be a vibrant market indeed! The same logic holds for other positional assets, such as vacation homes, but also for jobs and educational degrees. All goods that have an inherent social consumption character, that is, goods that are more valuable as long as they are not widely shared, follow the same logic, as Hirsch explains. To protect their inherited privileges, the rich tend to withdraw their assets from general market competition, thus diminishing the total amount of goods in circulation, or at least effectively in circulation, as most of this market withdrawal is achieved through pricing. The "upper crust," in other words, has created separate markets for themselves and shields it from the average wage earner through high pricing. While housing provides an obvious example, the job market follows the same logic: the fact that almost all American presidents and senators are graduates from the same universities (the Ivy League) points to a general pattern—the "truly good" jobs are reserved for those able to attend an Ivy League university, where Ivy League attendance is shielded from average people through high pricing. The fact that today the superrich hold 50 percent of all assets tells us that those 50 percent of assets are no longer available to the rest of us. They are not on the market.

The current scenario is thus one in which average people with average incomes and average wealth only have a fair chance on most competitive markets if they entered them early—before they became crowded—and then held on to them for generations, which is highly unlikely, or if the playing field was leveled for them by a severe crisis. In other words, the current capitalist system is so irrational that crisis is the only hope we have to gain access to most disputed goods and assets. To find decent housing for an affordable price, average people must wait for a natural disaster. Only if Los Angeles is halfway destroyed by an earthquake or Manhattan victimized by life-threatening events making most rich people either lose their assets or leave will average earners have a fair chance at decent housing. As Joseph Schumpeter (1976) already explained, capitalism relies on "creative destruction."

Today, seventy million superrich people compete on markets containing $185 trillion, while the "rest" of us, some seven billion people, complete on markets of the same size. Who do you think competes harder? Asset concentration and asset withdrawal from regularly accessible markets thus creates artificial scarcity, poverty, and exclusion.

Not surprisingly, a 2013 study conducted by a group of distinguished economists and other social scientists about the situation of poverty and social exclusion in the United Kingdom found that:

> The situation is worse today than it has been for the past thirty years. Independent surveys of poverty using modern scientific methods were first conducted in 1983 and again in 1990, 1999, 2002/03 and 2012. Comparing the surveys shows that, in Britain:
>
> – The number of people falling below the minimum standards of the day has doubled since 1983
> – More children lead impoverished and restricted lives today than in 1999.
>
> (*Living Standards in the UK* 2013)

Asset concentration over generations has thus distorted most markets to the point that no fair competition is possible. According to Piketty, the United States has become an inheritance society: "a society characterized by both a very high concentration of wealth and a significant persistence of large fortunes from generation to generation" (Piketty 2014, 249). Piketty further explains that

> Whenever the rate of return on capital is significantly and durably higher than the growth rate of the economy, it is all but inevitable that inheritance (of fortunes accumulated in the past) predominates over savings (wealth accumulated on the present). In strict logic, it could be otherwise, but the forces pushing in this direction are extremely powerful. The inequality $r > g$ in one sense implies that the past tends to devour the future: wealth originating in the past automatically grows more rapidly, even without labor, than wealth stemming from work, which can be saved. Almost inevitably, this tends to give lasting, disproportionate importance to inequalities created in the past, and therefore to inheritance. (Piketty 2014, 267)

The fortunes the rich inherited from the past not only buy them large houses and a place on the beaches of this world, but also better educations for their children and with it, it cements privilege firmly into a family history. Before they go to Harvard, Princeton, Yale, Oxford, or Cambridge, the rich send their children to private preschools, middle schools, high schools, or boarding schools, where their offspring get groomed for their bright futures. A

Harvard law degree costs US $164,500 in tuition alone (assuming three years of attendance at currently $54,850 of estimated tuition costs for nine months). According to Piketty, "the average income of the parents of Harvard students is currently about $450,000, which corresponds to the average income of the top 2 percent of the US income hierarchy" (Piketty 2014, 339–40).

Access to education, knowledge, training, and skills is the most widely recognized path toward undoing inequality—if historically underprivileged groups and individuals actually had access to high-quality education. What we witness instead in most countries is just the opposite: privileged education tends to be reserved for the already privileged, while poor education is extended to the poor. Inherited privilege becomes entrenched, together with inherited exclusion.

Following this logic it is clear that the main market distortions happen at the extreme ends: excluded groups are forced out of markets and the extremely wealthy have found ways to shield their assets from open market competition through high price mechanisms. It is also clear what the general policies to combat this must achieve: they must push back the market capture of the rich and expand the market participation of the poor so that more people can effectively participate with equal opportunities, that is, fairly. After all, on many markets, there is only one pie for all of us.

It is also clear that any attempt at creating fairer markets, or markets that are more embedded in local communities and subjected to democratic regulation, cannot exist without a political-institutional environment that supports them and allows for their existence. The many examples of social or solidarity economies, documented by such authors as Ash Amin (2009) and J. K. Gibson-Graham (2006), all highlight that such experiments cannot survive outside a supportive political environment. This is also the lesson that can be drawn from Quebec, where social economies have expanded the most. Margaret Mendell, reporting on the experiences from Quebec, thus writes:

> We have learned in Quebec that an enabling environment that is not limited to accessing existing public policy tools and resources is essential for the social economy. Policy innovation for the social economy requires new *processes* of policy formation and *institutional innovation*. This means designing *intermediary inter-sectoral dialogue spaces* that represent the numerous actors involved in the social economy and those that share its objectives. Social economy actors must be and are the co-authors of numerous policies that have emerged in the last decade in Quebec. The development of this political capacity is critical. (Mendell, in Amin 2009, 182; emphasis in original)

In other words, economic democratization depends on political will. Economic experiments, while interesting and important for all those involved and affected, are circumscribed by the political environment into which they are embedded. Thus, instead of searching for new economic models in isolation, my own search is for innovative ways that political communities constitute themselves and, by doing so, create the possibilities for organizing markets according to their needs and preferences. This approach rests on the insight that it is precisely the decoupling of the economy from society and politics that causes its excesses in the first place—and insight that goes back to the work of such classics as Karl Polanyi (1977).

Brazilian economist Celso Furtado explains in his book *In Search of a New Model* (*Em Busca de Novo Modelo*, 2002), "development policies have to be formulated based upon an explanation of the substantive ends we seek to achieve and not based upon the logic of the means set forth by the accumulation process controlled by transnational enterprises" (Furtado 2002, 36; my translation). Furtado thus places himself with all those who have long critiqued the working of different markets, demonstrating their tendencies to undermine themselves, to erode social trust and sociability, to produce increasing inequalities and concentration of power, and to destroy the environment. We need to urgently rethink what kinds of markets we want and we need to devise ways to keep markets competitive and accessible to the majority—every generation anew. The group we need to focus on the most, as I have shown, is not the poor but the rich and the superrich, as it is because of them that our markets are distorted and exclusive. They are also the ones who are responsible for diminishing the amount of goods available to the majority. Instead of focusing our attention on "welfare" and assistance policies for the poor, we need to spend much more energy thinking about curbing the assets, earnings, and political influence of the rich.

THE CASE FOR WEALTH DISTRIBUTION

The proposal to limit the concentration of wealth is as old as the very idea of democracy. It is also at its core, as I will demonstrate here. To put this into precise language, I argue that addressing inequality by limiting the amount of assets the rich can hold as well as providing equal opportunities to all by granting the majority equal access to high-quality education has always been at the core of democratic thought and is by no means radical or outlandish. Making such a proposal appear radical is the result of concerted propaganda against it by the rich and those able to bestow a better education onto their own children while withholding it from the rest. While I think it is time to claim "a different kind of radical," in this section I want to demonstrate that seeking ways to ensure equal distribution and access to assets and wealth as well as guaranteeing equal access to high-quality education for all are not radical at all. These proposals are rather mainstream.

The theme of limiting economic inequality and avoiding that wealth spills over into the political realm has been termed "Greek" or "Athenian" by such authors as Eric Nelson (2004), as it can be traced back to ancient Greek sources. From there, it reemerged almost everywhere that republics were established and where democracy was debated.

Plato writes in his *Laws*:

Honour is not to be given to the fair body, or to the strong or the swift or the tall, or to the healthy body (although many may think otherwise), any more than to their opposites; but the mean states of all these habits are by far the safest and most moderate; for the one extreme makes the soul braggart and insolent, and the other, illiberal and base; and money, and property, and distinction all go to the same tune. The excess of any of these things is apt to be a source of hatreds and divisions among states and individuals; and the defect of them is commonly a cause of slavery. And, therefore, I would not have any one fond of heaping up riches for the sake of his children, in order that he may leave them as rich as possible. (Plato 348 BCE, 97f)

For Plato and his world, property and wealth were strongly related to land-ownership, and the concentration of land in but a few hands was perceived as the source of misfortune. Plato offers his solution to this problem in his *Laws*:

How then can we rightly order the distribution of the land? In the first place, the number of the citizens has to be determined, and also the number and size of the divisions into which they will have to be formed; and the land and the houses will then have to be apportioned by us as fairly as we can. (Plato 348 BCE, 105)

According to Nelson (2004), Plato suggests that to ensure happiness to all, "the *polis* must—on grounds of justice—either abolish private property (as in the Republic) or sharply restrict its accumulation (as in the *Laws*)" (Nelson 2004, 13).

Aristotle agrees with his teacher Plato in his assessment of the corrupting influence of wealth and the need to limit it. According to Fred Miller,

Aristotle's theory of property rights also allows for the regulation of property. Newman remarks that the defence of private property in *Politics*, II 5, is not expressly coupled with qualifications, but Aristotle elsewhere endorses various social policies which limit private property rights. The qualifications upon private property rights should probably be understood in the light of the fact that they are, for Aristotle, subordinate to political rights. His defence of private property is not intended as a case for total privatization. Presumably on similar grounds, he advocates coercive taxation for the purposes of defence and internal needs (VII 8 1328^{b}10–11; III 12 1283^{a}17–18). He also recommends support for needy citizens, as virtuous acts carrying out his policy of "private ownership, common use" (VII 10 1329^{b}41–1330^{a}2; VI 6 1320^{b}2–11). The provisos which he attaches to natural acquisition can explain his advocacy of legal limits on the amount of land any citizen can own (see VI 4 1319^{a}8–10). He also recommends that individuals do not have the liberty to sell and bequeath land however they please (II 9 1270^{a}18–21). He even admits that the ostracism of very rich or powerful citizens may be justified by a sort of political justice (see III 13 1284^{b}15–34; VI 8 1308^{b}19). The point here is probably that the excessive exercise of property and other rights by some persons jeopardizes the political rights of the other citizens, and that the political rights of the latter should override the property rights of the former. (Miller 1997, 329–30)

In his *The Constitution of Athens*, Aristotle quotes Solon, called upon by the Athenians after civil war had broken out between the rich landholders and the common people. Solon, himself a commoner, lived from 638 to about 558 BCE, thus a good century before Plato (428–348 BCE) and Aristotle (384–322 BCE) and has this to say on the issue of limiting the assets of the wealthy and their influence on politics:

> But ye who have store of good, who are sated and overflow,
> Restrain your swelling soul, and still it and keep it low:
> Let the heart that is great within you be trained a lowlier way;
> Ye shall not have all at your will, and we will not for ever obey.
> (Aristotle 2001, Book 1, Part 5)

And Aristotle continues:

> Indeed, he constantly fastens the blame of the conflict on the rich; and accordingly at the beginning of the poem he says that he fears "the love of wealth and an overweening mind," evidently meaning that it was through these that the quarrel arose. (Aristotle 2001, Book 1, Part 5)

To end the war of the nobles against the commoners and, in Aristotle's words, "the oppression of the many by the few," Solon ended slavery among citizens, canceled debts, and created the Council of 400. The Athenians were thus decisively opposed to the concentration of wealth in few hands and favored policies that either protected equal access to land or, once lost, restored it. Most treaties focus on land, as it must be thought of as the main asset a man or a family could hold, thus bequeathing unequal opportunities to the head of the family and his offspring.

While the Romans living under the republic differed in their approach to justice and liberty from the Athenians, they nevertheless shared their concern for the evils growing out of excessive wealth and power. Here, as in Athens, wealth was strongly associated with landownership and the dispute over land is one that characterizes the entire duration of the republic, culminating in the reforms proposed by the Gracchi brothers.

Tiberius Gracchus was elected tribune in 133 BCE and proposed a law making it illegal for any person to possess more than 500 *iugera* (about 300 acres, or 121 hectares) of public land and for any family to own more than 1,000 *iugera*. He was killed in that same year by opposing senators and their supporters. His brother, Gaius, subsequently served two consecutive terms as tribune, which he used to advance an agenda very similar to his brother's. He was also killed, together with 3,000 supporters, without trial (Le Glay 2009). The violence and the extralegal ways the Gracchi brothers were dealt with by powerful Roman senators and their followers point at the level of contestation the question of limited landownership faced. While for the Gracchi brothers, land reform was essential and a sine qua non condition to protect Rome from civil war and rural decay, the benefitting senators and latifundio owners, while they might have agreed with the diagnosis, acted in defense of their own privileges.

Throughout the republic, ordinary Roman citizens made several attempts at limiting the power of the aristocratic senators, at times formally, through their tributes, and at times through protest and violence. I will discuss in more detail the different legal proposals advanced during this time shortly. For now, it is enough to highlight that in Rome, just like in Athens, the citizenry was weary of the concentration of wealth and power in few hands and advanced different proposals to limit it.

Eric Nelson (2004) provides a detailed analysis of how Greek thought on equality and justice has influenced republican thought in general and the American republican tradition in particular. From his detailed account it becomes clear that not only the founding fathers, but also a whole array of American public leaders active around the time of American independence, had subscribed to the ideas of Plato and Aristotle, as well as those of Machiavelli and James Harrington. Many of the proposals advanced during the late eighteenth and early nineteenth centuries favored imposing limits to wealth accumulation, limits to intergenerational wealth transfer, and institutions, as well as laws, able to fend off the undue influence of the rich onto politics and public affairs in general. This topic was also discussed in the Federalist Papers (particularly Federalist No. 10) and preached by different republican-minded clerics in the young American republic.

In fact, when the Pennsylvania Declaration of Rights was discussed by the Philadelphia Congress in July and August of 1776, it originally contained an article (No. 16) that stated:

> That an enormous Proportion of Property vested in a few individuals is dangerous to the Rights, and destructive of the Common Happiness, of Mankind; and

therefore every free State hath the Right by its Laws to discourage the Possession of such Property.[4]

Article 16 of the Pennsylvania Declaration of Rights, which acted under the leadership of Benjamin Franklin, was later deleted and substituted with another quite different article that contained no more references to large and excessive property. However, the fact that it was part of the Declaration of Rights at one point highlights the importance and the centrality of this concern among the American founders. Thomas Jefferson was particularly outspoken about the undue influence of wealth in politics. He took inspiration not just from Plato, Aristotle, and Montesquieu, but also from James Harrington (1611–1677), who himself based his claims on Plato, Aristotle, and Machiavelli and argues:

> For equality of estates causes equality of power, and equality of power is the liberty, not only of the commonwealth, but of every man. (Harrington 2006 [1656], 8)

The solution, for Harrington, to existing inequalities in wealth and power was to limit access to them. In his utopian Oceana, he ordains:

> That every man who is at present possessed, or shall hereafter be possessed, of an estate in land exceeding the revenue of £2,000 a year, and having more than one son, shall leave his lands either equally divided among them, in case the lands amount to above £2,000 a year to each, or no near equally, in case they come under, that the greater part or portion of the same remaining to the eldest exceed not the value of £2,000 revenue. And no man, not in present possession of lands above the value of £2,000 by the year, shall receive, enjoy (except by lawful inheritance) acquire, or, purchase to himself lands within the said territories, amounting, with those already in his possession, above the said revenue. (Harrington 2006 [1656], 60)

Harrington also defends universal access to education, which he argues should be free of charge to the poor. Harrington greatly influenced Thomas Jefferson, who in his autobiography favored an inheritance law able to break up family fortunes and thus avoid the emergence of a money aristocracy. In a letter to John Adams, Jefferson writes,

> At the first session of our legislator after the Declaration of Independence, we passed a law abolishing entails. And this was followed by one abolishing the privilege of Primogeniture, and dividing the lands of intestates equally among all their children, or their representatives. These laws, drawn by myself, laid the axe to the root of Pseudo-aristocracy. And had another which I prepared been adopted by the legislature, our work would have been compleat. It was a Bill

for the more general diffusion of learning. . . . Worth and genius would thus have been sought out from every condition of life, and compleatly prepared by education for defeating the competition of wealth and birth for public trust. (The Adams-Jefferson Letter, quoted in Nelson 2004, 203)

To James Madison, Jefferson writes,

I am conscious that an equal division of property is impractical, but the consequences of this enormous inequality producing so much misery to the bulk of mankind, legislators cannot invent too many devices for subdividing property, only taking care to let their subdivisions go hand in hand with the natural affections of the human mind. (Jefferson, *Writings*, quoted in Nelson 2004, 204f)

John Locke is equally supportive of imposing limits to ownership of land, stating in his *Second Treatise on Government* that in the state of nature, men did not hold more land than they could use.

James Madison agrees and argues:

The great object should be to combat evil: 1. By establishing political equality among all. 2. By withholding unnecessary opportunities from the few, to increase the inequality of property, by an immoderate, and especially an unmerited, accumulation of wealth. 3. By silent operation of laws, which, without violating the rights of property, reduce extreme wealth to a state of mediocrity, and raise extreme indigence towards a state of comfort. (*The Papers of James Madison*, quoted in Nelson 2004, 207)

Adam Smith approaches the same subject, even if not so much from a moral standpoint, but in terms of economic efficiency and market distortions resulting from monopoly pricing—the unavoidable result, he thought, of hoarding great amounts of land in but a few hands. Smith argues that primogeniture affects markets negatively in that it withholds land from markets, concentrating it in the unproductive hands of the few. He states:

The small quantity of land . . . which is brought to the market, and the high price of what is thither, prevents a great number of capitals from being employed in its cultivation and improvement which would otherwise have taken that direction. (Smith 1976 [1776], 384)

Smith further argues that "if landed estates . . . were divided equally among all the children, upon the death of any proprietor who left a numerous family, the estate would generally be sold. So much land would come to market, that it could no longer sell at a monopoly price" (Smith 1976 [1776], 423).

John Adams is equally supportive of making land accessible to all by limiting the amount of land one person can hold. He writes,

The only possible way, then, of preserving the balance of power on the side of equal liberty and public virtue, is to make the acquisition of land easy to every member of society; to make a division of land into small quantities, so that the multitude may be possessed of landed estates. (Adams, *Works*, quoted in Nelson 2004, 209)

Arguments about imposing limits on property and asset holding were, at least during the early days of the American Republic, rather commonplace, even if they were controversial and perceived as such. To many of the participating debaters, be it Jefferson, Madison, or the young John Adams, imposing limits on the ownership of land seemed inevitable if the protection of virtue and justice were the goal. The way to achieve a broader spread of property was to abolish entail and primogeniture inheritance, which was achieved by Jefferson. As he explains, this strategy relied on the then common reality of families counting on a large group of offspring among which the land could be divided. It also focused on the main asset available for the accumulation of wealth: landownership. To Henry George, the American worker turned thinker and philosopher and author of *Progress and Poverty* (first published in 1879), it was clear that asset concentration undermined equal opportunity for all and created poverty. He argued, "Poverty deepens as wealth increases; wages fall while productivity grows" (George 2006 [1880], 180). George understood that this was caused by the undue accumulation of assets, which provided undue privileges and rents, undermining the opportunities of all those who could not count on such wealth privileges. The only solution, to George, who during his lifetime was the third most famous person in the United States (after Mark Twain and Thomas Edison, according to Agnes George de Mille, his daughter), was to make land common property. According to his daughter,

Georgists believe in private enterprise, and in its virtues and incentives to produce at maximum efficiency. It is the insidious linking together of special privilege, the unjust outright private ownership of natural or public resources, monopolies, franchises, that produce unfair domination and autocracy. The means of producing wealth differ at the root: some is thieved from the people and some is honestly earned. George differentiated; Marx did not. The consequences of our failure to discern lie at the heart of our trouble. (Agnes George de Mille, in George 2006, 308)

Thus Henry George, similar to the American founding fathers, recognized the long-term distortions growing out of asset concentration and monopoly capital. Undue privilege and rent seeking, to him, lay at the heart of poverty amid progress and richness. Similar to the founding fathers, his focus was on land. Transferred to our days, with reduced family sizes and asset holding no longer grounded in land, the set of policies proposed then translates today into the need for general limitations on asset holdings and the splitting up of property and assets in general after the death of a family head, be it for the sake of protection of justice, democracy, and general happiness (Jefferson) or to protect markets from monopoly pricing on assets artificially made scarce through hoarding (Smith). All involved debaters were also well aware of the kind of opportunity hoarding that results from entering competitive markets already endowed with assets and of the negative effects the rich exercise on politics.

This theme did not die with the American founding fathers. It was picked up in Europe by communists and anarchists around the time of Karl Marx and Mikhail Bakunin and the First Communist International in 1919. Anarchists in particular spoke out for strong inheritance taxes as a way to limit the passing on of privilege from one generation to the next. Such iconic figures as Pierre-Joseph Proudhon, Mikhail Bakunin, and Peter Kropotkin made history when they opposed the state- and party-led proposals of the communists. The utopian socialists also contributed significantly to this history of the idea of asset limitation. Charles Fourier, Robert Owen, and the followers of Leo Tolstoy all sought to create societies without hierarchies and without rule over others. The French Communards were able to put these principles into practice, if only for some two months, in 1871. In Germany of 1918, soldiers and citizens established councils inspired by anarchism and libertarian socialism defending the idea that private property needs to be limited (or abolished) for the sake of general happiness. Anarchism had another chance in 1936, when the Spanish civil war dealt a blow to the monarchy and opened the door for the formation of local councils and associations. All the while, in parts of Africa and Latin America, indigenous groups practiced communal landownership, land rotations among community members, and collective land holding. In Europe, commons and other forms of collective land- or forest ownership were very present in rural communities and continue to exist to this day (Ostrom 2015).

On December 15, 1868, the International Alliance of Socialist Democracy was founded by Mikhail Bakunin and given a program. This program states:

1. The Alliance declares itself atheist; it wants abolition of cults, substitution of science for faith and human justice for divine justice.
2. It wants above all political, economic, and social equalization of classes and individuals of both sexes, *commencing with abolition of the right of inheritance*, so that in future enjoyment be equal to each person's production, and so that, in conformity with the decision taken at the last workers' congress in Brussels, the land, instruments of labor, like all other capital, on becoming collective property of the entire society, shall be used only by the workers, that is, by agricultural and individual associations.

3. It wants for all children of both sexes, from birth, equal conditions of development, that is, maintenance, education, and training at all degrees of science, industry, and the arts, being convinced that this equality, at first only economic and social, will increasingly lead to a great natural equality of individuals, eliminating all kinds of artificial inequalities, historical products of a social organization as false as it is iniquitous.
4. Being the foe of all despotism, not recognizing any political form other than republican and rejecting completely any reactionary alliance, it also rejects any political action which does not have as its immediate and direct aim the triumph of the workers' cause against capital. (Emphasis mine)[5]

Communists, anarchists, and libertarian socialists, while differing greatly in their analysis and approach, all saw the accumulation of wealth in a few hands as harmful to the general happiness, to widespread economic prosperity, and to broad self-rule. Similarly, the provision of free public education was perceived by all as a prerequisite for freedom.

While communism and anarchism were quickly bedeviled and labeled "radical" and antithetic to democracy, the American founding fathers, as I have demonstrated, were equally committed to the same goals of avoiding the concentration of wealth and power in a few hands. They were also equally committed to passing laws that actively worked against this concentration of wealth and political power and for the broader distribution of these assets and the opportunities they provided. It is thus too easy and wrong to dismiss these proposals as "communist."

PROPERTY-OWNING DEMOCRACY AND PRE-DISTRIBUTION

Contemporary mainstream economists and philosophers continue to debate this theme and they continue to propose new and innovative ways to protect equal opportunity, fairness, and political equality.

James Edward Meade, a British economist (1907–1995), received the Nobel Prize in Economic Sciences in 1977 after having published *Efficiency, Equality, and the Ownership of Property* in 1965. In this book, Meade introduces the concept of "property-owning democracy." Meade explains:

Arrangements which encourage the accumulation of property by those with little property are certainly as important as those which discourage further accumulation or encourage dispersal of their fortunes by large property owners. . . . We have already noted (p. 30–32 above) the extreme importance of education as a form of investment which affects earning power. (Meade 1965, 59)

Meade was hardly a radical. He served as a lecturer and later professor at Oxford, the London School of Economics, and Cambridge University, and his proposals resonate strongly with those proposed by the ancient Greeks, the American founding fathers, and many libertarian socialists and anarchists

Meade's proposal of a property-owning democracy also did not die with him. John Rawls integrated his approach into his own *A Theory of Justice* (1999). Rawls, to be sure, focuses his attention on the institutional requirements able to protect justice and fairness. In his book *Justice as Fairness: A Restatement*, Rawls aims "to sketch in more detail the kind of background institutions that seem necessary when we take seriously the idea that society is a fair system of cooperation between free and equal citizens from one generation to the next" (Rawls 2001, 136).

Rawls finds that only two systems are able to create the necessary background conditions for ensuring his two principles of justice: fairness and equal opportunity. These are liberal socialism and property-owning democracy. He rules out laissez-faire capitalism, welfare state capitalism, and state socialism. When comparing those two, he concludes that only property-owning democracy is able to secure fairness and equal opportunity. It is worth quoting him at length:

> The background institutions of property-owning democracy work to disperse the ownership of wealth and capital, and thus to prevent a small part of society from controlling the economy, and indirectly, political life as well. By contrast, welfare-state capitalism permits a small class to have a near monopoly of the means of production. Property-owning democracy avoids this, not by redistribution of income to those with less at the end of each period, so to speak, but rather by ensuring the widespread ownership of productive assets and human capital (that is, education and trained skills) at the beginning of each period, all this against the background of fair equality and opportunity. The intent is not to simply assist those who lose out through accident or misfortune (although that must be done), but rather to put all citizens in a position to manage their own affairs on a footing of a suitable degree of social and economic equality. (Rawls 2001, 139)

While John Rawls is notoriously vague about the concrete steps a society must take to institute justice, fairness, and equal opportunities, Amartya Sen (2009) points at capabilities and freedom as the ultimate goals where societal and individual development must meet. With this, Sen opens the door for thinking about the specific needs and opportunities concrete individuals and groups encounter and require fulfilling their wishes and needs. Similar to Rawls, the only system that can provide equal and fair opportunities for all in every generation is one in which investments in education and assets are distributed equally *before* individuals and groups enter into competitive situations. As Martin O'Neill and Thad Williamson (2014) have recently demonstrated, the proposals of both Rawls and Sen point to a system of "pre-distribution" rather than one of post-factum redistribution. Accordingly, Sen writes, in his *The Idea of Justice*:

> Equality was not only among the foremost revolutionary demands in eighteenth-century Europe and America, there has also been an extraordinary consensus on its importance in the Post-Enlightenment world. . . . Equality is demanded in some basic form even by those who are typically seen as having disputed the "case for equality" and expressed skepticism about the central importance of "distributive justice." For example, Robert Nozick may not lean towards equality of utility (as James Meade does), or towards equality of holding of primary goods (as John Rawls does), and yet Nozick does demand equality of libertarian rights—that no one person should have any more right to liberty than anyone else. (Sen 2009, 291)

In this, the liberal proposals advanced by Rawls and Sen meet the socialist approach advanced by Marxist economists Samuel Bowles and Herbert Gintis (1998), who argue that smart asset distribution can achieve the twin goals of enhancing economic efficiency and equality. This is, in turn, where Marxist scholarship meets the Yale economist Jacob Stewart Hacker (2011), who coined the term "pre-distribution." He argues:

> To protect and restore the hallmarks of a well-functioning market democracy, progressives in the United States and elsewhere must rebuild its institutional foundations and shift back the uneven organisational balance between concentrated economic interests and the broad public. (Hacker 2011, 1)

Hacker is a member of the British Policy Network, which has close ties to the British Labour Party. In an even more recent treatment, Sir Anthony Atkinson (2015), the British economist, has argued for a lifetime capital receipts tax, which would, to some degree, work against the ability to pass on accumulated wealth to the next generation.

The theme of protecting equal opportunities in markets and politics thus has a long pedigree, reaching back to ancient Athens. It resurfaces among republicans of all sorts—from anarchists to liberals and conservatives. All of them have given asset limitations some thought, as all of them have understood that to protect equal opportunity and fairness in competitive markets, all participants must enter those markets equipped with the same assets and capital. Universal education, and sometimes universally provided health care, also play central roles in the thinking of all those concerned with equal opportunity and fairness. Those who have pressed these questions the furthest all seem to agree that the inheritance of assets provides those who benefit from them with unfair advantages—ultimately not justifiable in a democracy. They all seem to agree that for the sake of equal opportunity, it is not enough to first let inequality and unfairness play out, only to address them later through some sort of redistribution. At that late moment, the damage inequality causes is already done and it is too late to address and undo the moral hazards created. Instead, the central concern of all the authors discussed earlier is how to pre-distribute in order to level the playing field before people enter the public realm, which necessarily contains competitive markets.

Debates about asset limitations are thus far less radical than they seem at first sight. The most common policies addressing them are progressive income taxes, taxes on wealth, taxes on inheritances, and taxes on capital transactions (Piketty 2014). In fact, many countries have progressive income tax regimes, thus charging more taxes to those earning more money. Several countries also tax wealth (France, Spain, Switzerland, Norway, The Netherlands, and India), applied in different ways to assets exceeding certain levels, sometimes calling it "solidarity tax" (in France). In addition, most countries have different tax regimes in place for inheritance, gifts, real estate transfers, and endowments. Belgium, the Czech Republic, Denmark, Finland, France, Germany, India, Ireland, Italy, Japan, Luxembourg, The Netherlands, Norway, Philippines, Poland, Portugal, South Africa, South Korea, Spain, Switzerland, Turkey, the United Kingdom, and the United States all levy taxes on the transfer of assets from one person to another, upon death or before, using different criteria and allowing for different tax-free minimum and maximum asset amounts. (A good source of information on inheritance, asset, and gift taxes is provided by financial planning organizations and investment banks, for example, by Ernst & Young, whose 2013 International Inheritance and Tax guide served as a source for this list. It is available at http://www.ey.com/Publication/vwLUAssets/2013-international-estate-and -inheritance-tax-guide/$FILE/2013-international-estate-and-inheritance-tax-guide.pdf).

Different versions of the "Tobin Tax," that is, a tax on financial transactions initially proposed in the 1990s, continue to surface in today's political debates, advocated by such politicians as Bernie Sanders and like-minded others. The European Commission proposed a financial transaction tax in 2013, but was blocked from imposing it in 2014, 2015, and 2016, mostly by Europe's financial heart: the United Kingdom.

What all of these attempts have in common is that they seek to protect equal opportunity and fairness over generations by curbing the influence and power of multinational corporations and the rich. The case for asset distribution and limitation is core to the democratic ideal.

POLICIES FOR FAIRNESS AND EQUAL OPPORTUNITY

If open and fair markets and equal economic opportunities and chances are our goal—and they should be—then the main question we need to ask is: How can we counteract that some people have been able to first accumulate tremendous amounts of assets and then effectively withdraw them from common markets while passing them on to their descendants? In other words, how can we defend and ensure fair and open markets in which everybody has an equal chance to succeed? This is, after all, the original promise of markets: that everybody has an equal opportunity and chance to win independent of one's starting position. So again, what sorts of policies are required to counteract this phenomenon? Marxists would say: end free markets. At this historical moment, however, it seems that this is a rather unattractive option. Wherever markets were ended, powerful parties and states have stepped in, contributing to instead of alleviating the power of inequality, elite capture, and opportunity hoarding.[6] Anthony Atkinson (2015) and Thomas Piketty (2014) both suggest a series of tax, welfare, and redistribution policies, some of which have been tried and continue to be applied to some extent in many social welfare state systems. However, welfare state–type redistribution schemes can been criticized for first allowing some people to take advantages of unfair starting positions only to take part of their earnings away from them and redistributing them to the less fortunate. Such a model not only perpetuates a sense of deserved winning among those at the top—even if they are only there due to their better starting positions—but also stigmatizes the recipients of such redistribution, marking them as charity receivers. The solution to equal opportunity and fairness on markets cannot rely on charity and favors. The kind of negative incentives created through schemes of redistribution must also be avoided. The only possible solution must lie in the "pre-distribution" area.

The proposal advanced here starts from the premise that markets can be efficient mechanisms for the interchange of goods and services as long as distortions are avoided and actively counteracted. This, it seems to me, is much in tune with the tenor of both Adam Smith (1976 [1776]) and Amartya Sen (1999), as well as Thomas Piketty (2014), as all of them have plausibly argued that bartering and thus participating in markets is a genuine human right.

What sort of policies would we need to counteract the market withdrawal and distortion caused by the affluent? Some policies seem inescapable if fair markets are the desired outcomes: asset accumulation would have to be limited. The ability to pass on assets from one generation to the next would have to be altogether eliminated. The resulting utopia would be one in which everybody is equipped with the same assets *before* entering markets. This also includes the provision of free high-quality education and health care to everyone. In addition, and bearing in mind that assets are essential for succeeding in markets—even if those markets are controlled and limited—governments should provide startup funds to every citizen in the form of a government loan or donation (Kretzmann and McKnight 1993; Yunus 2003; Ackerman and Alstott 1999). Anthony Atkinson has recently included this policy in his treatment of the subject, under the heading "Inheritance for All" (Atkinson 2015, 169), demonstrating that making such a capital endowment available to all citizens when they reach early adulthood would enable all to become active stakeholders and participants in different markets. Atkinson (2015) suggests financing such a policy with a tax on capital gains. Others have suggested financing it through a tax on personal wealth (Ackerman and Alstott 1999). Either way, providing graduates with startup funds in order to increase their capabilities and enlarge their agency seems particularly relevant for those who have been pushed to the back of the line through systematic exclusion and stigmatization. It is in this context that a serious debate about reparations for the descendants of slaves and dispossessed native people should be initiated.

If justice, fairness, and equal opportunity are to be achieved, such policies would have to be combined with absolute restriction on any personal inheritance. Assets left behind after death could then also be used to cover the costs of an "inheritance for all." Only when everybody has similar assets when entering competitive markets can we talk of fairness and equal opportunities. The struggle over positional goods would thus be limited, if not avoided.

However, to effectively secure fairness and equal opportunity in the long term, maximum earnings and asset holdings would have to be enforced because they are the only way to secure long-term sustainability, given the absolute limits of consumption imposed by limited resources (Klein 2014). To rely on constant and ever-expanding growth as the sole recipe to secure a sustainable future has proven insufficient. The enactment of maximum asset holdings and earnings, coupled with the inability to pass assets on to the next generation, would actively counteract the construction of family empires and dynasties, while leaving intact the incentives to excel in general and fair market competition. The shielding of some goods, such as realty, from average markets via excessive prices would come to an end, as nobody would have the millions now required to secure a place among the superrich.

Maximum asset holdings and earnings, coupled with the kind of up-front asset distribution recommended by Samuel Bowles and Herbert Gintis (1999), also have the potential to provide a concrete step toward a zero-growth or degrowth scenario in which all participants are well off. As such they are preferable to welfare systems that apply post-factum redistribution and create negative incentives and moral hazards.

If upper limits to income and asset holding, together with (tax) measures to end inheritance, universal access to high-quality education and health, and startup funds for graduates, would be enacted, several things are very likely to occur:

1. Frozen assets, inherited from generation to generation and thus effectively shielded from markets, would reenter the market, thus significantly increasing its total size and accessibility for average earners.
2. Prices of luxury goods would have to follow and come down. Nothing worth $10 million would be sold anymore and luxury goods would become accessible again to the majority.
3. These policies are also the only ones able to effectively address the problem of a sustainable future with limited natural resources. A public policy regime that limits the amount of maximum asset holdings and earnings and prohibits the passing on of assets to the next generation while at the same time providing free education, health care, and startup money to their young is not only able to protect equal opportunities for all, but also able to provide a path toward a sustainable future and a break from the cycle of more growth, more expansion, more excess, more waste, more destruction, and more competition over more and more limited natural assets. Given the limited availability of most resources, only when an asset owned by one person is reintroduced back into the general market after he or she dies can we maintain a market that provides new opportunities for the next generation.[7] Instead of waiting for "creative" destruction of assets, values, and prices, such a regime would be able to continuously provide for opportunities in a rational way.
4. By focusing on up-front asset distribution instead of posterior welfare taxation, the moral hazards and disincentives resulting from post-hoc redistribution policies could also be avoided. People will still have incentives to enter markets, compete, and succeed. "Donations" would not be needed. Bowles and Gintis (1999) have explained the advantages of asset distribution at length.

CONCLUSION

Markets can be anything we collectively and politically decide them to be. Our most ardent task today is to look for ways to curb the undue influence of a few rich individuals and groups or corporations onto the political process. This is not to say that our main strategy must be to cut back on government, as the libertarian faction argues. Their arguments do not aim at improving governance, let alone democracy, but at providing free license to entrepreneurs in hopes that somehow, miraculously, more capitalism will fix it, in which "it" includes, in their account, justice, fairness, and equal opportunity (Doherty 2008). There is, however, not one good reason to assume that, but myriad evidence on how unrestrained capitalism does just the opposite (Harvey 2011). In short, we must find ways to ensure and protect that ordinary citizens can have a say in the kind of laws and rules they have to live under. Political apathy and alienation can only be fought back when and if ordinary citizens know and feel that they have something at stake in politics. The direction of reform, therefore, must necessarily be one that brings the state and government back to the people. Doing so bears the promise of also reining in the economy, bringing it back under the control of the many by taking it away from the authority of those powerful actors that have been able to escape the control of the collective.

While the concentration of wealth is perceived by some as morally degrading in itself, others focus on its moral effects on the larger community or on its potential to spill over into politics. Wealth leads to more wealth—that is the core insight driving all these debates. Wealth also leads to a hoarding of opportunities in that economic wealth easily translates into other realms and provides those entering competitive markets with large assets with undue advantages. These advantages are ultimately unjustifiable. To others, this is not a question of morals, but of fair competition, or even economic efficiency. From Adam Smith to James Meade, Samuel Bowles and Herbert Gintis to Fred Hirsch, economists have highlighted the dangers of monopolies, a tendency greatly enhanced by high asset concentrations. If a small group of people—let's say the richest 1 percent of adults who, according to Oxfam (January 2015) own 50 percent of the world's wealth—has already brought most goods and assets under their control, then these goods and assets are no longer on the market for the 99 percent who are not rich. The 99 percent as a result have to complete in a market that is not only reduced by 50 percent, but also a market in which all the most desirable goods and assets have already been bought up and are shielded against the competition of the 99 percent through high prices.

Concretely, this means that the vast majority of average-earning people will never gain access to houses on the beach or to apartments in New York City, London, Frankfurt, or Hong Kong. Nor will they ever gain systematic access to high-quality education. Never—unless those goods are reintroduced back into the market of average-earning citizens.

The very broad spectrum of authors discussed here represent only a fraction of authors and average people who have reached the same apparently inevitable conclusion: to protect equal opportunity and fairness while also protecting against tyrannical states and their apparatuses asset holding has to be limited, asset inheritance has to be radically undermined, and education and health services have to be made available to all in the same way and with the same quality. Those who press this further, like John Rawls and Amartya Sen, have argued that those who enter competitive situations with a disadvantage need to receive more assets and education so they can reach a position of equal opportunity *before* they start competing with everybody else. These conclusions are inevitable if democracy, fairness, and equal opportunity are the goals. These proposals are, as I have demonstrated, not radical or utopian, but practical and realistic in their necessity.

I am unaware of any current concrete proposals to enact upper limits of income and wealth possession other than in Bolivia, discussed shortly. This topic is, however, of the utmost importance and central to any attempt to protect equal opportunity and fairness, as I have demonstrated. While discussing minimum wages has much merit, a much more important and urgent discussion we need to have is about maximum wages and, even more importantly, maximum asset holdings, be it in the form of land, real estate, securities, or any other form of asset.

How to enact such policies and what sort of specific policy proposals promise the most efficient way to control and counteract high asset concentration should become one of the core discussions of any democracy concerned with fairness and equal opportunity. In its absence, war and destruction provide the only mechanisms able to level the playing field for future generations. So far, most Western societies have relied precisely on those destructive forces to provide the young with new opportunities (Schumpeter 1976). As a result, most post-war societies experienced growth and opportunities. Death and destruction thus allowed for new opportunities and space for expansion for those who survived. We cannot, however, wait on the destructive forces of war, nature, or capitalism to provide new generations of people with economic opportunities. Or maybe we should not. Asset limitations, coupled with high-quality universal education and high-quality health care, make it possible to entrust new generations to themselves and their communities without having to provide them with unfair privileges so they can prevail over all others. Such a model is not sustainable in the long run, as not all can win, and even if a few win due to their inherited privileges, the majority will always lose.

NOTES

1. The Ethnographic Atlas is a database on 1,167 societies coded by George P. Murdock and published in twenty-nine successive installments in the journal *Ethnology*, 1962–1980. It gives ethnographic codes and geographical coordinates but no actual maps (maps were later added by the World Cultures electronic journal's

MAPTAB program, by Douglas R. White, along with an electronic version of the codes and the codebooks). A summary volume of the Atlas was published by the University of Pittsburgh Press in 1967. It contained the data on 862 of the better described societies in each of 412 cultural clusters of the world. Murdock published a new edition with Pittsburgh Press in 1980 titled *Atlas of World Cultures* and included 563 of the better described societies in the atlas, classified in 150 more linguistically based clusters (http://eclectic.ss.uci.edu/~drwhite/worldcul/atlas.htm).

2. To illustrate: if you start out with a $1 million inheritance and invest this money in securities that grow at a 5 percent average rate every year, you will have earned $50,000 interest in the first year. If you do not spend all the $50,000, but reinvest $20,000, then you will earn (assuming the same 5 percent interest rate with now $1,020,000) $51,000 in year two. If you keep your expenses at $30,000 and reinvest $21,000 in year three, your $1,041,000 will now earn you $52,050 in year three and allow you to invest $1,063,050—thus earning you $53,152.50 in year four. In only five years, assuming a steady average interest rate of 5 percent and a constant spending of $30,000, you will have augmented your capital by over $86,000, earning more interest every year. If you started with $10 million and kept your expenses at $300,000 every year, your capital would have earned you $860,000 before taxes.

3. "Figures show that doctors in some countries are writing prescriptions for more than one in 10 adults, with Iceland, Australia, Canada and the other European Nordic countries leading the way. Separate data from the US shows that more than 10% of American adults use the medication. In China, the antidepressant market has grown by about 20% for each of the past three years, albeit from a lower base. Global rates of depression have not risen to the same extent, even though more people are being diagnosed in some countries" (Boseley, Chalabi, and Rice-Oxley 2013).

4. The document including Article 16 before its alterations can be accessed at http://founders.archives.gov/documents/Franklin/01-22-02-0314.

5. Document available at https://www.marxists.org/history/international/iwma/documents/1868/iasd-program.htm.

6. I am aware that there are more subtle Marxist, neo-Marxist, and post-Marxist approaches and indeed answers to the crisis of capitalism and I am indebted to some of them, particularly those advanced by such authors as J. K. Gibson-Graham, Ernesto Laclau and Chantal Mouffe, David Harvey, and Slavoj Žižek, but my own proposal differs from these approaches in that I do not seek to elaborate a theoretical response to the crises of capitalism. Instead I seek to employ theory only to the extent that it can help me guide my empirical research and direct my gaze toward those empirical sites where alternatives are likely to be found and observed. Of all the authors mentioned here, my efforts come closest to the work of Gibson-Graham (2006), but focus on empirical examples of political not economic innovation.

7. A complicating factor for this possibility is populational growth, which must come to an end if zero-growth is our long-term goal.

Part II

EMPIRICAL CASES

The empirical studies presented here constitute the core of this book. They are the basis upon which I draw my conclusions because I do not aim to make a theoretical argument here. As stated earlier, I simply use theory to direct my gaze at those empirical phenomena that are relevant to this general endeavor and my specific research question and interest. Theory, beyond allowing us to look at reality a certain way and from a certain angle, also presents reality a certain way by putting it in order. Theory is thus more than a lens; it is a filter to look at the world, allowing some information to pass through while keeping some out. Theory helps to make sense of the world.

The theory I have presented so far is aimed at presenting the world in a certain way. This is not a neutral or objective exercise. It is done with a specific interest in mind. My interest here is to first detect viable alternatives to capitalism and political representation and then to seek empirical examples in which some of these alternatives have been practiced. My gaze is geared firmly toward political institutions. This is so, I suspect, in part because I am a political scientist and hence interested in political institutions over other potentially relevant categories and ways to think about society and power. It is also driven by my conviction that the different political institutions I will show present different answers or solutions to universal problems.

The universal problem I am interested in analyzing is "how to organize collectives so that fairness and equal opportunity prevail over generations." My assumption is that the bundle of political institutions making up the Western liberal democratic way to achieve this is not the only possible way to address this problem. Maybe Western-type political institutions at one point came close to addressing this problem successfully. But times have changed and most institutions and regulations have not, so it is not surprising that they no longer live up to their promises (if anybody even remembers their promises).

Instead, many have become ossified and ineffective at securing and protecting fairness and equality. Maybe they have never achieved this goal because from the very beginning the political institutions created to organize political communities were tainted by elite interests. The Greek city-states, Athens in particular, not only accepted slavery, but apparently relied on it for its democratic advances. The American founding fathers did the same, and so did the French revolutionaries, as the case of Haiti demonstrates. Be that as it may, changing times require changing political institutions and political institutions have to constantly be adapted, as any set of political institutions aimed at establishing fairness and equality will by default face the onslaught of elite interest as soon as elites have formed.

It is easiest to organize and respond to attempts of elite rule at the beginning, before elite rule can become consolidated and thoroughly institutionalized. Once elite rule has achieved this, legitimation will follow, making it more and more difficult to even think about, let alone propose, alternative political institutions (Berger and Luckmann 1966). This is the state of affairs today. Liberal democracy has become so highly institutionalized and legitimated that any debate about possible alternatives appears utopian in the worst sense, that is, impossible and naïve.

The solution to this problem of lack of possible alternatives I have embraced is to point out empirical examples or practiced alternatives. All of the cases presented here are real-life and practiced experiences. As such they represent possible solutions to the universal problem of political organization. It is worth taking a closer look at the specific political institutions enacted at one time or another, in one place or another, as all these institutions show promise. They were all designed to hold elite rule at bay, to protect equal opportunity, and to ensure and enshrine fairness among members of a collective. I will thus provide a description of the political institutions relevant in each case.

My descriptions are necessarily scant and limited, as I do not have the space to provide thick descriptions of twenty-two cases. Those readers interested in more detailed descriptions should look for ethnographies about them. Many exist, and those ethnographies provided the empirical material I used to extract from them what is relevant for my current purpose. I only conducted primary empirical research on three cases: Palenque de San Basílio, the Wintukua, and participatory budgeting, and I have published thicker descriptions of these cases elsewhere (Reiter 2007; 2008; 2015; 2017).

The main question, to me, is not *if* an institutionalized solution to a political problem invented and developed in one place and at one time can help solve a similar problem at another, it is *under what conditions*. This is so because to some extent the political problems human communities face are universal. We all face the risk of some to abuse others and then justify it with reference to being better qualified, more gifted, smarter, or otherwise better suited to rule than others. We all face structural economic dynamics that tend to lead to the concentration of different forms of assets and wealth and we are all faced with the attempts of those who have been able to acquire advantages over others seeking to secure and protect them—and pass them on to their own children. These are, again, universal problems. Their attempted solutions are not. Solutions instead grow out of local knowledge, experience, culture, and what has become tradition. Political solutions to this universal problem in fact *become* culture and tradition if successful, whereas "success" only means achieving broad acceptance and legitimacy. Because political institutions can become culturally embedded and solidified, they can also travel and be adopted elsewhere or maybe be adapted to another reality.

How, then, can we learn which institutions hold the most promise for holding political and economic elitism at bay? This question is an empirical one. We can describe different more or less promising political institutions, created at different times, in different places, and under different circumstances. This is part of my approach here. The reader will find the distilled political institutions of "anti-elitism," developed in different parts of the world over the past 2,500 years. As such, the case studies presented here represent great human wisdom and experience and it is worth learning about each single case, as each one offers promising institutional designs.

I was able to collect information from twenty-two cases, but of course there are many more. Virtually every society at one point or another had to respond to the attempts of some in their midst to elevate themselves and become despots over others. All societies at some point face the problem of the concentration of assets and wealth, particularly over generations. Call this the "Iron Law of Oligarchy" or simply "Market Mechanisms at Work"—inequality, asset concentration, and despotism are likely to appear at some point. It is the actions taken to fight back against despotism and to protect fairness and equality that are of interest here, and political scientists should spend much more time collecting these different institutional responses, analyzing them, and sharing them. Sadly, I am certain that some of the most effective institutions to fight economic and political elitism are lost forever, as they were simply not recorded or written down—and if so, then not given any attention by Western colonial science. This is the case in most African and Asian egalitarian political institutions. We simply do not know much about them, particularly because colonialism has ensured that Western institutions were adopted in non-Western societies, displacing local ones.

African village democracy can look back at a long history, but most of these traditions have been distorted by colonialism (Mamdani 1996) or forgotten even by local elites, most of whom were trained in Western institutions in which they learned how to dismiss and disregard local wisdom. The *kgotla* village democracy system of Botswana represents an exception, as there is some knowledge about its workings, but even here our knowledge about specific institutional design is very scant—so scant that I have not included this case here. Other cases are very promising, but have been highly politicized, such as the post-Revolutionary Soviets created in such cities as Petrograd, on which almost too much literature exists. This literature, however, does not provide enough valid information on the institutional design of the soviet formed there in 1915. I have thus only included cases in which I found reliable information on the political institutions created to fight back against political and economic elitism.

None of the twenty-two cases presented here are perfect and I am well aware of their limitations, both in terms of their degree of democraticness and the degree to which they have created and sustained fair markets and equal opportunities. Some cases only score highly on one dimension, while others contain several factors that are of relevance to this study. Accordingly, some cases are given more space than others. The descriptions given of each case are thus far from complete. Instead I focus on what I found relevant to the interest of this study, where "relevance" is established in accordance with the preceding chapters. I am exclusively interested in innovative and promising institutions and I thus focus only on those, neglecting to a great extent the broader contexts, the drawbacks, and the limitations of each innovation. This is justifiable, I think, given my specific and rather narrow interest. Each case could have a footnote stating something like "while very participatory, women were not allowed and slaves played a large role in this society" (Athens) or "despite its progressive design, many of the changes these new rules foresee have not translated entirely into reality" (Bhutan, Bolivia). For the most part, I have not added such footnotes and again want to remind the reader that I am interested in finding and isolating successful and promising laws, regulations, institutions, and constitutions, even if they are present together with other less promising ones or if they are submerged in rather dire realities.

Chapter 4

Classic and Medieval Cases

Athens is an obvious starting point in this search for empirical learning. Not because it is where democracy started. It did not. Democracy started much earlier, before human communities settled on fixed leaders and hierarchical structures (Service 1975). However, classical Athens is the place that allows us to read about the institution of democracy as self-rule as they were instituted in the late sixth and early fifth century BCE—and thus learn from it. The same is true for Republican Rome, where direct democracy was also a practice and where several institutions and laws were crafted to keep a balance between rich patricians and poor plebeians. Finally, we can learn from some European medieval city republics at precisely the moment when the Roman Empire broke apart, creating a power vacuum, and before the new European dynasties were able to form. Power, after all, cannot be administered by the people and the state at the same time, as I have argued earlier.

All three cases presented in this chapter point to innovative political institutions, laws, and regulations aimed at holding elitism and elite domination at bay. They also allow us to glimpse the importance of political community—how it emerged and what it meant originally. All three cases furthermore point to active citizenship as the main ingredient of democracy. Citizenship in Athens, Republican Rome, and the European medieval city republics was characterized first and foremost by duties and responsibilities. It meant being an active member in a political community that sought and fought for ways to retain control over the state and the government. Some of the solutions devised 2,500 years ago have not lost their appeal and currency for today's problems. It rather seems that we have lost much of the democratic spirit that inspired and motivated citizens back then.

CLASSICAL ATHENS

The descriptions of ancient Greek democracy by Aristotle, Plato, Xenophon, Herodotus, Polybius, and Pericles, and the many modern and contemporary scholars who have made ancient Greece their field of study, allow us to reconstruct how democracy was practiced in Athens and surrounding Attica between 507 BCE, when Cleisthenes reformed Athenian governmental institutions in such a way as to avoid the concentration of power among the elites, and 338 BCE, when Athens came under the control of Philip II of Macedon, after the battle of Chaeronea, and joined the League of Corinth in 337 BCE, effectively ending its independence.

The ancient Greek polis sought to nurture its members' sense of moral responsibility toward the collective. Accordingly, the chief benefit of living in a polis was justice and moral improvement as, according to Aristotle, the polis "enunciates what is just, thereby allowing man's best qualities to flourish" (Manville 1997, 45).

Aristotle explains in his *Politics*: "To be fellow citizens is to be sharers in one polis, and to have one polis is to have one place of residence" (*Pol.* 1260b40–1261a1). According to Aristotle, the citizen of the polis is one "who enjoys the right of sharing in deliberative or judicial office" (*Pol.* 1275b18–20). Thus according to the words of one analyst, Athenian citizens were not taxpayers, but shareholders in a corporation whose profits were moral excellence (Manville 1997, 45).

To be a full Athenian citizen did not mean to have influence in the doings of the state, but rather to be part of the state. Athenian democracy provides not only the strongest example of direct democracy, but also an example of a political system in which ruling and being ruled overlapped considerably. The core of Athenian democracy consisted of not separating rulers from ruled. Indeed, Athenian citizens all participated in the ruling of their polity. To ensure that this setup remained in place, Athenian statesmen devised several means, such as appointment to office by lot. In addition, several institutions were created for the purpose of avoiding a concentration of power among state officials. The strong commitment to avoiding a system in which something like a political ruling class emerged becomes evident from many of the formulations Aristotle uses to describe Athenian democracy; for example, when he explains that because some people are not superior to others, "it is clear that, for a variety of reasons, all must share alike in the business of ruling and being ruled by turns" (*Pol.* 1332b12).

THE CHARACTER OF ATHENIAN CITIZENSHIP

According to Manville, "Citizenship was membership in the Athenian polis, with all that this implied—legal status, but also the more intangible aspects of the life of the citizen that related to his status. It was simultaneously a complement of formal obligations and privileges, and the behavior, feelings, and communal attitudes attendant upon them" (Manville 1997, 7).

In fact, Athenian full citizens had plenty of rights and even more obligations. Once they reached legal adulthood, all young Athenian male citizens were expected to serve in the military. Citizens were entitled to participate in public cults, festivals, and religious worship. They had the right to attend, speak, and vote in the popular assembly (*ekklesia*). They could serve (after the age of thirty) as jurors in the law courts (*dikasteria*). Very importantly, depending on age and eligibility, they could exercise elected and allotted offices (*archai*). They were entitled to redress and receive protection from the laws. They were allowed to own land in Attica. Finally, they were entitled to receive public disbursements for services provided (Manville 1997, 9).

Thus, Athenian citizenship consisted of a set of rights, obligations, and duties toward the collective. It was not a set of legal entitlements only, but rather a political system of breaking down the barriers between ruling and being ruled as much as possible. For Ostwald, "the Greeks tended to see citizenship more in the context of sharing and being part of a community on which the individual depends for his or her sense of identity" (Ostwald 1996, 49). In Athens, citizens ruled themselves.

According to Josiah Ober, "For the first time in the recorded history of a complex society, all native freeborn males, irrespective of their ability, family connections, or wealth, were political equals, with equal rights to debate and to determine state policy" (Ober 1989, 7).

To clarify: Classical citizenship, rather than a right, instead focused on responsibilities and duties. In his famous speech, Pericles emphasizes the duties and responsibilities of Athenian citizenship when he states, "For we alone regard the man who takes no part in such things not as one who minds his own business (apragmona), but as one who has no business here at all (achreion)" (2.40.2, quoted in Manville 1997, 15).

Athenian citizenship thus meant a lot to all those who were citizens. It made them power holders and rulers of their own destinies. How could such a system be achieved and sustained? The successive reforms conducted under Solon, Cleisthenes, and Ephialtes provided the institutional framework that made Athenian democracy possible.

SOLON, CLEISTHENES, AND EPHIALTES:
COUNTERBALANCING SOCIETAL INEQUALITIES
THROUGH POLITICAL INSTITUTIONS

Aristotle says of Solon (c. 638–558), "By setting up courts drawn from the entire body of citizens, he did establish democracy in Athens" (Aristotle 1992, 161). For Aristotle, popular participation in the courts (*dikasteria*) was the core element in which popular sovereignty ultimately rested. Martin Ostwald, the renowned scholar of ancient Greece, agrees, arguing that "Solon established popular power by opening membership in the law courts to all" (Ostwald 1986, 5). Ostwald further explains that "from pre-Solonian times on, there were in Athens two kinds of law courts. Most private litigation fell within the jurisdiction of one of the nine *archons*, each in charge of his own tribunal and each within a well-defined sphere of competence, authorized to judge lawsuits in their own right, and not, as they do nowadays, merely to conduct the preliminary inquiry" (Ostwald 1986, 6).

Other cases regarded as private were tried before the Areopagus, that is, the council of ex-*archons* with considerable power across several jurisdictions that had at all times in Athenian history jurisdiction in all cases of homicide, wounding or poisoning with intent to kill, arson, and such religious matters as the care of the sacred olive trees (Ostwald 1986, 6f; also Sealey 1964, 12).

Most specialists agree that the core of the Solonian reforms consisted of three measures. First, the prohibition against giving loans on the security of the person of the debtor, thus providing important safeguards against losing one's freedom and establishing very basic rights of unalienable personhood for Athenian citizens; second, the right to take legal action on behalf of an injured party, independent from one's social standing; and third, the institution of an appeals procedure (*ephesis*) and a new court (*heliaia*) to hear appeals, which provided a check against the arbitrary administration of justice on the part of the aristocratic establishment and made the people the court of last resort (Ostwald 1986, 14f).

Democratic reform in Athens was advanced even further by Cleisthenes (c. 570–507). The historian Herodotus, who credits him with the true establishment of Athenian democracy, mentioned Cleisthenes's reforms. The central question that Cleisthenes addressed was how to prevent societal inequalities from spilling over into the public realm. In contrast with modern reform proposals that target societal inequalities and seek to achieve equitable political influence by equalizing society, Cleisthenes took societal inequalities for granted and instead sought to devise ways to diminish their importance in the political realm. The main way Cleisthenes pursued this goal was by breaking ethnic and regional, as well as tribal and clan-based loyalties and replacing them with civic ones. This was achieved in the main by dividing

Attica into three regions—city, coast, and inland—and then creating small administrative units called *demes*.

Above the *demes*, Cleisthenes created thirty *trittyes*, and above those ten *phylai*. Each *phylus* (tribe) contained three *trittyes*, one *trittye* from each of the three regions (Jones 1999, 155). Power rested with the general assembly (*ekklesia*), which met every ten days. "Each a fraction of the Athenian whole, tribe succeeded tribe in the administration of the city" (Leveque and Vidal-Naquet 1996, 15). According to Pierre Leveque and Pierre Vidal-Naquet, "Thenceforth, no room was left for the old "regionalist" parties dating from the middle of the sixth century. The reform drew the logical conclusions of at least two centuries of evolutionary change in the polis, which at first had been centered on the Acropolis, then on the Agora and the Prytaneum" (Leveque and Vidal-Naquet 1996, 10).

This institutional design provided a way to neutralize the political influence of dynastic clans, family factions, and regional loyalty by diluting them and forcing different regional groups (*pedieis*, the faction of the plains; *paralioi*, the faction of the coast; and *hyperakrioi*, the faction of the hills) together into new associations (Ellis and Stanton 1968, 98). Furthermore, Cleisthenes created six new *trittyes*, that is, regional associations, amplifying them from the previous four and populating those new *trittyes* with *demes* from different regions with different social and economic standing. This is the mixed form of government that Aristotle talks about in his treatise on politics (Ostwald 1986, 19).

However, according to Ostwald, even after Cleisthenes's reforms, the Athenian upper class still controlled several important political institutions, thus giving it supremacy and control over the ordinary citizens. Particularly, the treasurers still had to be members of the highest property class, and the nine *archons*, or governors, of the highest two. Furthermore, the Aeropagus, the high court of appeal for both criminal and civil cases, was still dominated by societal elites (Ostwald 1986, 26f). Considered as a whole, the Cleisthenian reforms created the basis for political equality among citizens through institutionally enforcing the principles of political equality or *isonomia* (Ober 1989, 70).

The final measures toward establishing true political equality among citizens are associated with the third of the Athenian reformers, Ephialtes. Ostwald explains, "Just as political *isonomia* implied that no legislative measure could be valid without the approval of the Assembly, so a judicial *isonomia* was introduced, either by Cleisthenes himself or soon after his reforms, in crimes against the state, in which the verdict of the people as a whole acted as a counterweight to what had been the sole jurisdiction by a body composed of the rich and well born. Ephialtes' achievement was to complete the process by giving the people full sovereignty in handling crimes against the state" (Ostwald 1986, 39f).

According to Ober, "In 462, an important, if somewhat obscure, series of reforms crippled the direct political power of the elite. A certain Ephialtes led a movement to strip the 'extra powers' from the Areopagus council . . . the Areopagus probably lost some of its legal powers, including the authority to review and set aside as 'unconstitutional' decisions of the Assembly" (Ober 1989, 77; also Rihil 1995). Ostwald provides some more detail on the reforms introduced by Ephialtes. He explains that the transfer of judicial powers in political cases from an aristocratic body, the Areopagus, to the Council of 500, in which every deme of Attica was represented to the Assembly, and of which every adult male citizen was a member, and eventually to the jury courts, on which every adult male was eligible to serve, did not, to be sure, place executive power into the hands of the *demos.*

The highest offices in the state remained the preserve of the higher property classes, and even the opening of the archonship to the *zeugitai* as of 457/456, which was a further step toward a more complete democracy, meant only that this office no longer ranked as a major magistracy. Still, by transferring jurisdiction in political cases from the Areopagus to popular organs, Ephialtes gave the *demos* an effective control over the executive offices that is tantamount to guardianship over the state; by extending to judicial proceedings the *isonomia* that Cleisthenes had given the people in legislative matters, he created popular sovereignty, which was justly called *demokratia* (Ostwald 1986, 49).

Each *deme* annually sent a fixed number (based on its population) of individuals to serve on the new advisory Council of 500, which replaced the Solonian Council of 400, and by doing so, the elite lost its veto power over the decisions of the masses (Ober 1989, 78). In this Council of 500, every Athenian citizen had the right to speak, called *isegoria*, thus making it the basis of popular sovereignty.

After 462, Athenian democracy saw a lowering of property qualifications for office holding, as well as the introduction of pay for government service. In 457 all offices, including the archonships, were opened to the *zeugitai*, that is, manual workers. This movement away from property qualification was indeed gradually expanding during the fifth century BCE, so that by the fourth century there were no more property qualifications for office holding, and even *thetes*, landless peasants and agricultural laborers, could hold public office—and in fact many did (Ober 1989, 80).

Athenian citizens learned, through practical political participation, how to rule themselves and their polity, leading Ober to the conclusion that "at Athens the masses ruled, and the decisions of the majority were binding upon the minority . . . the absence of property qualifications for the exercise of citizenship rights was a basic principle of the Athenian political order. Pay for office holding and for political participation, selection of magistrates by lot, and the right of free speech in the Assembly—all of which were guaranteed by the binding nature of mass decisions upon the entire populace—made domination of the state's political apparatus by rich citizens more difficult" (Ober 1989, 193).

THE INSTITUTIONS OF DEMOCRATIC ATHENS

Athens, after the reforms of Solon and Cleisthenes, had a general assembly open to all, roughly 30,000 citizens. This assembly met forty times a year.

The judicial system was composed of courts (*dikasteria*) that met daily. Its 500 jurors were chosen randomly among all men citizens above thirty years of age. Athens also had an appellate court (*helaia*) with 6,000 members, also chosen by lottery among men over thirty. Above these two, there still was a court of elders (Areopagus), all former officials of the executive (*archons*).

The executive system was composed of a council of 500 men (*boule*), composed of fifty members from each tribe (*trittye*). The service time in this executive council was one year. The *boule* met every day.

Importantly, the ten tribes were not composed of bonds of family, ethnicity, or social status. The main merit of the reforms of Cleisthenes (570–507 BC) was precisely the creation of these artificial tribes, composed of people from different family groups, wealth, and regions. Cleisthenes's main aim was precisely to break family solidarity and social status and replace it with a civic solidarity.

This, to me, is to this day the most radical example of how to deal with differences between various groups and individuals. Instead of abolishing the differences and trying to make people equal, which will necessarily impact their individual freedom and limit their agency, Cleisthenes mixed, different from Marx, different people of different economic, family, and regional backgrounds together and made them make decisions together. With that he created a system and institutions that counterbalanced existing inequalities and prevented the stark inequalities of economic and political status from penetrating the political sphere (Leveque and Vidal-Naquet 1996). In other words, Cleisthenes created institutions that protected the political sphere from the undue influence of the economic sphere. This solution, contrary to Marx's proposal, helped Cleisthenes achieve two goals simultaneously: political equality and economic freedom. As a result, Athens, unlike socialist systems, did not have to become an authoritarian political system to safeguard equality.

Holding political and economic power apart also was a concern of the American founding fathers and it was one of the reasons to place state capitals away from economic centers. But Cleisthenes created much more effective and exemplary institutions to protect democracy from the influence of economic elitism. He created civic alliances, which replaced ethnic and economic alliances. He went so far as to replace family names with the names of the civic tribe one belonged to.

In addition, all the young men of Athens had to serve in the army, which was another measure to strengthen civic and national alliances. As a result of these reforms, civic patriotism grew very strong in Athens, to the point where it became more and more hostile toward non-Athenians and ultimately led to war (Thucydides 1954).

With this, in the ancient Greece of Cleisthenes, citizens were the state and sovereignty was truly popular. There was no representation in the legislative and everyone was involved in the executive and legislative process (Manville 1997). According to Josiah Ober, "For the first time in the recorded history of a complex society, all native freeborn males, irrespective of their ability, family connections, or wealth, were political equals, with equal rights to debate and to determine state policy" (Ober 1989, 7). It is worth noting that 30,000 citizens were able to do this without phones, e-mail, or cars.

THE ROMAN REPUBLIC

Well before the beginnings of the Republic, commonly dated at 509 BCE, Roman society was divided into patricians and plebeians. Adcock explains that "the patrician body . . . was united in tradition and social consciousness; small as it was, by its military and landowning character and its clientele it went far to justify the position of privilege which it enjoyed" (Adcock 1969, 20).

The Roman Republic was established when the early monarchy was terminated in 509, and it lasted until the year 27 BCE, when Octavian was named Augustus and became emperor. Under the Roman Republic, sovereignty rested with SPQR, "*Senatus Populusque Romanus*"—the senate and people of Rome (Shotter 1994, 4). However, the people of Rome were highly stratified and divided into several property classes (Vanderbroeck 1987, 18). According to specialist Paul Vanderbroeck, "At the bottom of society were the (male) free citizens, who had the right to vote and who participated in the popular assemblies. Among this group large differences could exist. . . . A special phenomenon of Roman society was that freed slaves were enfranchised. The relationship between members of the upper strata and the lower strata is mostly to be qualified as a patron-client relation. Vertical ties permeated all status groups and existed in multifarious forms" (Vanderbroeck 1987, 20).

Roman citizenship was thus split into two groups: patricians and plebeians. Plebeians had access to sovereignty and could be elected to the senate, but political office was not remunerated, which made it practically impossible for average plebeians to serve. Popular sovereignty rested in the assemblies: three *comitia* and the *Concilium Plebis*. However, according to Shotter, "There was neither freedom of debate nor power of initiating business from the floor. The people's function, in other words, was limited to that of voting" (Shotter 1994, 5).

The senate, dominated by the rich, exercised broad clientelistic power over the common people, and "senatorial endorsement (*senatus consultum*) was considered a necessary prerequisite to the exercise of popular sovereignty" (Shotter 1994, 5). Plebeian citizens had the right to protest senate decisions (*provocatio*) and they could elect their own tribal leaders, called tribunes. In the Concilium Plebis, binding decisions could be made that became law once the two consuls elected from within the senate agreed. However, in the third century BCE the decisions of the plebeian assembly were given the independent force of law (Shotter 1994, 7). This strengthening of popular sovereignty has led one of the foremost scholars of Republican Rome, Fergus Millar, to conclude that "the *populus Romanus* was not a biological descent group, but a political community defined by rights and duties (the latter consisting predominantly of military service in the legions), and it was formed above all by the progressive extension of Roman citizenship throughout Italy, and by the distinctive Roman custom of giving citizenship to freed slaves. Participation as a citizen was not limited by considerations of wealth or class (though the holding of elective office certainly was), but it will have been far more profoundly affected by distance. The unaltered convention that the citizen could exercise his rights only in person, by voting in the Forum or the Campus Martius, gave an overwhelming predominance in the politics of the late Republic to those 'representatives' of the wider *populus Romanus* who lived in and around the city" (Millar 1998, 211).

The Social Wars of 90–87 BCE between Rome and its Italian allies (the *socii*) were resolved largely by Rome's extending citizenship to all those south of the river Po in 90 BCE. A census conducted in the year 70 BCE indicates that by then, Roman citizenry had reached 910,000 (Millar 1998, 28).

Thus, whereas the Athenian polis categorically excluded women, slaves, and foreigners from being active citizens, during the Roman Republic property was the main, even if not the only, criterion for exclusion from the political community. Plebeians, however, had legislative authority in their conciliums, and the tribunes elected from these had significant power. They could veto laws, elections, and the actions of other magistrates they felt were against the interests of the plebeians. In the middle of the fifth century, Rome passed a legal code that added protection to plebeians.

THE PLEBEIAN STRUGGLE FOR POLITICAL RIGHTS

Patrician power did not go uncontested. Throughout the Roman Republic, ordinary Roman citizens—plebeians—sought and found ways to challenge and contest the power of the patrician elites. Between 494 and 88 BCE, that is, from the passing of the Lex Sacrata, which formally established the Concilium Plebis, the forum of the common people, until the date when Sulla took Rome and ended the power of the tribunate, we can analyze several laws and democratic institutions that characterized the Roman Republic. Of course, what we had in Rome was no true democracy in the sense that the Greeks gave the word. It was rather an oligarchy or aristocracy, with a strong concentration of power in the hands of the nobles and patricians, who claimed for themselves control of the senate at all times of the republic. Still, there was no representative system and sovereignty was popular and belonged to all Roman citizens throughout the time of the republic. During all this time, Roman citizens had the power to declare war, choose administrators, and pass laws. Throughout the period of the republic, political decisions were taken in public and in the open with the participation of Roman citizens.

To enable and protect the influence of ordinary people in Roman politics, several laws and institutions were put in place:

- The Comitia Curiata was the first assembly, created, according to legend, by Romulus. It had a representation by families and clans (of the thirty *curiae*) of the Roman people. With the emergence of the republic, this *comitia* lost almost all its power and took an increasingly symbolic role.
- The Comitia Tributa was an assembly of tribes by place of residence. With the expansion of Rome, this *comitia* grew from four to thirty-five tribes represented there.
- The Comitia Centuriata was the general assembly where the Roman people were represented by groups of status and wealth. Determined by the census that was conducted every five years, the Romans were divided into five groups, plus equestrians and *proletarii*. The equestrians, who were rich, together with the Class 5, the richest of the pedites, controlled 98 of a total of 198 votes. In 241 BCE the Comitia Centuriata was reformed so that from then on the richest citizens did not control an absolute majority, but the influence of the poorer classes remained low.
- In 494, with the Lex Sacrata, the Concilium Plebis was formally created, a public assembly open only to ordinary people (and not aristocrats). The Tribunis Plebis was elected by the people and represented the interests of ordinary people.

With the Lex Hortensia, passed in 287 BCE, all bills proposed in the Concilium Plebis, the plebiscites, were considered law and did not need, as before, to be approved by the senate or to pass through another comitium (Brunt 1971).

The supreme executive power was given to the consulate, but there were always two consuls who had to agree and service was restricted to one year— the same for other administrative and executive positions (*praetors, aediles, quaestors,* tribunes).

Reelection was forbidden (although it happened) and, importantly, after the service ended, the parting administrators and executives were held accountable for what they had done and could be taken to court.

Consuls, censors, praetors, and tribunes could all propose laws, but the people gathered and represented in the Comitia Centuriata had the last word and Roman law was thus an expression of popular sovereignty and relied on the active political participation of the Roman people (Brunt 1971).

There were other measures to ensure the sovereign power of the people and to limit the power of the patricians. Between 494 and 88, a total of 236 laws, proposed legislation (*rogationes*), and plebiscites all sought to protect or increase equality, popular participation, mutual consultation, and protection of the poorest groups—the four categories that according to Charles Tilly (2007) characterize a process of democratization.

Among these were:

- 367, reserving one consulship for plebeians;
- 357, which limits interest rates;
- 342, prohibiting a consul to be reelected to office after ten years have passed and prohibiting anyone from holding two public offices simultaneously;
- 342, which states that the two consuls might be plebeians;
- 218, which limits the number and size of vessels that a senator can own;
- 209, setting limits on gifts one can make to one's patron;
- 189, giving freed slaves citizenship;
- 123, regulating the distribution of grain to poor citizens;
- 89, opening of the courts to ordinary people, with fifteen jurors from each tribe;
- and many laws, at different times, on land reform, the use of public land, and debt forgiveness.

In addition, during the Roman Republic, the richest and most powerful citizens, the patricians, had concrete and formal obligations toward the most vulnerable because these were their clients.

MEDIEVAL EUROPEAN CITY STATES: *ARENGOS*

European city republics emerged from the power vacuum left by the crumbling Carolingian empire toward the end of the ninth century. The communes slowly wrested power from kings and bishops via concessions. Such was the case, for example, with Lucca, which secured a concession from Henry IV in 1081 not to build castles within six miles of the city and no building within its city limits. "Henry also renounced jurisdiction within the city of Pisa and promised to name no new marquis in Tuscany without the consent of the Pisans" (Waley and Dean 2010, 9f). Apparently, such concessions were preferable to the violent uprisings that some cities had organized when their claims were denied. To Waley and Dean, "Communes filled these gaps, providing effective connections between political power and local elites" (Waley and Dean 2010, 10).

The ways other communes emerged in this region are very similar. "First, we have the Marquis, or his representative the viscount, of Teutonic origin, presiding in the courts, surrounded by his *Scabini*, or judges, who, although in one sense imperial officers, seem nevertheless to have been chosen usually from among the inhabitants of each town and territory, and not to have travelled about in the suite of the overlord" (Duffy 2011 [1892], 3). According to Duffy, these relatively independent *Scabini* gave the starting impulse for further independence. Duffy also highlights the fact that such a development occurred in northern Italy precisely because the bishop was less influential than elsewhere and the German overlord, in the figure of the marquis, was relatively distant.

What emerged in Tuscany as a result was a relatively small commune of free citizens, who regularly met in a popular assembly and, so assembled, elected "twelve principal citizens, who are variously distinguished as *Buoni uomini*, *Sapientes*, or *Majores*. Thirty years or so later, these Buoni uomini are fewer in number, and have received the title of Consuls" (Duffy 2011 [1892], 6).

Once these communities had reached maturity, the people of the lower classes were able to challenge the dominance of the richer merchants and craftsmen, especially by creating powerful guilds. Social parties and associations also started to emerge. In fourteenth-century Florence, for example, social parties formed around income and social standing, thus constituting a party of the upper middle class (Grassi), one of the middle class (Mediani), and one of the lower class (Minuti). High-ranking officials were now elected from those three. According to Duffy, "In little more than one year Florence had undergone four changes of government, the final result of which was to strengthen the power of the two lower classes at the expense of those rich and powerful members of the community who, whenever the *grandi* succumbed, had remained the dominant faction" (Duffy 2011 [1892], 162f).

Indeed, in the first half of the fourteenth century, Florence's rich and powerful citizens lost so much influence in the administration and management of city affairs that many withdrew to the countryside out of frustration. However, this rise of the lower guilds was soon met by concerted efforts of the higher guilds, who sought to control the power of the lower classes by establishing an oligarchy.

According to Duffy, "In 1371, the supremacy, thus obtained, of the Ricci and Albizzi, was felt to be so intolerable that the people named a commission, or Balia of fifty-six members, for the express purpose of excluding those two families entirely from office" (Duffy 2011 [1892], 174). Continued discontent among the people of Florence finally led to a violent popular uprising in June 1378, through which the lower classes of Florence secured their influence in city politics. Their influence lasted until 1433, when Cosimo de Medici's tyranny finally ended the communal republic of Florence. Toward the end of the fifteenth century, all of the citizen republics of northern Italy finally succumbed to the competing influences of Pope Francesco della Rovere, Sixtus IV, and Lorenzo de Medici the Magnificent (Duffy 2011 [1892], 298f).

One of the core features of these free cities was their relatively small size. Very few had more than 20,000 inhabitants. This small size was also grounded in the conviction that for a community to work, its members had to know and be able to discuss daily affairs with each other. Just like Plato and Aristotle, medieval city leaders thought that 100,000 inhabitants was the upper limit of viability for a republic (Waley and Dean 2010, xxi).

Weber also explains the principle of *Stadtluft macht frei* ("city air makes free") because the economic opportunity that cities offered allowed many to purchase their freedom from slavery or serfdom and join the commune of free citizens (Weber 1968, 1238). Indeed, according to Weber, "The urban citizenry therefore usurped the right to dissolve the bonds of seigniorial domination; this was the great—in fact, the *revolutionary*—innovation which differentiated the medieval Occidental cities from all others. In the central and northern European cities appeared the well-known principle that *Stadtluft macht frei*, which meant that after a varying but always relatively short time the master of a slave or serf lost their right to reclaim him" (Weber 1968, 1239).

In most cases, the time it took to actually become a free member of the city commune was not so short—typically one year and one day, but sometimes much longer than that—and it was also bound to a series of conditions, such as buying a house and thus becoming a resident and being able to pay a minimum amount of taxes. It was also conditional upon a whole list of duties and responsibilities. Still, free city communes offered a way to escape the rule of the feudal lord and to become a free citizen.

In fact, citizenship in the early Italian city republics implied more duties than rights, and it was not enough to be a formal citizen in order to be eligible for administrative office (Waley and Dean 2010, 62). The requirements and duties of citizenship included loyalty to the commune, obeying its laws and officers, performing military service, attending meetings, and paying taxes, among other things. Citizens in these city republics were required to regularly participate in the great assemblies, called *arengos*, that met regularly to decide major collective matters. The size of such *arengos* varied from some 200 up to 4,000 (Waley and Dean 2010, 36). In addition, citizenship meant active office in one of the many civic and military organizations responsible for conducting and regulating city life. Waley and Dean stipulate that similar to the Athenian democracy, in the medieval north Italian city republics, about one-third of citizens held office every year (Waley and Dean 2010, 65f).

The Arengo of San Marino, for example, was formed during high medieval times, around the year 1000.[1] It was the first form of government of the republic. It was instituted as a result of the need to create a political organ capable of governing and managing the community that had been formed. The term *arengo* originally indicated a gathering of all heads of families, who were summoned together by ringing the main bell tower of the church, to decide on and deal with important matters regarding the functioning of the State of San Marino. This body detained all powers, legislative, executive, and judicial, that were previously in the hands of one man only, the Abbot feudatory.

The *arengo* nominated persons to the highest positions in the state, including the consuls (latter called regents). From 1244 on, the regents (captain regents) took over both executive and judicial activities. The *arengo* also began to draw up the statutes, that is, a series of laws to regulate the life of the community.

To Peter Kropotkin, who wrote in 1902 on the centrality of mutual aid as a universal motive among humans and animals alike,

> With a unanimity which seems almost incomprehensible, and for a long time was not understood by historians, the urban agglomerations, down to the smallest burgs, began to shake off the yoke of their worldly and clerical lords. The fortified village rose against the lord's castle, defied it first, attacked it next, and finally destroyed it. The movement spread from spot to spot, involving every town on the surface of Europe, and in less than a hundred years free cities had been called into existence on the coast of the Mediterranean, the North Sea, the Baltic, the Atlantic Ocean, down to the fjords of Scandinavia; at the feet of the Apennines, the Alps, the Black Forest, the Grampians, and the Carpathians; in the plains of Russia, Hungary, France and Spain. Everywhere the same revolt took place, with the same features, passing through the same phases; leading to the same results. Wherever men had found, or expected to find, some protection behind their town walls, they instituted their "co-jurations," their "fraternities," their "friendships," united in one common idea, and boldly marching towards a new life of mutual support and liberty. (Kropotkin 2014 [1902], 86f)

Kropotkin argues that feudalism had not destroyed the village community, which lived on and found a new framework in the city community and the guild. The emerging medieval cities, even though they selected or elected leaders, never gave up on their right to self-administration and self-jurisdiction (Kropotkin 2014 [1902], 87).

LESSONS LEARNED FROM CLASSIC AND MEDIEVAL EUROPE

As already discussed, according to Jean-Jacques Rousseau, "The idea of representation is modern; it comes to us from feudal government, from that iniquitous and absurd system which degrades humanity and dishonors the name of man. In ancient republics and even in monarchies, the people never had representatives; the word itself was unknown. It is very singular that in Rome, where the tribunes were so sacrosanct, it was never imagined that they could usurp the functions of the people, and that in the midst of so great a multitude they never attempted to pass on their own authority a single *plebiscitum*" (Rousseau 2003 [1762], 65).

In antiquity there was courage and initiative to limit the concentration of political and economic power in a few hands through institutions that protected the common interest. Popular sovereignty was never given up on, especially when it came to making laws. The concept of political representation when it comes to proposing and discussing laws was not known. The legislative process in all of antiquity and not only in Athens and Rome, but also between peoples considered "primitive" and "barbaric" by the Greeks themselves, was always a task for either the many or sometimes the few, but these few never claimed to "represent" the people (Service 1975; Shapiro et al. 2010).

For the citizens of the classical republics, just as for those of the medieval European city republics, the legislative process was and had to be public and direct. It was only with the American and French Revolutions that we get political representation, and we know very well that representation was a measure to mitigate and reduce the influence of the people and not to protect it. It thus comes as no surprise that it was Thomas Hobbes (1588–1679), fearful as he was of his fellow citizens, who is credited with first proposing this idea (Shapiro et al. 2010).

The lessons from Athens are clear: smart laws, regulations, and institutions can avoid the spilling over of economic power into politics. A politics of the common good does not depend on voting, but on self-rule. Self-rule is possible. It was possible for 30,000 Athenian citizens who had no technical or logistic support. Their interaction was face to face. They moved by foot or on horseback. Athenians practiced direct, deliberative democracy and they did not have representatives. Their executive was made up by 500 people. Their courts were independent and staffed by lottery. Despite all of this, they were able to act swiftly and aggressively to foreign threats, particularly after having won victory against the Persian empire in 449 BCE.

The shortcomings of Athens are also clear. Given the extension of the territory and the frequency of meetings and assemblies, actual participation of all citizens must have been limited. Still, a great number of citizens did participate in the general assemblies, which gave rise to the power of oratory and rhetoric—where both must be seen as distortions of the democratic process. Another shortcoming certainly was the high degree to which citizenship was regulated in Athens, at times dependent on double descent, making Athenian democracy highly exclusive.

According to John Pocock, in Rome, "citizenship has become a legal status, carrying with it rights to certain things—perhaps possessions, perhaps immunities, perhaps expectations—available in many kinds and degrees, available or unavailable to many kinds of persons for many kinds of reasons" (Pocock 2007, 36). It no longer meant what it had in Athens, where "citizenship is not just a means to being free; it is the way of being free itself" (Pocock 2007, 32). For Pocock, the Romans legalized citizenship and thus changed its character from the political to the legal. For this distinguished author, this was the beginning of possessive individualism and the rise of "homo legalis," a person whose rights and political power were defined by the amount of assets he commanded. It was also the beginning of stripping citizenship of its aspects of obligation and responsibility. The more citizenship came to solely mean access to rights and entitlements, the more it became subject to the logic of competitive markets, where most assets were worth more if others did not possess them. More than the legalization of citizenship, this transformation meant a gradual commodification of citizenship and its mutation into a possession and a good that only the rich and powerful could afford. In 1981, Pocock wrote: "It begins to look, however, as if the characteristic tendency of jurisprudence was to lower the level of participation and deny the premise that man is by nature political. . . . As the polis and res publica declined toward the level of municipality, two things happened: the universe became pervaded by law, the locus of whose sovereignty was extra-civic, and the citizen came to be defined not by his actions and virtues, but by his rights to do things" (Pocock 1981, 359f).

Despite this critique, the Roman Republic instituted several laws that successfully held the power of the patrician elites in check. Here, as well as in Athens, lawmaking happened in open, public assembly. Deliberation was a built-in feature of its democracy. Popular sovereignty prevailed. Political representation was unknown. Executive power was limited and divided between two consuls. Incumbency was outlawed. The law of 218 imposed limits on the assets rich people could command. Public office holders were required to provide an account of their time in office, which was limited to one year, and they could be sued if their rendering of accounts was off. In other words, accountability of public office holders was ensured and enforced. Roman citizens sought and found ways to protect and extend their influence on public affairs against the powerful senators, and they never handed over sovereignty to them.

The limits of democracy in the Roman Republic are quite clear: rich aristocrats dominated the political process. As the republic grew larger and larger, direct participation became less and less viable for ordinary citizens, particularly those residing outside of Rome. As this happened, Roman direct democracy became more and more exclusive and elite-dominated.

Medieval city republics emerged as a response to abusive elitism and aristocratic control. They provided a way to escape slavery and serfdom. Once instituted, the characterizing element of these city republics was their sense of community—Weber's "Verbandscharacter." Citizens wielded and controlled sovereign power. To uphold and defend it against the many foreign enemies, citizenship was active, direct, and very involved. To a great extent, it also was constituted by active military or militia duty aimed at defending the city. The city walls we can visit today provide strong reminders of this reality.

The real threat to this kind of community-based, direct democracy was, however, not coming from outside the city walls, but from emerging elitism within. As some citizens became rich, they also found ways to become politically important, thus gradually wrestling popular sovereignty away from their fellow citizens. What started as a movement against elites ended up succumbing to the new elites emerging from within.

Nevertheless, as long as these democratic experiments lasted, they provide rich examples for how cities can organize democratically, namely through public assemblies or *arengos*. One more time, the principle of direct democracy, particularly when it comes to the making of laws, is what makes these examples important. And again, it was not their focus on rights and entitlements that kept them alive and strong, but their sense of shared duty and responsibility, which were the very basis of their community.

At the same time, direct democracy in these city republics was highly circumscribed and limited. *Arengos* gradually lost power to the city grandes—powerful merchants or guild leaders. Step by step, these started to reproduce within the city walls exactly the kind of inequalities they had originally ran away from when they escaped their feudal lords.

NOTES

1. See http://www.sanmarinosite.com/eng/arengo.html.

Chapter 5

Anarchism

Another set of telling and informative cases comes from different historical attempts to institute anarchism, anarcho-syndicalism, or Räte (Council) Republics. The sort of institutional designs informing this approach were spelled out by such authors as Mikhail Bakunin, Peter Kropotkin, Gustav Landauer, Erich Mühsam, and many others, depending on the national background. They all shared common skepticism against the state, hierarchical organizations in general, and political representation, but they differed on how exactly collectives should organize and based on which principles. The institutions they developed were nevertheless highly effective against elite rule, even if none of the anarchist experiments lasted long. Once states were destroyed, free communities became vulnerable to foreign attacks, as well as internal dissidence, ultimately ending what some have called the "short spring" of anarchism (Hans Magnus Enzensberger, when referring to Spain). In this chapter, I will describe the cases of the Paris Commune of 1887, the German Räte Republics of 1918, and the Spanish Anarchism of 1936–1937. My main focus is, as always, on the kinds of political institutions proposed and enacted by anarchists and during the short periods of time when anarchism was the dominant system.

THE PARIS COMMUNE

When the German Coalition army, led by Prussia, won the Franco-Prussian War of 1870 and besieged the city of Paris, many Parisians followed the call to end the empire and establish a republic. The Third Republic came to power on September 4, 1870, but Paris was still under siege and the masses of Paris started organizing around their twenty neighborhoods, or arrondissements.

Arrondissement councils were created, as well as many political clubs. The arrondissement councils created a central committee. Vigilance committees did the same and the National Guard, which was composed mainly of working-class Parisians, was supportive of ending the rule of elites and establishing municipal autonomy, in which power rested with local communes.

Socialists, Jacobins, Marxists, and Blanquists were all very involved in these local organizations. When the German siege was finally over, leaving Paris starved and demoralized, the Republican Government of National Defense called for elections. On February 8, 1871, after the French capitulation and the agreement to surrender Lorraine and Alsace to Germany, the new elections returned "overwhelmingly conservative, monarchist deputies to the National Assembly, which would meet in Bordeaux, not Paris" (Merriman 2014, 16). One month later, they moved to Versailles, the old seat of the French monarchy. While France was relieved that the war was finally over, the situation was different in Paris. To many Parisians, the end of the war meant the reinstatement of rents, the suspension of payments to the National Guard, and the end of the moratorium on pawned goods in the state-owned pawnshops. Many poor Parisians were still starving, while the rich and powerful were frolicking in Versailles. They were outraged at the conservative government and agitated by the many radicals among them. Many still remembered the 1848 revolution, some also the July revolution of 1830. Ordinary Parisians, mostly from the poor quartiers, started taking to the streets in protest. The government sent in troops to restore order, but they failed. On March 18, 1871, the citizens of Paris defeated the French army, who retreated. According to John Merriman,

> Thiers realized that the army did not have enough troops to crush the insurrection. He first ordered Vinoy to pull his troops back behind the Seine and to occupy the bridges of the Left Bank; then he ordered a complete evacuation of Paris by all government officials, followed by troops. Of about 4,000 policemen, more than 2,500 joined the line troops heading for Versailles. Paris was left with virtually no officials or functionaries, no magistrates or police. Many Parisians of means had already begun to desert the city. The next day, Thiers cut all correspondence between Paris and the provinces. (Merriman 2014, 29)

The Paris Commune was born. It lasted until May 28 of the same year—a total of seventy-two days. The day after the victory, its central committee sent a letter to the government in Versailles demanding the right to elect mayors for each arrondissement, the abolition of the prefecture of the police, the right for the National Guard to elect its own officers, the continuation of the moratorium on rents, and the proclamation of the republic. Elections were held in Paris for the Central Committee of the National Guards and on March 28, the Paris Commune was officially proclaimed. In mid-April, the Commune began to mint its own money. During its seventy-two days of existence, the Commune Council, "which included about sixty-five men, many of whom were also officials in their own arrondissements, met fifty-seven times" (Merriman 2014, 41).

Parallel to the Commune, pre-commune local administrations continued to exist and exercise power. Mayors, deputy majors, and commissioners continued to work. Next to those, the National Guard also exercised influence through its own federation and, to make things even more complicated, the Commune established executive commissions, taking on the authority of ministries, each under a delegate.

As the army regrouped and started to attack Paris from Versailles, the Commune also had to expend efforts toward its defense and survival. Some 20,000 National Guards were assembled to this end.

After taking power of the city, the Central Committee of the Commune issued a statement to the *Journal Officiel*, the official government newspaper. It stated:

> The proletarians of the capital, faced with the incompetence and treachery of the ruling classes, have understood that the hour has come for them to save the situation by taking direction of public affairs. . . . Will the workers, who produce everything and enjoy nothing in return, who endure poverty in the midst of wealth which they have produced by the sweat of their brow, always be subjected to abuse? . . . The proletariat, faced with a constant threat to its rights, a total denial of all its legitimate aspirations, along with the imminent destruction of the country and of all its hopes, has realized that it is its imperative duty and absolute right to take its destiny in its own hands by seizing political power. (Quoted in Bookchin 1998, 224)

FREEDOM

According to the account of Merriman, "The Commune was something of a 'permanent feast' of ordinary people who celebrated their freedom by appropriating the streets and squares of Paris" (Merriman 2014, 52). After the Commune took over the city administration, city life continued as normal. The Louvre opened and even the stock exchange functioned normally. Shops and stores functioned regularly. The difference was mainly perceived in the parks and squares, filled with working-class people. Working-class people from poor neighborhoods also strolled down the avenues of the rich, looking at all the luxury goods they could not afford, but also breaking the invisible barrier that normally kept them out of these neighborhoods. The publication of daily newspapers exploded during the Commune and artists found new freedoms under it.

The communards were a sample of the average Parisian: relatively young and mostly born elsewhere. Only 2 percent of them had secondary education, but only 11 percent were illiterate. Most of them were artisans and craftsmen (Merriman 2014). Most communards did not want to abolish private property. Women participated heavily in the uprising and, according to Merriman, "the status of women improved by leaps and bounds" (Merriman 2014, 64).

The program of the Commune did not seek to abolish private property, but instead focused on the liberty of work and to "universalize power and property according to the necessities of the moment" (Edwards 1971, 82). This was, then, not a socialist or communist revolution, but one based on reestablishing the dignity of work. First and foremost, it sought to support ordinary citizens against the abuses of the rich and powerful. Thus on its second day in office, the Commune council reinstated the moratorium on renting, as many ordinary Parisians could not pay their monthly rent due to the extraordinary situation Paris still found itself in. After six months of war and siege, paying rent was impossible to most. The council also reinstated the moratorium on overdue commercial bills, even if almost one month later. This moratorium was another measure in support of ordinary citizens unable to fulfill their financial obligation during times of war. According to Bookchin,

> The moratoriums were both popular, but the Council's qualms about rushing to reinstate the delay on overdue bills is a striking example of its economic conservativism, reflecting the awe in which the Proudhonists held property, credit, and banking practices. Indeed, it was not until April 25—nearly a month after its establishment—that the Council requisitioned vacant lodgings for the homeless. (Bookchin 1998, 232)

In April, the state-owned pawnshop was given instruction to hand back tools and household items to those workers who had pawned them during times of hardship, thus extending the previously enacted moratorium. The council also enacted legislation that protected workers against the abuse of factory owners. No more fines could be deducted from workers' salaries and the obligatory night shift of bakers was ended. According to Bookchin, "From a leftist perspective, the most celebrated of the Council's decrees was the one issued on April 16 that concerned the empty factories and workshops whose owners had fled Paris during the siege. These vacated premises, according to the new law, could be transformed into self-managed cooperatives" (Bookchin 1998, 233).

The Commune also tried to promote voluntary producers associations and some forty-three were created, but there was not enough time for this to actually materialize. To Bookchin, all of these elements indicate that the Paris Commune had a limited economic outlook and was too fixated on Proudhon's ideas around artisanal socialism. To him, as to other observers, the Commune was less class conscious than the June revolution of 1848. According to Roger Gould,

> The Central Committee of the National Guard Federation, in its own carefully drafted announcement of elections to the Commune, made it abundantly clear that the constituency on whose behalf it saw itself as acting—the constituency, in other words, of the revolution itself—was the entire city of Paris, irrespective of class position. (Gould 1995, 168)

This was, then, not a socialist, class-based revolution, but a civic revolution, more concerned about fair wages, democracy, and local self-administration. Instead of nationalizing the Banc de France, as they could have done, the council merely oversaw its activities as they continued to ask for small loans to keep the city accounts afloat.

The biggest internal problem of the Commune was its diversity in terms of convictions and outlooks, as well as the often redundant and overlapping authorities of the Communal Committee, the National Guard Federal Committee, the twenty arrondissement mayors who often disputed the legitimacy of the Commune, the different executive commissions created by the Commune (executive, military, labor and exchange, industry, and finance), and the many political clubs operating in the different neighborhoods, who at one point also created a federation. In addition to these competing instances of power, much energy was lost in internal struggles. Socialists, Proudhonists, Jacobins, Blanquists, and Republicans did not share the same outlook on what policies were best to enact. In the words of Bookchin, "The Proudhonists were embattled with the socialists, while the Jacobins dueled with almost everyone, including each other" (Bookchin 1998, 237). Among the most quarrelsome were the many intellectuals and Bohemians who also participated in the Commune.

The lack of coordination, maybe of centralization, became an important weakness in the face of the military onslaught that the army brought down on Paris in May 1871. Decentralized libertarianism, it turned out one more time, is not suited to face a centralized army. When the army took Paris and in the trials and court martials that followed, the total number of casualties among the communards reached 25,000, by most accounts. The army lost a total of 877. Thousands of communards were sent into exile. The brutality of the slaughter of poor, working-class Parisians was so outrageous that the foreign press reported it with revulsion and foreign nations put pressure on France to stop it. John Merriman (2014) refers to it as a massacre.

GERMAN RÄTE REPUBLICS

German Räte Republics emerged as spontaneous responses to the societal, economic, and political crisis caused by World War I. According to Ernst Däuming (1866–1922), journalist, revolutionary, and co-founder of the German USPD, "The storm of November 1918 saw workers' and soldiers' councils emerge all over Germany, spontaneously and without any preparation. The revolution created its own expression with elementary force. The council idea does not come from the mind of a particular individual. It can be found in any revolution in which workers lead the struggle for freedom and pursue proletarian and socialist goals" (Däuming 1920, in Kuhn 2012, 51).

From the beginning, this movement was aimed at establishing self-rule by workers and soldiers, the two groups that had been used as "cannon fodder" not just during World War I, but also in general during this time of general industrialization and rapid economic expansion.

According to Volker Arnold, "because of the willingness of the masses to self-organize, gradually, regional and supra-regional councils were formed at the municipal, regional, provincial, and state levels. All this happened without the involvement of political party leadership" (Arnold 1985, 48; my translation). Arnold also highlights that in 1918, at least by law, Germany constituted itself as a Council Republic, composed of autonomous and self-ruling local councils (Arnold 1985, 49). Däuming explains, "The council organization strives for socialist production and self-managed communities" (Däuming 1920, in Kuhn 2012, 51).

The same Däuming, who was an active participant in the short-lived German Council Republic of 1918–1919, further explains,

> The workers' and soldiers' councils that formed during the first days of the revolution were, as already stated, improvised. They remained improvisations for almost a year. Yes, the soldiers' councils disintegrated after a mere six months due to their own incompetence and the political short-sightedness and spinelessness of their leaders. Today, as these lines are written, it will be decided whether the leading sections of the German proletariat have the insight, the will, and the force to build a council system that lives up to its historical calling, or whether the council idea shall be warped in pitiful employee's organizations that carry the council label in order to consciously deceive the masses. (Däuming 1920, in Kuhn 2012, 52)

Under the anxious leadership of the social democratic party (SPD), which incorporated the revolutionary proposals from the radical wing, but then used them to coopt and control revolutionary workers, worker councils became institutionalized spaces within companies, giving workers a very limited and circumscribed say in the management of the firm. This was, of course, far less then what "workers' councils" had meant originally, when the revolution broke out and "All Power to the Councils" became the slogan of the streets. In fact, the principles of the council idea, according to Ernst Däuming (1920), are,

1. Proletarians, not citizens, as actors;
2. Anti-capitalism;
3. Anti-parliamentarism;
4. No long-term powers to delegates and permanent possibility of instant recall;
5. Anti-political party (proletariat as a whole). (Kuhn 2012)

The statements and writings by Kurt Kautsky and Rosa Luxemburg during and immediately after the November Revolution all reflect the historical moment they were involved in: the need to win the revolution and the need to establish a new socialist order. Under those conditions, it is not surprising that Kautsky argues for a national assembly and against an extension of workers' councils. It is also not surprising that Luxemburg's program includes repeated calls for representation at the national level. Given their communist agenda, it is also clear that both advocated not for general councils, but for workers' and soldiers' councils.

Even though there was a great divide among communists like Luxemburg, and anarchists like Pannekoek, Däuming, Ruhl, Gorter, and Pankhurst, Rosa Luxemburg's critique of parliamentarism captures the critique of both groups against political representation: "England can look back at 700 years of parliamentarism, but it can hardly claim having established democracy with parliamentarism" (Luxemburg 1918). Also in 1918, Rosa Luxemburg explains, "Parliament is, among other things, a means of the ruling class to exercise and uphold their political power" (Schneider and Kuda 1969, 123).

Another core member of the 1918 uprising was Gustav Landauer (1870–1919). He explains,

> I do not believe that we need the central government of Berlin or a national assembly based on the old party system and parliamentarism for the sake of the Entente. We rather need a constitution and a democratic structure based on the people's direct participation in all the individual republics. Hessen (Rheinhessen and Kurhessen), Frankfurt, the Rhine Valley, and Westphalia shall separate from Prussia and form an autonomous republic. Hanover will follow. Then, the union of the southern German, western German, and Austrian republics must form. Then the rest of Brandenburg-Prussia must follow. Each republic must be sovereign and based on participatory democracy, strong municipal autonomy, and cooperatives. The current workers', soldiers', and peasants' councils are the right beginning. (Gustav Landauer, in Kuhn 2012, 175f)

Landauer, who was a pacifist and theorist, proposed a new beginning after the disaster of 1914–1918. According to him, "There are two very different understandings of council democracy. One wants to use the current, insufficient and spontaneous, form of the councils to establish a 'dictatorship of the proletariat.' The other trusts the councils as a new instrument and the spirit that fills these bodies enough to make them the basis of public administration, whereby local activity is crucial, not the replacement of parliament by a council congress" (Gustav Landauer, in Kuhn 2012, 193).

Similar to other anarchists and certainly inspired by the writings of Mikhail Bakunin (1814–1876) and Peter Kropotkin (1842–1921), Landauer argued that

> Democracy as self-determination of the people, and of individual groups among the people, is something entirely different to the nonsense of elections, which means abdication of power by the people and governing of an oligarchy. Our revolution has already begun returning to the true democracy we can find in the medieval constitutions of municipalities and provinces, in Norway and Switzerland, and especially in the meetings of the sections of the French Revolution. No longer shall there be atomized workers abdicating their power. Instead, there shall be municipalities, cooperatives, and associations determining their own destiny in big assemblies and through delegates; delegates who are in constant exchange with their constituencies, who can be recalled and replaced at any time. The principle of imperative mandate will be crucial, not only in the fields of government and legislation but regarding all motions presented to the people by executive bodies. (Gustav Landauer, in Kuhn 2012, 200f)

For Landauer, "There must be equality and freedom. There must be federative structures, and they must form from the bottom to the top" (Gustav Landauer, in Kuhn 2012, 201).

Erich Mühsam (1878–1934) was another important member of the 1981 German Revolution. He writes,

> The revolution in Munich started two days before the one in Berlin, on November 7, 1918, the anniversary of your victory! Its political dynamics carried it far beyond any of the plans that Eisner had made with the counterrevolutionary social patriot Auer. . . . It [the first workers' council] constituted itself spontaneously from about fifty proletarians actively involved in the revolution. These proletarians gathered around Eisner who was at the time immensely popular. The Revolutionary Workers' Council (Revolutionaere Arbeiterrat) (RWC) that they formed remained the strongest force of the Bavarian Revolution until April 1919. Its regulations included the right to expel unreliable members and to appoint comrades of their own choosing. (Erich Mühsam, in Kuhn 2012, 213)

Similar to his fellow anarchists, he was also convinced that parliamentary politics could not be the solution to the problem of persistent exclusion and alienation, but was, in fact, part of the problem: "I feared that forming a party would have the same consequences it had always had in Germany: the submission of the proletarian revolutionary will to party interests" (Erich Mühsam, in Kuhn 2012, 216). And, "I am convinced that the rapid revolutionization of Munich's proletariat happened because of the decision to boycott the scheduled elections for the national assembly and the Bavarian Landtag" (Erich Mühsam, in Kuhn 2012, 217).

Mühsam saw the failure of the revolution and its shortcoming of implementing a Räte system in Germany caused in part by the failure to change the entrenched German bureaucracy: "Generally, the bourgeoisie could have been content with Eisner. In one of his resolutions, he reinstalled all officers and civil servants driven out by the masses" (Erich Mühsam, in Kuhn 2012, 218).

The German Council Republic did not survive long. Too heavy were the financial burdens resulting from the lost war. There was not enough food to feed the people, not enough raw materials to feed the industries, and not enough time to organize and carry out the post-war demobilization and to change from war to peace economy. There was not enough time to integrate all the unemployed and to repair the infrastructure necessary for a well-functioning economy. It also appears that the revolutionaries were not revolutionary enough, handing power over to the moderate, bourgeois SPD leadership, who used the masses as support, but quickly found ways to rein them in and appease them with minimal concessions. State power was not thoroughly wrestled from traditional groups, nor was the bureaucracy changed. In addition, a national revolutionary government was put in place that brokered power centrally, while the true power and the momentum of the movements rested in local councils (Arnold 1985).

Still, during the few months—and sometimes years, depending on the place—when the councils ruled in Germany, the core proposals and institutions created offer rich insight into the possibility of councils.

SPANISH ANARCHISM, 1936

When fascist troops under General Francisco Franco started to wage war against the elected republican government in Spain in July of 1936, peasants in such regions as Catalunia, Aragon, Huesca, and Andalucia filled the power vacuum created by the conflict to put in practice structures of self-organization, creating "colectividades." This development was particularly pronounced in those regions where anarchism and anarcho-syndicalism had a strong presence and history—as in Catalunia. According to Murray Bookchin (1994),

> While the republic's institutions lay in debris, abandoned by most of its military and police forces, the workers and peasants had created their own institutions to administer the cities in Republican Spain, formed their own armed workers' squads to patrol the streets, and established a remarkable revolutionary militia force with which to fight the Francoist forces—a voluntaristic militia in which men and women elected their own commanders and in which military rank conferred no social, material, or symbolic distinctions. (Bookchin 1994, 5)

Wherever the republican forces were able to expel the invading fascists, mayors, clerics, and large landowners (latifundistas) became the main targets of popular uprisings. Popular tribunals were erected, replacing the traditional judicial system. In fact, the republican government in Madrid had enacted laws that sought to establish popular tribunals as early as in 1935 (Casanova 2006). However, during the civil war and immediately after it, local committees, war committees, and militias or "columns" all exercised justice. In January 1937, the Security Council of Aragon (Consejo de Seguridad de Aragon) was created under the leadership of anarchists. Its task was to enforce revolutionary law, which also meant the expropriation of large landownerships and their distribution among peasants organized in collectivities. According to anarchist or libertarian communist doctrine, small family farms were left untouched and participation in the collectivities was free.

On September 15, 1936, in the national assembly of the General Confederation of Labor (CNT) in Madrid, it was decided that all of the freed territories form regional councils (Consejos Regionales de Defensa) that, by ways of federation, gave rise to the national council. Those regional councils were to take over administrative functions.

In February 1937, Aragon saw the emergence of the Regional Federation of Collectivities (Federacion Regional de Colectividades), where the 450 collectivities of Republican Aragon, representing some 300,000 peasants, came together for their first Congress on February 14, 1937 (Casanova 2006, 178).

According to Julian Casanova, "The judicial powers were taken over by revolutionary committees and by the collectivities, but it was not always the popular assembly that spoke justice and decided on the verdict; in some occasions even a slight suspicion of having 'developed fascist activities' was enough to provoke murder" (Casanova 2006, 161; my translation).

Indeed, in Aragon, "once the insurgent forces were defeated, in all the villages local antifascist committees were created, sometimes also called defense committees or revolutionary committees. Those organizations were created to fill the power vacuum, even if in some places they only pretended to maintain order, and to avoid bloodbaths among the local people" (Casanova 2006, 119; my translation).

In January 1937, the first action the newly-founded council undertook was "the substitution of the revolutionary committees by municipal councils" (Casanova 2006, 120; my translation). Next to the council of Aragon, there was a Regional Federation of Collectivities (Federacion Regional de Colectividades), thus following the libertarian recipe of imposing control over administrative power by relying on two types of organizations: regional and thematic. The anarchist and anarcho-syndicalist factions of this movement demanded a radical land distribution and the abolition of waged rural labor, which could be achieved by limiting landownership to the size that a family could cultivate. The communists, on the other hand, sought to advance more political goals and demanded expropriation of the lands of the fascists (Casanova 2006).

In the city of Barcelona, anarcho-syndicalists took over factories and shops and created workplace councils, as well as city-wide confederations. Behind the civil war front lines, in the liberated zones, "power lay essentially in the hands of the trade unions and their political organizations" (Bookchin 1994, 24). In some rural places, money was eliminated and replaced with schemes of allotting food by need and family size. According to Bookchin, "The administrative apparatus of 'Republican' Spain belonged almost entirely to the unions and their political organizations. Police in many cities were replaced by army workers' patrols. Militia unites were formed everywhere—in factories, on farms, and in socialist and anarchist community centers and union halls, initially including women as well as men" (Bookchin 1994, 24). Where the anarchists dominated, they established a network of regional councils and took over not only law enforcement, but also lawmaking and jurisdiction.

Barcelona and some rural areas of Aragon, Huesca, and Andalucia were able to advance furthest in this process of self-administration. In those regions dominated by anarchists and their organizations, such as the General Confederation of Workers (UGT), the General Confederation of Labor (CNT), and the Iberian Anarchist Federation (FAI), up to three-quarters of factories, shops, and agricultural production units were placed under direct control of workers and farmers, often after killing the landlord, latifundist, factory or shop owner.

In the department of Huesca, for example, several rural villages used the opportunity provided to them by the civil war to create collectivities. Pelai Pages i Blanch (2013) documented the creation of such colectividades in the villages of Altorricon, Benabarre, Capdesaco, and Penalba, all small villages of some 1,000 to 2,000 people each. Most of them started to form village councils in October 1936. Among the central actions were land reform and the kicking out of large landowners and the priests.

Diego Abad de Santillan, a participant, described the operation of collectivized companies the following way:

> In every factory, workshop, or workplace, a new administrative body was elected among the workers, administrators, and the technical staff. The factories of the same industry became associated at the local level, forming a federation for each industry. Local federations formed a regional federation—and those culminated in the national federation. The linking of federations gave birth to a national economic council. (Quoted in Alba 2001, 87; my translation)

Víctor Alba also explains that "the assembly of all workers and employees of a company chose committee members to control the company, which used to consist of five to ten people. Theoretically members of the two central union were also present in those councils, in proportion to the number of members in the company" (Alba 2001, 87).

Alba provides another telling quote from a participant:

> The committees were often composed of people over 30 years; younger people were rarely in front. This deprived many companies of the imagination, enthusiasm and devotion of the youth. In general, all members of the committee were men, although in the least worse of cases and when it was a company with a majority of female workers, there were some women. The committee chose the director of the company—the manager in business terms—but this manager was much more scrutinized than the ones of private companies and he was required to follow the guidelines of the committee and not only be accountable to it, but to consult it on important issues and to accept and implement its decisions. The choice of director was always a problem. (Alba 2001, 87f)

In Aragon, after the anarchist, communist, and anarcho-syndicalist columns defeated fascism in July 1936, the political, administrative, and economic structures of the old regime broke down. Many industries were abandoned and transportation interrupted in what Julian Casanova calls a "global breakdown of authority" (Casanova 2006, 116; my translation).

Josep Termes explains that Spain has a long history of worker organization. During the 1860s and 1870s, Spain had a total of 149 worker societies (*sociedades obreras*) with 15,216 members (Termes 2011, 55). According to him, Spain already had 195 worker associations in 1869, with a total of 25,000 members. They decided for Barcelona as the place for the first Spanish workers' congress, as they were seeking to become a member of the First International, which was launched in 1864 in London. (The First International Workingmen Congress was held in 1866 in Geneva.) With the split of the First International and the expulsion of the anarchists in 1872, Spanish workers instead created the Spanish Regional Federation of the

First International and associated themselves with the AIT, the International Workers Association (Termes 2011, 55; my translation).

According to Frank Mintz, "Self-organization from the bottom up occurred spontaneously, or rather, it immediately applied the anarcho-syndicalist propaganda, i.e. its three orientations: statistics (to control the economy), new techniques (for economic restructuring) and culture (for a new world view)" (Mintz 2006, 125).

According to historian Alejando Diéz Torre, the collectivization of urban companies and of rural farms produced astonishing results and very high yields, as now workers and farmers were working for themselves and were thus highly motivated. He explains,

> Over the course of collective experience, the small tenants and sharecroppers who joined the Communities, saw their living standards rise and for the first time, embraced mechanization in rural areas of this deep-Spain of the 20th century. In addition to everybody finding work, all rural sectors of those collectivities—including women and elderly farmers—the age-old hidden unemployment among small farmers were abolished. (Torre 2009, 18)

This was possible, according to Torre (2009), because of the rotation systems the collectivities put in place. Less desirable work was rotated, as was supervision and technical work. Work teams were formed and sent to different areas to help those unable to manage by themselves. Women were integrated into the work process and all workers, independent of their tasks, including administrative and office or managerial personnel, received the same salary.

Some collectivities replaced individual wages with family wages, which varied according family size and need (Torre 2009). This same author also explains that average wages rose during this time by up to 50 percent for women and 15 percent on average. This was possible because a new system of collective security was implemented, as profits, instead of accumulating in single hands and withdrawing them from the collective, now remained in the community. With this extra money, new social services were created, such as collective eateries, medical, and educational services. All of this was possible, according to Torre (2009), because all power now rested with the public assemblies that replaced the previous authorities at the city, the village, and the company level. In fact, the Spanish Anarchists, once they took power, killed many company owners and priests, perceived as the allies of the parasitical señorial class. They were replaced with cooperatives and collective ownership structures. Torre finds that overall, agricultural production rose by 20 percent during the time of collective ownership (Torre 2009, 23).

Confederation was a central element of the Spanish Anarchist period. As soon as workers' councils took over farms, they sought to cooperate with other farms, creating associations. The same was true for urban industries in such cities as Barcelona, which the local anarcho-syndicalists controlled during most of 1936 until May 1937, when the anarcho-syndicalists were brought down by the USSR-backed communists. After the communists won the upper hand, the war against the nationalists under General Franco continued until the war against fascism was finally lost in April 1939.

In Bookchin's careful analysis, "Spanish anarchism . . . sought out the pre-capitalist collectivist traditions of the village, nourished what was living and vital in them, evoked their revolutionary potentialities as liberatory modes of mutual aid and self-management, and deployed them to vitiate the obedience, hierarchical mentality, and authoritarian outlook fostered by the factory system" (Bookchin 1994, 7–8). By doing so, Spanish Anarchists continued a tradition that took shape among Parisian communards and again in early Russian soviets, such as the Petrograd Soviet. While this movement toward collectivization, councils, council confederations with imperative mandates, and recall of delegates emerged out of practice and the power vacuums created by civil war, they were also influenced by anarchist and libertarian socialist theories and leaders who adhered to these positions. According to Bookchin, "The assembly form comprised the organizational ideal of village anarchism from the days of the first truly Bakuninist congress of the Spanish IWMA in Córdoba in 1872, stressing the libertarian traditions of Spanish village life. Where such popular assemblies were possible, their decisions were executed by a committee elected from the assembly. Apparently, the right to recall committee members was taken for granted and they certainly enjoyed no privileges, emoluments, or institutional power" (Bookchin 1994, 9).

The Spanish Anarchists sought to transform the workplace and the very way work was organized. They also sought to change the state's bureaucracy and the way their country was administered. According to some analysts, it was precisely their stopping short of replacing the state apparatus with libertarian councils that undermined their success, as the socialists and communists who controlled parts of the state bureaucracy between 1936 and 1939 ended up betraying them.

LESSONS LEARNED FROM ANARCHISM

The absence of a uniting ideology able to provide orientation when it came to favoring one policy over another created much attrition among the Paris Commune. So did its convoluted administrative apparatus. Instead of replacing old administrative structures with new ones, the Commune added new structures on top of the old ones, thus doubling the bureaucracy. The protection of private property ensured the continuity of business as usual during the Commune, but it also did not alter the power structures of the city and the country.

Creating a libertarian, decentralized utopia while under siege from foreign nations and their own French army, it turns out, is not a practical route toward a better future, as the state represents and controls violence, but the Commune, while able in theory to assemble and organize power, diluted it, thus becoming vulnerable to the onslaught of concentrated and organized violence. The artisan socialism of anarchist and libertarian bent that was erected in Paris in 1871 was thus doomed from the beginning, as it faced concentrated and hierarchically-organized, state-led military violence.

During the short-lived German Räte Republic, local council republics were enacted, taking advantage of the power vacuum created after World War I. They did not last long and were unable to erect a system structured according to their beliefs. External threats were constant from right-wing conservatives and from the dogmatic, socialist left, which ultimately undermined the anarchists. While they lasted, the German councils had a shared vision and guidance (even if not religious, but very spirited) from their different leaders. They strongly felt that they had to take matters into their own hands and thus participated actively and strongly.

The core proposal of this movement was self-organization of workers and soldiers, mostly at the fabric level. In practice, the German revolution never eliminated the parliamentary system, despite the critique of some of its core anarchist proponents. However, core to the idea of the council republic was (and is) the imperative mandate, that is, parliamentary deputies can only enact policies in accordance with concretely transmitted preference by their electorate.

As explained earlier, the five principles of the council idea, according to Ernst Däuming (1920), are:

1. Proletarians, not citizens, as actors;
2. Anti-capitalism;
3. Anti-parliamentarism;
4. No long-term powers to delegates and permanent possibility of instant recall;
5. Anti-political party (proletariat as a whole).

Core is also the idea espoused by Gustav Landauer, namely of direct, local participation in the legislative process. "Each republic must be sovereign and based on participatory democracy, strong municipal autonomy, and cooperatives. The current workers', soldiers', and peasants' councils are the right beginning" (Gustav Landauer, in Kuhn 2012, 175f).

Political parties have no place in a council republic. Erich Mühsam warned against them repeatedly: "I feared that forming a party would have the same consequences it had always had in Germany: the submission of the proletarian revolutionary will to party interests" (Erich Mühsam, in Kuhn 2012, 216).

Finally, state bureaucracies must be changed if a community seeks to change the way power is brokered and administered. The failure to do so was probably the main cause for the demise of the German Council Republics.

During the "Anarchist Spring" of Spain, the places where direct democracy worked the best and longest were in the rural communities of Aragon and Andalucia, where power vacuums were created by the civil war. Direct democracies were practiced there as long as the absence of external threat allowed for it. They came to an end when the Nationalist troops led by General Franco took power. The direct democratic experiments were local and sought to construct a federalist system, but they were unable to achieve this goal. The accounts we have thus stem from local communities organizing themselves.

Similar to what happened in Germany in 1918, Spanish Anarchism was not given much of a chance. It was able to install itself only briefly during times of turmoil and war, which made it impossible to execute its core principles. Similar to Germany, councils emerged in Spain spontaneously, as the first response by frustrated workers and farmers who had long suffered from the exploitation of abusive landowners, company owners, and governments. Protest and rage was directed at once against formal state institutions and their representatives, as they represented the oppression from which ordinary people had long suffered.

Once established, collective ownership was among the first measures taken, followed by collective decision making in open assemblies. Confederation followed. Wages were equalized and work teams were formed. A rational distribution of tasks and a need-based distribution of profits in the form of family wages were quickly instituted in most places, particularly in the countryside, where anarchism had more time to take root and where it also found more peace to be implemented, lasting for several years in some Aragon and Andaluce municipalities.

It is worth noting here that Spain counts on a long tradition of open assemblies, called "cabildos," which reaches back to the sixth century, after the decay of the Roman Empire in this region. Open cabildos were village assemblies that met to make collective decisions, but particularly to pass laws.

Those parts of Spain controlled by the Anarchists in 1936–1937 formed a dual organizational structure consisting of local trade organizations (*secciones de oficio*), which together formed larger, federal unions for each occupation (*unions de oficio*), and regional federations, irrespective of the specific trade or occupation (*federaciones locales*). According to Bookchin,

"This dual structure forms the bedrock of all syndicalist forms of organization. In Spain, as elsewhere, the structure was knitted together by workers' committees, which originated in individual shops, factories, and agricultural communities. Gathering together in assemblies, the workers elected from their midst the committees that presided over the affairs of the vocational *Secciones de oficio* and the geographic *Federaciones locales*. They were federated into regional committees for nearly every large area of Spain" (Bookchin 1994, 11).

The kind of liberal anarchism established by Comuneros in Spain emerged during times of war and turmoil, which created a power vacuum, promptly and eagerly filled by peasants and workers. Their decentralized organizations, however, were no match for the onslaught of the fascists under Franco or even the much more centrally organized communists. Libertarian anarchism is able to provide freedom by abandoning the state, but it cannot resist the onslaught of centralized state and military power.

Chapter 6

Religious Communes and Intentional Communities

All over the world, at some point or another, groups of people have joined to form their own community and live by the convictions they share. These communities are often referred to as "intentional communities" or "communes." There are many historical and contemporary examples, most of which offer some interesting insights into the ways they constituted and organized themselves. Some of these communities are religiously inspired, others secular. Some allow for private property, some don't. For the purpose of this book, I have selected those for which some information on their constitution was available. As always, the focus of the analysis is not so much on how long they actually lasted or how many people were able to live under these regimes, but on what sorts of institutional designs and proposals these communes developed and put into practice. Here again I contend that we can learn from the often innovative ways these communes sought to combat elitism, elite abuse, and elite domination. Some of them have achieved remarkable results in their attempts to protect self-rule, and it is this aspect of their histories that should interest us the most.

OWENITE COMMUNES

According to the Encyclopedia Britannica, Robert Owen (1771–1858) was a "Welsh manufacturer turned reformer, one of the most influential early 19th-century advocates of utopian socialism. His New Lanark mills in Lanarkshire, Scotland, with their social and industrial welfare programs, became a place of pilgrimage for statesmen and social reformers. He also sponsored or encouraged many experimental 'utopian' communities, including one in New Harmony, Indiana, U.S." Indeed, in the United Kingdom, a total of ten communities were created based at least in part on Robert Owen's principles. In the United States, a total of sixteen communities were founded during the 1820s, inspired by the same principles (Harrison 2009). None of these communities survived beyond the 1840s.

Robert Owen expressed his views in his collection of essays, written between 1813 and 1816 and published under the title *A New View of Society, or: Essays on the Principle of the Formation of the Human Character, and the Application of the Principles of Practice*. In them, Owen advocates for the rational organization of humankind into well-organized communes. He was also a strong advocate for education. In his first essay, Owen writes:

> This principle is, that "Any general character, from the best to the worst, from the most ignorant to the most enlightened, may be given to any community, even to the world at large, by the application of proper means," which means are to a great extent at the command and under the control of those who have influence in the affairs of men. (Owen 1816, 6)

With this, Owen argues against the then-dominant assessment that some people, particularly the poor and uneducated, are condemned to eternal backwardness. Instead, he believes that everybody can achieve growth and become a functional member of society if given the proper training, education, and task. He explains in an address prefixed to the third essay,

> Many of you have long experienced in your manufacturing operations the advantages of substantial, well-contrived, and well-executed machinery. Experience has also shown you the difference of the results between mechanism which is neat, clean, well-arranged, and always in a high state of repair; and that which is allowed to be dirty, in disorder, without the means of preventing unnecessary friction, and which therefore becomes, and works, much out of repair. In the first case the whole economy and management are good; every operation proceeds with ease, order, and success. In the last, the reverse must follow, and a scene be presented of counteraction, confusion, and dissatisfaction among all the agents and instruments interested or occupied in the general process, which cannot fail to create great loss. If, then, due care as to the state of your inanimate machines can produce such beneficial results, what may not be expected if you devote equal attention to your vital machines, which are far more wonderfully constructed? (Owen 1816, 3)

Owen further argues that individual happiness can only be increased if and when the happiness of all around that individual also increases. Through rational organization of labor and inactive structures that favored work and orderly conduct, while also investing in education and training, Owen was able to transform a cotton mill in Scotland, which he bought in 1799, into a new model of organizing work and community life. Following his example, other communities were created and Owen himself founded a new community in the United States in 1825, calling it *New Harmony*.

While much was achieved in New Harmony, making it the birthplace of the first free library and of public education open to boys and girls, the experiment did not last long. In March 1827, after several attempts to save it through different measures of restructuring, it finally broke up.

According to Josiah Warren, a participant,

> It seemed that the difference of opinion, tastes and purposes increased just in proportion to the demand for conformity. Two years were worn out in this way; at the end of which, I believe that not more than three persons had the least hope of success. Most of the experimenters left in despair of all reforms, and conservatism felt itself confirmed. We had tried every conceivable form of organization and government. We had a world in miniature. —we had enacted the French revolution over again with despairing hearts instead of corpses as a result. . . . It appeared that it was nature's own inherent law of diversity that had conquered us . . . our "united interests" were directly at war with the individualities of persons and circumstances and the instinct of self-preservation . . . and it was evident that just in proportion to the contact of persons or interests, so are concessions and compromises indispensable. (*Periodical Letter II* 1856, quoted in Martin 1970)

Joseph Clayton quotes Robert Owen's son, Robert Dale Owen, who stated that the New Harmony community was "a heterogeneous collection of radicals, enthusiastic devotees to principle, honest latitudinarians, and lazy theorists, with a sprinkling of unprincipled sharpers thrown in" (Clayton 1908, 92). According to another analyst, William Wilson, New Harmony attracted "crackpots, free-loaders, and adventurers whose presence in the town made success unlikely" (Wilson 1967, 116).

Robert Owen is credited with the foundation of cooperativism and his principles have influenced communitarians and believers in the possibility to organize communities rationally for the sake of the common good, which in return provides the grounds for individual freedom and happiness. However, the experiments of establishing such communities in the United Kingdom and the United States all failed. In the United States, New Harmony lacked organization, internal agreement, and the necessary skills among its participants to succeed (Wilson 1967). In the United Kingdom, the communities analyzed by R. G. Garnett (1972) also did not last beyond the 1850s for similar reasons.

Garnett sums up his study of three Owenite communities in the United Kingdom with these conclusions:

> Owen and the Owenites had no satisfactory answer to the problem of production in a community setting, nor were they consistent in their views on equality of

reward of property. Perhaps the most intransigent problem was that of devising an efficient form of democratic government: the Owenite experiments, although short-lived, provided some evidence that without a resolution of this problem the model community would degenerate into patriarchy or anarchy. . . . Once the communities were established, it was difficult to select suitable lines of production not requiring large-scale equipment and yet having a readily marketable output. Strong social cohesion could have been achieved if it had been possible to incorporate a sufficiently wide range of craft skills to enable communal self-sufficiency to be possible, but the communities never accomplished this norm. (Garnett 1972, 220–21)

TOLSTOYANS

During the late nineteenth century, Leo Tolstoy, Russia's foremost writer, turned away from novel writing and focused his energy on developing a doctrine of alternative community life, called "Christian anarchism" by most. According to William Edgerton, "The heart of Tolstoy's message was what he called the Law of Love, as expressed in Jesus' commandments to love God with all one's heart and one's neighbor as oneself, and to 'resist not him that is evil'" (Edgerton 1993, x). Tolstoy rejected all forms of coercion, which made him reject the state, the police, the military, and the legal system. Tolstoy became an advocate for simple, rural life, self-sufficiency, pacifism, and vegetarianism. His disdain for the rich and wasteful and his teachings about nonviolence became an inspiration for many to follow, including Mahatma Gandhi.

Agricultural communities were founded in different parts of the world, taking inspiration from his teachings. In Russia, by 1900 Tolstoyans were called a sect with adepts in eight provinces (Edgerton 1993, xi). When the Bolsheviks took power in October 1917, Russia had an estimated 5,000 to 6,000 Tolstoyans (Edgerton 1993). According to Boris Mazurin, one of the founders of the biggest Tolstoyan communes ever to exist, the Life and Labor Commune, and a personal acquaintance of Tolstoy's (through his parents), the first Tolstoyan commune emerged in Russia in 1918 (Mazurin, in Edgerton 1993, 70).

After the October Revolution and particularly after the New Economic Policy took effect in the Soviet Union in 1921, Tolstoyans and other pre-Soviet believers in communalism and rural communism were allowed to put their beliefs into practice, as the USSR was facing a shortage of food supply and thus had to rely on the experience of the "Old Believers and sectarians." Many of these Old Believers were indeed old practitioners of village communism based in the *mir*, a form of village self-government that administered the common-held farmland, redistributing it periodically among peasant households depending on their family size and hence need. In pre-revolutionary

Russia, village authority lay with the village assembly and the village elders. Tolstoyans and anarchists could thus count on a tradition of village autonomy and local self-rule, even if limited by the presence of the overarching state, which, under the tsar, was minimal in its capacity and reach.

According to Edgerton, "The Tolstoyan colonies had a reasonably good life during the period of the New Economic Policy (NEP), from 1921 to the end of 1928" (Edgerton 1993, xv). This changed with the collectivization of agriculture during the first five-year plan, 1928 through 1932.

They were expelled and granted refuge in Siberia, and by 1931, about 1,000 Tolstoyans had settled there. Their peace, however, did not last. By 1936, the Soviet Union arrested all leaders of the Siberian "Life and Labor Commune," sending them to prison. Tolstoyan communes formed in the United Kingdom, the United States, Japan, Bulgaria, and India. For the purpose of this book, I shall focus on the experiences in Russia as described by its survivors, Boris Mazurin, Dimitry Morgachev, Yakov Dragunovsky, and Ivan Dragunovsky. These accounts were first edited, commented on, and published by the Russian journalist Mark Popovsky in 1983 and they serve as the canvas for the publication of the English-language translation and publication by William Edgerton (1993). In what follows, I will provide brief descriptions of different Tolstoyan communities.

The New Jerusalem Tolstoy Commune

According to one of its co-founders, Yelena Shershenyova, this agricultural colony was created in 1922, some thirty kilometers outside of Moscow. By 1923, the commune had some thirty members, among peasants and intellectuals with no prior agricultural experience. They were all vegetarians and anti-militarists and some pursued other idealistic goals (such as not drinking milk, not wearing leather boots, or even not wearing clothes). They strived to bring about world brotherhood and were inspired not only by the writing of Leo Tolstoy, but also by such authors as Henry George. They embraced simplicity and shared all daily tasks, including child rearing. Food supply and money was shared and distributed among all members according to need. They organized in a general assembly, which elected a chairman. This chairman held executive power, but served only as long as he found support among the commune. His mandate, in other words, was open to recall. According to Yelena Shershenyova,

> We were all vegetarians; none of us drank, smoked, or used foul language. We understood very well that the harmony of our social structure was maintained thanks to the community of convictions among the majority and our mutual confidence and respect for one another. We understood that we could not sustain our

Leo Tolstoy Commune, that is, maintain its free and peaceful spirit, if people poured into the commune who not only did not share our convictions but tried in every way to oppose them. (Shershenyova, in Edgerton 1993, 17)

In 1929, the commune was forced to merge with a local state farm and was rebaptized "Red October." The Tolstoyan commune New Jerusalem was over. In 1931, most of their members moved to western Siberia, where the government had given another Tolstoyan commune land so the Life and Labor Commune, originally also located outside of Moscow, could resettle there. Because of their committed anti-militarism, some members of the New Jerusalem commune were sentenced to prison and hard labor, as they had refused to join the army or even pay toward military efforts. Many died during their imprisonment and while serving hard labor.

Tolstoyan Communes in Siberia

The Life and Labor Commune, meanwhile, flourished from 1921 to 1931 on the outskirts of Moscow. They produced milk for sale and supplied themselves with different agricultural produce. According to Boris Mazurin, a founding member, the commune strived after the initial year of taking over an abandoned farm. "We lived happily and worked with great enthusiasm. We got up at daybreak and went to bed as soon as it was dark" (Mazurin, in Edgerton 1993, 30). Mazurin also explains that they had a community house where they shared vegetarian meals. "We would discuss all our work together around the table at breakfast, dinner, or supper. Nobody was the official leader. We tried to make sure that all members of the commune kept up with everything, and we decided that each one in turn, a day at a time, would be responsible for managing current affairs. At the beginning, absolutely nobody bothered us. We knew nothing about residence permits, regulations, taxes, any kind of agricultural instructions, and so on. And our work went well. Our organization was not very large but it was full of life, truly collective, hard working, of high quality, and socially useful. Our expenses for administration, management, and office needs amounted to zero" (Mazurin, in Edgerton 1993, 31).

Some of their early members were anarchists and referred to themselves as "extarchists—that is, extragovernmentalists" (Mazurin, in Edgerton 1993, 31). Mazurin, even though he was not an anarchist but a Tolstoyan, greatly admired these anarchists because, according to him, they were "industrious, quick to learn, sociable, and always merry. They would not allow any tobacco, vodka, cursing, or debauchery, which, along with their vegetarianism, antimilitarism, and rejection of the state, paved the way for their closeness to us Tolstoyans in practical life" (Mazurin, in Edgerton 1993, 32).

Mazurin further explains:

By 1925 we were provided with everything we needed. Our meals were communal and free; so were our living quarters, lights, and heat; and for clothing and shoes everybody received twenty-five rubles a month to be spent as they thought best. (Mazurin, in Edgerton 1993, 33)

In 1927, when the collectivization of the countryside began, Tolstoyans all over Russia faced problems, as their philosophy and practice did not allow for a smooth merging with state farms. According to Boris Mazurin, it was Vladimir Grigoryevich Chertkov, Tolstoy's most famous and influential disciple, who suggested that all Tolstoyans should come together and be given land apart from the state land.

In March 1931, Tolstoyans from all over Russia moved and settled in western Siberia, creating three different communities and numbering about one thousand in total. In general assembly, the newcomers decided that

The Uralians would form an agricultural cooperative named "Peaceful Plowman" and settle along the Aspen Ravine, with their lands to the west of the Aspen Creek. The Stalingraders would form the World Brotherhood Community and settle along the Diving Duck Ravine, with their lands to the east of the Diving Duck Creek. And finally, the Life and Labor Commune from the Moscow area would remain as a commune, with their housing along the Tom River and their lands in the center of the whole resettlement plot. (Mazurin, in Edgerton 1993, 50)

Each community had a council and a chairman, elected among them. Whenever major collective decisions had to be made, a general assembly was called in. During the first years, the men had to work outside the commune to earn money for food. All the money earned was handed over to the general treasury of the commune. According to Mazurin,

The free spirit of enterprise—not capitalistic but collective, peasant enterprise—is stifled when you work for wages and on orders from above. In the commune there were no directors, no work superintendents, no approved lists, projects, bank accounts, allocations, estimates, transfers, cadre problems, production norms, categories, economists, no platoons of bookkeepers, no sick lists. We had none of all that creaking, cumbersome bureaucratic apparatus, with its deadly effect on work and on any active initiative from the workers. (Mazurin, in Edgerton 1993, 65)

Collective decisions were made in production meetings or at the commune council. For bigger issues, a general assembly was called in. There was a weekly routine of meetings and gatherings. According to Mazurin, the commune rested on Sundays; met on Mondays for a production conference, open to all; on Tuesday, they sang and learned songs; on Wednesday, they had a philosophical study group; on Thursdays, a teachers' meeting, where parents also attended; on Saturday, they had a chorus rehearsal; and on Sundays they held a big general meeting.

The Siberian Tolstoyan Commune as well as its neighbors the World Brotherhood Community and the Cooperative all eventually ran into increased opposition to the state and its local apparatus. They were required to enlist in the military, which they refused, or pay a military tax, which they did not pay. They were given quotas of food and money to be paid and delivered to the local authorities, often in excess of what was possible. Their members were jailed and sent to prison and labor camps. Ironically, most of this action against the communes was done by the local village soviet, the formal, municipal structure put in place by the Soviet Union to administer its territory. Thus here, as elsewhere, genuine self-organization and community ran contra the formal collectivity ordained by the state. State power, after all, even if decentralized, could not tolerate the parallel power of extrastate communities and their structures. In the case of the Soviet Union, this was particularly ironic, as the expressed goal of the country was for the state to wither away and give way to genuine community. However, communist state officials argued that the times for this final step were not ripe. For Mazurin, however, the true reason was another. For him,

> The main thing was that the collective farm was a purely economic organization, with governing bodies to run it; but the commune took in a much wider circle of matters connected with its activity. The commune did not have a governing body over it; it had its own council, which decided not only farming questions but questions concerning the whole life of our commune. In essence, as long as such communes and commune councils existed, there would be no need of soviets as instruments of state power, since stateless communism would already have arrived, just as it said in the Party program. (Mazurin, in Edgerton 1993, 93)

Under pressure to integrate into the state-led collective farms, the Life and Labor Commune ceased to exist in January 1939. It became a state-owned and controlled agricultural cooperative.

KIBBUTZ

The word "kibbutz" stems from the Hebrew "kvutzah," meaning group. According to Dagana Baratz (1945), the first kibbutz was founded in Palestine in 1909. Most founding kibbutzim members were of Eastern European origin (Blasi 1978). According to Joseph Blasi, "The kibbutz provides a level of cooperation that critically alters social life and markedly eliminates gross social, economic and political problems, yet it does this in the context of a normal secular society of grandmothers, grandfathers, aunts, uncles, sons and daughters, with a strong respect for individual human rights and an attempt, albeit a complicated one, to relate responsibility to national obligations. Its members are diverse; their religious beliefs are mixed and are, in fact, distinctly secular; the lifestyle is comfortable yet radical, participatory but not intrusive, industrialized but not technocratic" (Blasi 1978, xv).

Some early kibbutzim members, particularly A. D. Gordon, who arrived in Ottoman Palestine in 1904 from Russia, were influenced by Leo Tolstoy. Gordon founded the kibbutz Hapoel Hatzair in 1905. He promoted a philosophy and practice of labor and a return to nature. After his death, his followers created the Gordonian movement, which founded several kibbutzim in Israel. Common to all kibbutzim, to this day, is a suspicion against individual wealth, even if contemporary kibbutzim have, for the most part, relaxed their regime of need-based and equal work compensation.

When Blasi wrote his book, he counted 250 communities and a total of 100,000 people involved in them, thus an average of 400 people per community, with a range of 50 to 2,000. In 2010, Israel counted 270 kibbutzim.

One of the founders of the kibbutz Blasi studied in the 1970s explained its origins:

> The youth movement from which this community sprung was founded in Poland in 1928. Many of our members even before then were reading a lot of philosophy, examining their conscience, and pursuing the issue of social life on a very high level. Ours, unlike other Zionist movements, put a great emphasis on kibbutz. Our newspapers stressed this theme. Some of preparation came from the Pfadfinder, an apolitical countercultural youth movement which developed in Germany in the twenties. It emphasized a return to nature through scouting groups, freer relations between people, and not simply following in the footsteps of our parents. The youth often asked themselves if this style was a game. How long could we play it without changing our lives? (Blasi 1978, 8)

The kibbutz researched by Blasi (1978) was atypical in that it had been founded in Palestine before the creation of the State of Israel in 1948, by people from Galitzia, Poland. They had not experienced the Holocaust and they all had a lower-middle-class background. For them, the kibbutz was not the answer to persecution, but to the alienation they had experienced in the Polish stetl. Life in the stetl, after all, was "radically hierarchical and inegalitarian. The Rabbis and the pious Jews were at the top and were keenly aware of their station and power" (Blasi 1978, 14).

According to Blasi, the kibbutz "solves social problems by changing social relations. It is built on mutual commitment and obligation among a group of people, a commodity within the reach of all. It calls for grouping human activities under 'one roof,' encouraging people to conduct most of their affairs within a fellowship based upon consistent rules, similar reference groups, and little hierarchy, and thus opposes the fragmenting tendency of modern society. It prescribes mutual aid that is free once the intention for fellowship is present; this costs little, requires minimum administrative supervision, promises a sure profit, and is something to which most people believing in its virtues can adapt themselves" (Blasi 1978, xxviii).

According to Michal Palgi and Shulamit Reinharz, "Kibbutzim opted to govern themselves with *direct* (rather than representational) *democracy* as well as rotation of officeholders both in kibbutz society and in the economic units" (Palgi and Reinharz 2014, 3; emphasis in original).

Raymond Russell, Robert Hanneman, and Shlomo Getz (2000) explain that after the heydays of kibbutzim of the 1960s and 1970s, the 1990s were a time of crisis and restructuring. By the end of this decade, many nonreligious kibbutzim had been transformed. These authors write:

> Changes in decision making transfer authority away from the egalitarian direct democracy of the General Assembly, and promote differentiation between leaders who specialize in holding offices and a rank and file that votes anonymously by secret ballot. In production, members who can earn more income outside the kibbutz than within it are now encouraged to work outside, while within the kibbutz, industrial ventures are now run by boards of directors with the freedom to fill both nonmanagerial and managerial positions with hired laborers. Consumption expenditures have been privatized, while the use of common dining facilities has been curtailed. Small numbers of kibbutzim are also now experimenting with various ways to create explicit links between individual efforts and material rewards, in contrast to the traditional kibbutz principle of "from each, according to ability, to each, according to need." (Russell, Hanneman, and Getz 2000, 2)

Indeed, most kibbutzim seem to have changed because of the onslaught of capitalism and the possessive individualism. According to Y. Don, kibbutzim members have lost their altruistic orientation, which provided the foundation for their success (quoted in Rosner 2000, 1). The "New Kibbutz" created during the 1990s was characterized by the introduction of market and hierarchical principles and mechanisms in the kibbutz (Rosner and Getz 1994).

Menahem Rosner groups the changes introduced during this time into three:

a. The first area is partial privatization of the communal household, through transition from direct supply of commodities and services to a system of allocation of monetary budgets to members, who can buy inside or outside the kibbutz. In almost all communities monetary budgets have replaced direct supply of commodities and services such as electricity, bus tickets, travel abroad, etc. Monetary budgets for clothing and furniture were already introduced at preliminary stage. In almost half of the communities, members receive money to pay for meals in the dining room.

b. The second area is introduction of a quasi-market system of work allocation, based on free choice of work places by members. On the other hand, managers of kibbutz branches are free to decide whom they want to employ and whom not. While in the conventional labour market the balance between offer and demand is realized—at least theoretically—through the mechanism of differential wages, the proponents of this change opposed such inequalities and favored equal wages. This basic inconsistency has created problems in the implementation of changes in this area. Free choice of workplace has been adopted by many kibbutzim and it has resulted in many cases in a sharp increase in the number of members working outside the kibbutz. A parallel development is a significant increase in the number of hired workers employed in almost all parts of the economy and community. (The percentage of hired workers in the overall workforce of kibbutz industry increased from 29% in 1990 to 60% in 1997.) On the other hand it is difficult to implement a labour market system without wages. It is especially difficult to create a fit between the demand for labour in the existing work branches and the work preferences of members. To overcome this difficulty some kibbutzim have introduced payment for specific types of work, e.g., overtime and nightshifts and monetary sanctions for not fulfilling work duties.

c. Third is the separation between community and economy. The rationale for this change was to "liberate" kibbutz economic organizations from restrictions due to kibbutz values or social considerations. The assumption was that the separation would lead to an opening of the economic branches to the Israel labour and capital markets, employing hired workers, and developing partnerships with private capital. Another related aspect of this separation is the introduction of more hierarchical forms of organization such as boards of directors and the enhancement of managerial authority, as part of a general trend toward deviation from kibbutz self-management principles (Tannenbaum A. and al. 1994) and conformity with conventional patterns. One third of the kibbutzim have wholly adopted the concept of separation between economy and community, but more have introduced specific changes belonging to this concept. Among these are an increase in the employment of hired labour, creation of boards of directors, and a decrease in members' participation in decision making. (Rosner 2000, 2–3)

A second set of changes has led a minority of kibbutzim to openly embrace market mechanisms and let go of communal principles, while the majority is seeking ways to reinstitutionalize the basic principles. Concretely, this second movement of change is splitting kibbutzim into market-based and communal in the fields of communal households, including shared responsibilities in health care, education, and care for the elderly versus family, or even individual responsibility. Another area of division is in the field of salaries, where a minority (7 out of 270 in 1997, according to Rosner [2000]) has opted for differentiated salaries. The majority has voted against such a scheme, but some kibbutzim have adapted a more controlled and regulated way to differentiate payments based on need and family size. Traditionally, all members of a kibbutz hold collective ownership of all assets. In fact, according to kibbutz by-laws, "the property of a kibbutz cannot be divided among the members, either during the existence of a kibbutz or after its liquidation" (Rosner 2000, 5–6). In recent years, some kibbutzim have decided to loosen this regime and have privatized consumption assets, such as housing. Others have shifted toward a cooperative model of private-owned assets. Rosner (2000) thus sums up the changes of kibbutzim since the 1990s into changes in consumption, work, and ownership.

The kibbutzim that are moving away from traditional practices are facing conflict with their regulatory frameworks, which is also supported in the federation. As they change, they most likely stop being kibbutzim. Those that have opted to maintain communal practices and collective ownership of all assets face other challenges, namely,

a. How to assure their economic future,
b. How to maintain and to develop the "utopian" and "altruistic" components of kibbutz ideology and to strengthen the commitment to these values by kibbutz members. (Rosner 2000, 8)

Blasi also already stated in 1978, "Having eliminated the most serious forms of social, economic, political and educational fragmentation and violence, the communal group is left with the complicated and mounting problem of keeping fellowship alive and well" (Blasi 1978, xv).

THE AMISH

The Amish are a religious group of some 300,000, living in small communities mostly in Pennsylvania, Delaware, Ohio, Indiana, and New York. There are also Amish settlements in Ontario, Canada. According to John Hostetler, "The Amish are a church, a community, a spiritual union, a conservative branch of Christianity, a religion, a community whose members practice simple and austere living, a familistic entrepreneuring system, and an adaptive human community" (Hostetler 1993, 4).

The Amish came to the Americas after a religious schism in Switzerland in 1693. Jakob Ammann was the leader of the splinter group, breaking away from the Alsatian Anabaptists. His followers are known today as Amish (Kraybill 2001).

Given their shared history of emigration, most Amish are born into the religion; however, Amish membership is regulated by baptism. Once a member, only endogenous marriages are allowed. The Amish are organized by church districts in groups of twenty to forty families. They abide by a set of laws and rules called the "Ordnung." The Ordnung ensures that the Amish practice a broadly shared set of rules and norms, renewing it twice a year during the general assemblies at church. According to Donald Kraybill (2001), the main aim of the Amish lifestyle is "Gelassenheit," that is, tranquility and serenity while surrendering to the will of God. In more concrete terms, the Ordnung asks the Amish to live reserved, modest, calm, and quiet lives; to submit to the will of God and be obedient, humble, and simple; to dress in specific ways and stay away from modern technology when possible; to organize in small communities; and to actively practice Mennonite Anabaptism (Kraybill 2001).

All Amish are farmers and work the land with horses. They make their livelihoods from working the land. According to Hostetler, "The charter of Amish life requires members to limit their occupations to farming or closely associated activities such a operating a saw mill, carpentry, or masonry. The Amishman feels contact with the material world through the working of his muscles and the aching of his limbs. In the little Amish community, toil is proper and good, religion provides meaning, and the bonds of family and church provide human satisfaction and love" (Hostetler 1993, 88).

According to Hostetler, "The congregation must agree on *how* to be different from the world, for the body of Christ must be 'of one mind.' Twice a year the members must express their unity before communion. This unanimous expression of unity implies satisfaction with the *Ordnung*, peace among all members, and peace with God. Unless there is a group expression of unity, the Lord's Supper is not held" (Hostetler 1993, 83).

The rules laid out in the Ordnung are intended to protect family life, piety, simplicity, and community. Status symbols are prohibited, as are tools that undermine direct communication (such as telephones and riding in airplanes). Amish houses have no electricity or central heating systems. They contain no TVs, radios, or computers.

The Amish, unlike the Hutterites, do not practice a community of assets, that is, communism. Families earn income and it is theirs to keep. However, those families do engage in several mutual aid practices. According to Hostetler, "intense interaction in the little homogeneous community makes members feel responsible for each other's welfare. Although community aid is often a form of economic sharing, the feelings are the result of intense social concern. While the Amish do not practice complete 'community of goods,' as do their Anabaptist cousins the Hutterites, they find many ways to help each other. Perhaps the most dramatic form of mutual aid is the barn raising. But there are many additional neighborly associations that result in an exchange of services" (Hostetler 1993, 249). Barn raising is the construction of a barn by the whole community. The sick and elderly are embraced and taken care of by the community.

All adult Amish meet in general assembly twice a year, holding a council meeting. These assemblies rely strongly on deliberation and even though voting is integral to it, veto power is very strong, requiring only two members to block a measure. Each church district falls under the spiritual guidance of a bishop. The church district effectively constitutes the local community. The Amish reject insurances and social welfare, as well as engaging with the national legal system.

If someone from the community sways from the prescribed ways, they are first shunned, then ultimately expulsed, thus insuring that the community remains uninfluenced by divergent thinking and practice. Marriage into the community by a non-Amish is also not possible—another way to avoid divergent ideas or practices infiltrating the community.

The Importance of Community

To the Amish, church, and more specifically the church community, which they call after the German *Gemeinde*, is the place for redemption. The belief is that theirs is the true church, whereas the other churches have fallen off from God's path and plan. As the true church, the Amish seek salvation in their communities. According to Hostetler, "Community-building is central to the redemptive process; salvation is not an individualistic effort to be practiced when convenient or in keeping with one's personal definition. The aim of the Amish is to incarnate the teachings of Jesus into a voluntary social order" (Hostetler 1993, 75).

This can only be achieved, as already stated, in small communities that allow for face-to-face interactions and by keeping distance from those that do not follow this path. Amish communities thus remain closed to outsiders and marriages are endogenous, that is, when an Amish wants to marry a non-Amish, the Amish person has to leave the community. The justification for this practice is found in biblical verse. According to Hostetler, "This doctrine forbids the Amishman from marrying a non-Amish person or entering into a business partnership with an outsider. It is applied generally to all social contacts that involve intimate connections with persons outside the ceremonial community" (Hostetler 1993, 75).

HUTTERITES

On the website of the Hutterian Brethren, one can find a general description of this community:

> Hutterites share a common ancestry with the Anabaptists, along with the Mennonites and Amish and as would logically follow, share many of the same beliefs and doctrine. Hutterites differ in one major aspect: they believe in sharing their possessions in commons as demonstrated by Christ and His Apostles and as later further refined and described in the Book of Acts. Christ commanded us to love one another, and Hutterites believe that living together is a wonderful and unique expression of love for their fellow man. (http://www.hutterites.org/history/)

Similar to the Amish and Mennonites, the Hutterites trace their origins to the religious schism among Anabaptists in Europe. Following the teachings of their religious founder, Jakob Hutter (ca. 1500–1536), an Anabaptist from Tirol, Hutterites practice pacifism, nonresistance, and community of goods. The first Hutterites arrived in North America in the 1870s. Since then, they have established and maintained communities in Western Canada and the northwestern United States. Their total number is estimated to be around 42,000. Hutterites live apart from other communities in their own colonies and practice mostly subsistence farming. They aim at being independent from the outside world.

On their own website, the Hutterites explain:

> It is important to remember that Hutterite communities are very diverse and that no two communities are identical in their organization and overall way of life. However, there are some characteristics and practices that are fairly similar for most communities. In every Hutterite colony, the minister is both the spiritual leader and the chief executive. He is also part of an advisory board that makes the day-to-day decisions affecting the community. The advisory board consists of the colony manager, the farm manager and two or three witness brothers or deacons. The colony manager receives and pays bills, does the banking and is the business manager of the colony. The numerous activities of each colony are managed by witness brothers (deacons) or other brothers. Most communities depend on mixed, large-scale farming as a livelihood. Many colonies also operate industrial shops, producing a wide range of products and services. Women serve many important roles in the community. A married woman is responsible for various housekeeping duties such as sewing, cleaning and caring for her family.

Women also manage community duties such as cooking, baking, gardening and food preservation. A female head cook works with several rotating pairs of married and single women who assist her on a weekly basis. Other management positions always filled by women are Gärtnerin gardener, Zeichschneiderin sewing materials manager, Klanaschuel-Ankela pre-school teacher, Essenschul-Ankela children's dining room supervisor and Kronka-Köchin special needs cook. It is quite common for women to serve as schoolteachers. Contrary to popular belief, Hutterites strongly advocate education. Although education was neglected during the first hundred years in North America, Hutterites are increasingly realizing its value. During the Golden Years, the Hutterite standard of education was so highly esteemed that lords and nobles brought their children to the colony to be educated. Centuries before governments introduced kindergarten, Hutterite parents sent their children between two-and-a-half and five years of age to a kindergarten maintained by the community. The young children learned prayers and songs, as well as how to live, play and eat together. Since the mid-nineties, over fifty Hutterite men and women have graduated from Brandon University's Hutterian Education Program (BUHEP) and received their teaching degrees. In many colonies, Grade 12 is a minimum education requirement. High school is delivered in various formats, including interactive television (IITV) broadcast via broadband Internet (HBNI). Most of the teachers on the HBNI-IITV system are Hutterites. Although Hutterites are primarily concentrated in North America, there are communities in Nigeria and Japan. Many communities are making an attempt to reach out to others beyond their immediate community through singing, volunteer work and financial contributions. (http://www.hutterites.org/history/)

As this excerpt demonstrates, Hutterites are hierarchically organized, and, according to John Hostetler and Gertrude Enders Huntington, "everyone must have the right position in a hierarchical world" (Hostetler and Huntington 1996, 21). Decisions are not made in public assembly, even though all full members regularly meet in assembly and all are part of the community. Only men have a vote and can elect the five- to seven-member council, which is the executive organ for the community while also performing judicial functions. Above the council, and himself a council member, stands the first preacher (Hostetler and Huntington 1996). According to Hostetler and Huntington, "the preacher receives no formal training prior to his election. He is elected by lot from nominations by his own colony (with the aid of other colony delegates). He is ordained to exercise full powers only after several years of proven leadership. . . . Ideally, he refers all weighty matters to the council" (Hostetler and Huntington 1996, 33).

The Wikipedia entry for the Hutterites provides some further helpful information on this recluse group of people. There one can read:

Each colony may consist of about 10 to 20 families (may not always apply), with a population of around 60 to 250, which falls within the limits of Dunbar's number. When the colony's population grows near the upper limit and its leadership determines that branching off is economically and spiritually necessary, they locate, purchase land for, and build a "daughter" colony.

The voting and decision-making process at most colonies is based upon a two-tiered structure including a council—usually seven senior males—and the voting membership which includes all the married men of the colony. For "significant" decisions the council will first vote and, if passed, the decision will be carried to the voting membership. This structure has resulted in a democratic culture in most colonies. Officials not following the democratically selected decisions can be removed by a similar vote of a colony.

Hutterites practice a near-total community of goods: all property is owned by the colony, and provisions for individual members and their families come from the common resources. This practice is based largely on Hutterite interpretation of passages in chapters 2, 4, and 5 of Acts, which speak of the believers "having all things in common." Thus the colony owns and operates its buildings and equipment like a corporation. Housing units are built and assigned to individual families but belong to the colony and there is very little personal property. Lunch and dinner meals are taken by the entire colony in a dining or fellowship room. Men and women sit in a segregated fashion. Special occasions sometimes allow entire families to enjoy meals together. Individual housing units do have kitchens which are used for breakfast meals. (http://en.wikipedia.org/wiki/Hutterite#Community_ownership)

Hutterers form small communes apart from the outside world, held together by a shared history, language, culture, and, most of all, religion. Executive and judicial tasks are administered by the council, with the first priest as the leader of this council. Legislative functions are not conducted by the community, as they rely on the Christian Bible as their book of law and the elders, the council, and the head priest as the guardians and defenders of their traditional ways and laws.

THE TWIN OAKS COMMUNITY

The Twin Oaks Community was founded in 1967 by a group of eight adults on a 123-acre farm in Virginia. It persists to this day, making it one of the longest enduring communities in the United States. Twin Oaks currently has some ninety adult members and fifteen children.

Similar to the Amish and Hutterers, the Twin Oakers live apart from mainstream society in a relatively homogenous group. They also share strong convictions and interests, and certainly the same language. However, Twin Oaks is not a religious community. On their website, they explain:

Twin Oaks is an intentional community in rural central Virginia, made up of around 90 adult members and 15 children. Since the community's beginning in

1967, our way of life has reflected our values of cooperation, sharing, nonviolence, equality, and ecology. We welcome you to schedule a visit. We do not have a group religion; our beliefs are diverse. We do not have a central leader; we govern ourselves by a form of democracy with responsibility shared among various managers, planners, and committees. We are self-supporting economically, and partly self-sufficient. We are income-sharing. Each member works 42 hours a week in the community's business and domestic areas. Each member receives housing, food, healthcare, and personal spending money from the community. Our hammocks and casual furniture business has generated most of our income in the past. Making tofu as of 2011 has become roughly equal in importance to hammocks. Indexing books and now seed growing are also significant sources of income. Still, less than half of our work goes into these income-producing activities; the balance goes into a variety of tasks that benefit our quality of life—including milking cows, gardening, cooking, and childcare. Most people prefer doing a variety of work, rather than the same job day in, day out. A number of us choose to be politically active in issues of peace, ecology, anti-racism, and feminism. Each summer we are hosts to a Women's Gathering and a Communities Conference where we welcome both experienced communitarians, and seekers who are new to community living. (http://www.twinoaks.org/)

Intentional communities are defined as co-residential communities sharing a common outlook and relying on mutual cooperation. The term was introduced to steer away from the idea that such a community was a utopia. In fact, the Fellowship for Intentional Community, a nonprofit umbrella organization for intentional communities worldwide currently lists 1,755 intentional communities in the United States alone. There are, of course, intentional communities in most countries of the world, many of which are not associated with the fellowship. On their website the fellowship lists a total of 722 intentional communities outside of the United States, in countries ranging from Argentina to Venezuela.

According to Kat Kinkade, co-founder of this commune and still a resident, "Communal life is for everyone" (Kinkade 1973, 13). Kinkade further explains that in 1972, when the community was five years old, "the average Community member, according to some statistics we took, is 23.5 years old and has two years of college. I would also add that he is likely to be quite intelligent, pleasant mannered, easygoing, familiar with counter-culture values and definitely not interested in the jobs that he could get working for corporations" (Kinkade 1973, 13).

Kinkade stresses the high responsibilities each member must take on when joining the community. To her, community life is thus not escapist. It is rather "take-it-on-ist" in that all participants must do their share for the community to prevail and strive. There is no liberal withdraw from one's responsibilities. Dishes must be washed, houses swept, floors cleaned, cows milked. Every day.

Twin Oaks has a labor credit system to assign different tasks and avoid that some members are stuck with only unpleasant work. However, as their numbers grew, what was unpleasant to one could be done by another and Kinkade finds in 1972 that "most of us these days, don't have to do a lot of unpleasant work" (Kinkade 1973, 44).

Beyond the search for a pleasing work experience, Twin Oaks is driven by a motivation to avoid the building up of individual privilege. Kinkade explains:

> Equality in labor is a large step towards social justice, but it is not the only step Twin Oaks has taken toward equality. Our financial and property policies reflect our determination to avoid a privileged class. Members get no cash income except a very small allowance which has ranged between twenty-five cents and a dollar a week [some $5 in today's value]. Any money which they might have owned before joining simply stays in the bank for their first three years unless they want to donate it to the Community. In any case, Twin Oaks receives the interest on it, as well as dividends on any stock and bonds, rents from real estate property, or any continuing income of any kind. (Kinkade 1973, 49)

While experimenting with consensus rule initially, Twin Oaks shifted the task of government to a board of three, who oversee task-specific managers. The term of board members is restricted to eighteen months (Kinkade 1973). Kinkade explains that "our bylaws leave us free to change our form of government any time two-thirds of the group wants it different. I personally think Twin Oaks would survive under a variety of governmental systems, including consensus or even democracy, as long as the managerial system was left intact" (Kinkade 1973, 55).

In fact, the current bylaws of Twin Oaks state in Article 3:

Paragraph One. In General.

The affairs of the Community are, in accordance with its Articles of Incorporation in the State of Virginia, managed by its Board of Directors. The Board of Directors has the authority and responsibility for making policy decisions for the Community.

Paragraph Two. Board of Directors and Officers.

A. The Board of Directors shall consist of the members of the Board of Community Planners ("the Board"). There shall be three regular members of the Board. An additional person may be designated as a stand-in member of the Board, and shall assume the responsibilities, duties, and powers of a regular member of the Board during the event of an absence of a regular member of the Board or in the case of a vacancy on the Board, and a second stand-in planner may be appointed when desirable because there are insufficient regular members of the Board due to absence or resignation or for other reasons, in order to maintain a full Board of three. All members of the Board shall be voting members of the Community. Upon termination of a person's term as a regular member of the Board or as a stand-in within six months of the termination of cos regular term, co shall not be reappointed to the Board for a period of at least six months, except that co may be appointed as a stand-in planner for up to three months in case the Board finds it desirable for reasons of continuity or for other reasons.

B. New members of the Board shall be appointed after the following general process with periods for and intervals between steps in the process being determined by the Board, except if there is no current member of the Board, in which case the procedure shall be as specified in subparagraph (D) below: The Board shall post public notice of each upcoming or current vacancy. The Board shall solicit the voting members for individuals interested in serving on the Board. A notice containing a list of the interested parties shall then be posted publicly, and any additional voting member may be added to the possible candidates by co placing cos signature on the notice. The Board shall then solicit the general membership for opinions of the candidates, after which the Board shall nominate an individual to fill the vacancy. A general ballot of the voting members shall then be held and all such voting members shall have the opportunity to accept or reject the nomination. If more than twenty percent of the members eligible to vote reject the nomination, the Board shall rescind the nomination, and, if not, the nominated individual shall be appointed to fill the vacancy. The term of regular members of the Board shall be eighteen months. The term of a stand-in member shall be three to six months. The term may end earlier by reason of resignation, death, or recall (method of recall is provided in subparagraph Three (A)(3) of this Article).

C. No member of the Board of Directors shall serve alone for a period of more than six weeks. Should this period pass without the appointment of at least one additional member of the Board of Directors, the remaining director shall resign and elections shall be called immediately by said director or any member of the Community, as provided for in subparagraph (D) below.

D. If there is no current member of the Board of Directors, due to resignation, recall, or for any reason whatsoever, elections shall immediately be called by any voting member of the Community. A request for candidates shall be posted in a public place in the Community for not less than 7 and not more than 14 days, and any member of the Community who wishes to be a candidate for the Board of Directors shall place cos name thereon. At the end of this period, elections shall be held. Any voting member may conduct this election; if no member steps forward within a week from the time at which there ceased to be a Board of Directors, then the election shall be conducted by the voting member who has been a member for the longest period of time. Each voting member of the Community may cast a vote for up to three of the candidates whose names appear on the slate, but no member may vote for the same candidate more than once. The three candidates who obtained the most votes shall be the new Board of Directors, provided that each of these candidates obtained votes from at least a majority of eligible voters voting in the election. If any of the three candidates did not obtain the necessary votes, then co shall not be appointed director; however, if one or two candidates did obtain the required votes, they shall be appointed the new Board of Directors and shall obtain additional members in accordance with the provisions of subparagraph (B) above. If no candidate obtained the required votes, runoff elections shall be held immediately.

E. The Board shall appoint three voting members of the Community to be the President (who shall also be a member of the Board), the Secretary, and the Treasurer of the Community, and the Board shall appoint such other officers and representatives as it deems necessary, all with such powers and duties as it finds necessary or convenient for the governance of the Community and/or the conduct of its external relations. Said officers shall be appointed for a term of one year, shall serve until their successors are appointed, and shall be removable at the will of the Board. The Board shall also designate an officer, a member of the Board, or a member of the Community to maintain a record of voting members of the Community. The Board may also appoint such groups as it deems appropriate to aid the Board in the performance of its duties.

F. The annual meeting of the Board of Directors shall be held directly after the annual meeting of the membership and at the same location, and no notice of the meeting shall be required. The Board shall appoint officers of the Community and conduct whatever business may be before it at its annual meeting.

G. A quorum of the Board of Directors shall be two members of the Board, except that if there is only one member of the Board, co may serve for up to six weeks by coself, as provided in subparagraph (C) above.

Paragraph Three. Participatory Governance.

A. In general, any reasonable means of managing the affairs of the Community may be entered upon and tried, without the necessity of amending these Bylaws, so long as such means shall be upon direction by and supervision of the Board, and providing:

1. That the governing body shall at all times manage and govern within the principles and policies of the Community as specified in these Bylaws;
2. That the government shall be participatory to the fullest extent possible, with general public forums to allow the consideration and input of the membership on all substantial policy decisions;
3. That the voting members of the Community shall always have the right to recall the governing body or a member of the governing body. A recall shall be preceded by a meeting of the membership called by any voting

member with at least ten, but not more than fifty, days of public notice prior to such a meeting. At this meeting, the member(s) of the governing body whom it is proposed to recall shall be given full opportunity to answer any accusations or to explain cos/their conduct or views. After the meeting, should the voting membership of the community desire to recall the member(s) of the governing body, it may do so by obtaining the signatures (including written or telephoned vote in absentia as provided in subparagraph (B)(2) below) of no less than a simple majority of the voting members of the Community on a petition of recall. Any voting member may initiate such a petition.

4. That the voting members of the Community shall always have the right to overrule any decision of the governing body. If any voting member of the Community wishes to overrule a decision of the governing body, co may attempt to do so by initiating a petition of overrule. To be successful, the petition must receive the signatures (including written or telephoned vote in absentia as provided in subparagraph (B)(2) below) of no less than a simple majority of the voting members of the Community. The Community may set a higher percentage for issues concerning the acceptance or rejection of members, as it deems wise. Said petition must be completed within three weeks of a decision's being made public by the governing body.

B. Provisions for Voting:

1. The record date for any notice shall be the date of the notice. The record date for eligibility to vote at any meeting shall be the date of the meeting. The record date for eligibility to sign a petition shall be the date for required completion of the petition, as per paragraph Three (A)(4) above.

2. No vote may be cast by proxy, but any voting member may submit a written or telephoned vote in absentia on an issue which is brought before a vote of the membership, and said written or telephoned vote shall be treated as a vote cast in person or as a signature on a petition, as appropriate. For a telephoned vote to be valid the member must speak directly to two voting members of the Community and state that co is casting a vote.

Paragraph Four. Meetings of the Membership.

A. The annual meeting of the membership shall be held on any day in November or December of each year on the property of Twin Oaks. An officer or member of the Board of Directors shall post notice of said meeting in a public place in the Community, which shall constitute personal notice to each voting member of the Community, at least 10 and not more than 50 days in advance of said meeting, except that if said meeting will be the official meeting with respect to a change in the Community's Articles of Incorporation, said notice shall be provided at least 25 and not more than 50 days in advance. If no notice is posted, then the meeting will be held on the first Friday of December at 3:30 p.m. in the normal place at which Community meetings are held, and no changes in the Community's Articles of Incorporation shall be discussed.

B. Any voting member of the Community may call a special meeting of the membership by posting notice of such a meeting in a public place at least 10, but not more than 50, days before the date of such a meeting. Such a meeting may be called for any purpose for which a general membership meeting is required or for any other purpose. (http://www.twinoaks.org/policies/bylaws#article-iii)

As these by-laws demonstrate, Kinkade was right in 1972 when she thought that Twin Oaks could survive even under democratic governance. For this to occur, limited terms, accountability, and a yearly general assembly must be deemed crucial.

LESSONS LEARNED FROM INTENTIONAL COMMUNITIES

The most important lessons that can be drawn from the Owenite communes all derive from their failures. While Owen's reforms were initially successful on his cotton mill in Scotland, the New Lanark Mills also stopped functioning after Owen left and started his international mission. His absence, it appears, produced a lack of guidance and let to internal disarray. Among the communities created in the United States and the United Kingdom, a similar phenomenon can be observed: the lack of shared commitment, shared vision, or philosophy strong enough to provide each participating individual with the moral and behavioral guidelines to act. As long as Robert Owen was present, his personal leadership could provide such guidance. In his absence, there was none. More than the need for personal leadership, the Owenite communes highlight the need for a strong and deeply shared culture or system of values and norms able to guide individual behavior and justify material sacrifices.

Owenite communities seem to never have created assemblies and other direct democratic mechanisms, instead relying heavily on individual, charismatic leadership. When this leadership was absent, the communes succumbed.

The Tolstoyan communes offer many lessons and they instituted many innovative institutions and laws all aimed at protecting equality while not stifling individual agency and entrepreneurship. In this, they were very akin to anarchist, anarcho-syndicalist, and libertarian socialist programs. The basis of their communes was collective ownership of land and equal distribution of profits according to family and individual needs. Their commitment to a simply life ruled out or sought to hold at bay individual tendencies toward the accumulation of privilege vis-à-vis others. Luxury and sloth were also controlled by this shared commitment to frugality and hard work, which was rooted in Leo Tolstoy's writings. While the Tolstoyans did not adhere to a sectarian religion, they did share strong cultural ties based on Tolstoy, which provided them with ethical and behavioral guidelines. Collective decisions were made in general assembly and involved everybody. Councils were elected and given executive power, but the elected delegates were recallable and did not serve fixed terms.

Tolstoyan communes emerged after the World War I in Russia and from there they spread around the globe. In Russia, the peasants who were the main agents in their creation could count on a history of village self-rule, the *mir*, in which village assemblies were held and village elders elected. After the Bolshevik takeover in October 1917, Tolstoyan communes were perceived as "too advanced," as they already presented the end stage of communist development. They were dismantled and their members were imprisoned and killed. The real threat to the USSR was not the futuristic aspect of the Tolstoyans, but their autonomy. State power could not tolerate parallel community power. Their strict anti-militarism, vegetarianism, and their insistence on schooling their children differently, according to the doctrines of peace and nonviolence, all provided plenty of justification for their persecution and annihilation.

Tolstoyan communes thus did not emerge in situations of crisis and war but became victim of a hostile environment against which they could not muster any resistance. The USSR did not tolerate the free and stateless communes the Tolstoyans established and ultimately destroyed them, killing hundreds and imprisoning the rest.

Among the kibbutzim, the importance of a strong belief, ideology, or vision seems necessary to provide the internal coherence, as well as the motivation to forsake comfort and privilege. As Israel is no longer in a phase of pioneering Zionism, the ideological force that was able to bring different people together at the beginning is evaporating. As a result, many kibbutzim are facing problems of disintegration caused by individual profit motives and the seeking of privilege and distinction.

Detailed information about the inner workings of Amish communities is scant. However, the evidence we do have is that the Amish have survived as a community to this day since their arrival in the late seventeenth century. The survival of this distinct community can be attributed to the set of rules and guidelines they follow (the Ordnung), as well as their conscious effort to stay separate from other different communities. Furthermore, they share a strong and binding religion that motivates and guides their actions. Amish community survival seems a direct result of the strengths of their community ties and their strong, shared culture.

The Hutterites, similar to the Amish and Mennonites, live apart and maintain the strength of their communities through a shared religion. This provides them with the kind of strong cultural ties that allow them to reproduce their own identity. It also provides them with the norms, values, and guidelines for their daily actions and interactions. Different from the Amish, the Hutterites share the ownership of all their lands, thus practicing communism. Their strong commitment to their own values and norms, as well as the maintenance of their separate identity, has ensured their survival and prosperity.

The members of the Twin Oaks Community all share a strong culture and interest. These shared interests are strong enough to ensure everyone's equal participation. Government is democratic, limited, held accountable, and legitimated by a general assembly. There is no legislator other than the commonly-agreed by-laws, reproduced in part here. Government thus rests heavily on the executive. Judicial functions are performed whenever necessary by the same elected board.

7

Native American and Indigenous Communities

Some of the most innovative institutions to hold elitism at bay come from first, native, or indigenous people. This fact indicates that, to a great extent, political and economic elitism is a Western disease, meaning introduced and sustained by Western-type political institutions, associated with modernization and modernity. If this is so, then we have even more reason to decolonize the world and free it from Western European hegemony, be it the hegemony of power or the hegemony of Western political models. The institutional solutions found in England to address the universal problem of power, rule, fairness, and equality occurred, after all, under the auspices of monarchy and aristocracy. It should not surprise us that Western liberal democratic political institutions remained mixed with aristocratic ones. Looking for democratic institutions among non-Western peoples promises to be a much more fruitful enterprise.

I conducted empirical research among the Wintukua and in Palenque de San Basílio, Colombia, in 2014, so the information on those two cases is richer than the information I have been able to obtain for most other cases. However, some of the cases described here, for example, the Zapatistas of southern Mexico, have long inspired researchers interested in alternative political models and institutions, so I was able to rely on a rich body of literature for them. Other cases, like the ones of Bhutan and Zomia, are less known, but they also point at innovative and inspiring institutional solutions to the problem of elite domination.

PALENQUE DE SAN BASÍLIO

Palenque de San Basílio is a Maroon community located in the department of Bolívar, Colombia. In the year 1600, a group of African slaves, brought to the port of Cartagena de las Indias, were able to escape. They created several free republics in the hinterlands of Cartagena, particularly in the territory of Montes de Maria—the Mary Mounts. They were never conquered by the Spaniards. Because of their defensive wall structures, these places were and are called "Palenques" in Spanish, as their defensive walls were made of stacks.

In the case of the Palenques in the Montes de Maria, we read that their independence and political autonomy were recognized in 1605 by the king after many struggles and many losses on the Spanish side. The first officially known Palenque was "La Matuna," located in the province of Cartagena. Runaway slaves led by Benkos Bioho thus created the first free town in the Americas—a village of Africans and their descendants. The freedom La Matuna offered attracted many runaway slaves, so that other Palenques formed in the near proximity.

Unable to conquer them, in 1691, the Spanish Crown granted, by royal decree, the following rights to the four Palenques of Montes de Maria, San Miguel, Matudere, Arenal, and Betancur: liberty, demarcation of their territory, legal and tax treatment equal to the free population, and self-government (Arrázola 1970).

After ongoing disputes and wars waged by colonial slave holders, another agreement was signed in 1713, this time between Governor Francisco Baloco Leigrave and the Palenqueros, again recognizing their freedom and autonomy (Arrázola 1970).

In 1772, the Palenque de San Basílio officially appeared as a part of the Mahates municipality, but with a certain autonomy. According to Bishop Peredo of Cartagena in a letter of 1772, "They appoint their own judge and a people's captain. They also control their own politics and the military. They have a mayor, who is only reporting to the Governor of the Province" (Peredo 1972, 140).

The information we have on the Palenques of Mount Mary, Colombia, tells us that in the colonial era, Palenques had political autonomy. This autonomy included legal, fiscal, legislative, military, and executive sovereignty. Palenques thus resembles the medieval European free cities described by Max Weber (1968). Everything indicates that, in the Palenques of Mount Mary, a form of open forums was practiced (*cabildos abiertos*), a millennial Spanish institution, which at this time had already lost its force in Spain and in the Americas, where its exercise was reserved to "neighbors" (*vecinos*), all of whom were white descendants of Europeans. The Maroons thus adopted and continued a Spanish tradition at a time when the same Spaniards had already stopped practicing popular participation by councils and public assemblies (Bayle 1952).

In the Americas, in Gran Colombia, and in the nation-states that were created after its breakup in 1831, different from the European towns, the

Maroon republics were not integrated and used as a model. To the contrary, the Colombian State, like the other American states, persecuted and destroyed these free republics when and where they could. When they failed, as in the case of the Palenques of Montes de Maria, they isolated them. The Creole political elites, blinded by racism, betrayed their own tradition of open councils and public assemblies and instead constructed exclusive and highly hierarchical states in the Americas, parallel to the Maroon republics, and finally they ended the black republics. The Colombian state only included these rebel territories after subjecting them to extreme poverty and having transformed what was once a political rebellion to a cultural curiosity, ready to be consumed by tourists.

Thus, the political autonomy Palenquera did not last. When Colombia, in 1821, after gaining independence from Spain, passed a constitution, Palenque and other previously independent territories become integrated to the nation—if not de facto, then de jure. The Constitution of Colombia 1821 created departments; each department was divided into provinces, cantons, and parishes. In 1886, with a new constitution, this time more centralist, municipalities were created, and Palenque became anchored into the structure of the Colombian State. The constitutional reform of 1968, after the era of violence (1945–1965), created citizen forums in municipalities and provincial departments, associations of municipalities, and metropolitan areas, allowing, at least on paper, citizen participation.

The 1991 constitution finally recognized thirty-two departments and 1,059 municipalities. It created indigenous territories and allowed municipalities to be divided into communes and districts. Thus with the constitution of 1991, Palenque de San Basílio became a township (*coregimiento*) of the neighboring municipality of Mahates, which in turn is attached to the department of Bolívar. In 2002, the Departmental Assembly of Bolívar, through Ordinance 07, recognized Palenque de San Basílio as a "zone of peaceful coexistence and an ethno-cultural territory." With this, the Colombian State sealed the loss of political autonomy and substituted political with cultural recognition, transforming a free people into a museum piece and a tourist attraction. In 2011, through the organic law on territorial organization, the Colombian government dedicated resources to Palenque de San Basílio for tourist development, highlighting their cultural particularity. This process was facilitated by the work of the group of scholars making the proposal to recognize Palenque de San Basílio as an Intangible Heritage of Humanity by UNESCO.

The Colombian government thus finally beat the Maroons—integrating them into the state and taking away their political, military, judicial, and executive autonomy—and replaced them with a highly circumscribed "participation," regulated according to government preferences. In doing so, the Colombian government ignored such Palenqueros institutions as the *kuagro* and it tamed the rebellious Cimarron forces, transforming them into minimal participation, organized to the taste of power, regularized, and highly circumscribed. The Colombian State achieved even more: with the shift in emphasis from the political to the cultural, it transformed Palenqueros into curious actors of their own history and Palenque into a kind of living museum. In this process, the *kuagro*, an ancestral association of military and political origin, has become a cultural institution.

Palenqueros, however, seek to resist this absorption into the nation-state and their gradual commodification as cultural curiosities. Here again, the *kuagro* plays a crucial function. Nina Friedemann and Richard Cross explain:

> According to the Spanish interpretation, [Palenque] had a war lieutenant, a sheriff, a treasurer, a religious leader and a supreme leader, who some considered to be a king, as in the case of La Matuna. In subsequent palenques they became captains following the command of a war chief. In 1693 Domingo Padilla was captain of Matuderé and founder of Tabacal in the Sierra of Luruaco and Francisco Arara was his war chief; Domingo Criollo was captain of Palenque de San Miguel and Pedro Mina was the war chief of that same palenque. This with a total of six hundred men organized into "escuadras" [squads] who, as in the case of San Miguel, were composed of eight to ten Mina blacks each. In these teams, who conducted ambushes, his warriors had their faces painted white and red. (Friedemann and Cross 1979, n.p.)

Thus after winning the war against the Spaniards, Palenque became a free city-republic. Accordingly, the *kuagros* stopped serving military functions and started to fulfill political and administrative roles. Then with independence Palenque became integrated into the national territory. Losing its political autonomy, the *kuagro* changed again into a predominantly social and cultural institution. A young Palenquero in an interview conducted in February of 2014 explains:

> We have established an organizational model where we start joining around the age of eight. The persons belonging to a *kuagro* are all contemporaries. Within this structure, we find our friends and marriage and we organize cultural events. We also collaborate with funerals. All our lives in the Palenquera community we live in *kuagros*. (Interview, Palenque, February 14, 2014; my translation)

Palenque, with its 4,000 residents and perhaps the same amount of Palenqueros living elsewhere, has, according to a local informant, "hundreds of kuagros." The exact number is difficult to determine. All interviewees confirm that any and all Palenqueros, men and women, with rare exceptions, belong to a *kuagro*, even those not living in Palenque. Assuming a total population of some 8,000 and an average number of twenty members per *kuagro*, the information obtained is not surprising. There are most likely hundreds of active kuagros among Palenqueros and Palenqueras.

A young Palenquero explains that today *kuagros* are for "social events, parties like birthdays or weddings, or financial support when a person dies or is sick" (interview, Palenque, February 14, 2014; my translation). Hence, one of the central functions of *kuagros* is solidarity—a solidarity that goes beyond death. Nina Friedemann and Richard Cross explain:

> The spirit of belonging, participation, and solidarity of the palenqueros reaches beyond parties and beyond life. When someone dies, their cuagro members, both male and female, accompany and contribute to the expenses incurred for the funeral ceremony of the nine nights. The same applies if the deceased is an infant. Cuagro members of the child's parents assist promptly. If it is someone who lives in Cartagena, Barranquilla and even towns like La Guajira and Rocha, San Pablo, Maria La Baja, San Cayetano or Gallo where there are palenquero colonies, the cuagros travel to the place of the wake. (Friedemann and Cross 1979, n.p.; my translation)

The *kuagro* is *the* central associational form of Palenque, but its function has changed to the extent that political autonomy was gradually removed from Palenque. From a military institution it first morphed into a political institution and then, after the loss of political autonomy, its main function became social, cultural, and recreational (Friedemann and Cross 1979).

From the *kuagro*, other initiatives of social organization and self-management have arisen. Palenqueros have created twenty to thirty thematic community *juntas*, where they gather to perform specific actions. Professor Carlos Arturo Cassiani, Palenquero and public school teacher in Palenque, explains:

> Well, we're seeing the juntas as a form of organization where different people come together mostly for economic purposes, that is: people who belong to different kuagros converge and form a *junta*. (Interview, Palenque, February 14, 2014; my translation)

Palenqueros created such a large number of community organizations that it is difficult for the outside observer to understand and capture the associative diversity of Palenque. Through interviews, it became clear that there are at least three types of *juntas* in the Palenque today:

1. Community action boards and municipal councils as part of land management process in the country (*ordenamiento territorial*);
2. Thematic *juntas* that are traditional to Palenque, especially to raise money; and

3. The directive *junta* (*junta directiva*) working with the community council, which in the daily life of the community is often referred to simply as "la junta" and which today plays a major role because of its interaction with the municipal council.

This is because the new law of 1991, which allows for the formation of community councils in black communities, was promptly implemented in Palenque. Thus in addition to *kuagros* and *juntas*, there is a community council, which has a distinct form of internal organization. An interviewee explains:

> Here in Palenque we have embraced the community council and we did not find it strange, because Palenque has administered its territory for more than three hundred years. (Interview, Palenque, February 14, 2014; my translation)

And:

> In 2002 the first *junta* was chosen; in 2006 a second *junta* was chosen and in 2009 the third *junta* was chosen. In December we chose another one, because the period is for three years. Basically we have a very similar organizational structure to that of the state. Sometimes people who come from other community councils wonder why we have such a large *junta directiva*. It is because each member is responsible for one aspect of the community. We have counselors for education, for identity and culture, recreation and sport, and we have councils for women, youth, public services, and for land and the environment. Each of the counselors responds to the internal dynamics we have here as a community. (Interview, Palenque, February 14, 2014; my translation)

Palenqueros are actively engaged in hundreds of *kuagros*, dozens of *juntas*, and a community council with twelve members, each one responsible for a specific area, all apparently based on the long tradition of the *kuagro*. To them, participation truly is a "habit of the heart" and strong civic engagement is everybody's reality. Furthermore, citizenship to them is not a set of rights and entitlements, but, similar to the classic and medieval European models, mostly a matter of responsibilities, in which rights are collectively constructed and defended.

THE WINTUKUA: GUARDIANS OF THE EARTH

The Wintukua people, known to outsiders as the "Arhuacos," is one of four indigenous groups living in the territory of the Sierra Nevada de Santa Marta, Colombia. The Sierra Nevada reaches 5,775 meters above sea level and extends to the edge of the Caribbean Sea. The Wintukua are about 50,000 people and tend to live in settlements composed of nuclear households and farms. A minority lives in larger agglomerates, especially in Nabusimake, the holy city, which is located at about 2,000 meters above sea level in the heart of the Sierra. Along with the Wiwa, Kaggaba (Kogi), and Kankuamo peoples, the Wintukua live in an indigenous reservation recognized by the Colombian State since 1980. Their reservation has 661,527 hectares. Among these four peoples, the Wintukua are the most numerous and the best organized, giving them a leadership role among the four groups. In their own words, they are the "older brothers."

The 1991 Constitution of Colombia states in Article 330: "indigenous territories will be governed by councils formed and regulated according to the customs of their communities." It recognizes the customary law of indigenous groups such as the Wintukua. In Colombia, most indigenous groups are organized into *cabildos* or town halls, a colonial Spanish form of municipal organization. In Spain and among the white and mixed settlers, these open assemblies succumbed to feudalism, but they survived and gained new strength of expression among indigenous people and Maroons. According to the Colombian Ministry of the Interior,

The Indigenous Cabildo is a special public entity, whose members are members of an indigenous community, elected and recognized by it, with a traditional socio-political organization whose function is to legally represent the community, exercise authority and carry out the activities attributed by the laws, their customs, and internal rules of each community.

Enrique Sánchez Gutiérrez and Hernán Molina Echeverri explain:

In the Andean region political authority rests in the cabildos. Each reservation has its own cabildo, and council members are elected periodically by members of the community. The role of the cabildo is to organize the work, divide the communal lands, settle internal disputes and represent the reservation to the white authorities. The cabildo was an institution imposed by the Spaniards onto the indigenous communities in the seventeenth and eighteenth century, but it adapted to our interests and traditions. It has been one of the main instruments for the defense of indigenous communities and is key for defending the land of the reservations and to recover the land stolen by big landowners. Experience has shown—both in the northern Cauca and throughout the country—that cabildos are our best weapon to organize, to recover the lands that have been taken from us and to maintain and develop our community life. (Sánchez Gutiérrez and Echeverri 2010, 215; my translation)

Parallel to the cabildo, the Wintukua have another internal structure of sacred and wise people, who have great authority: the Mamos. According to Romero Infante and Guzman Barrios, the Wintukua "administer themselves through a dual system of traditional authorities or Mamos and civil authorities or cabildos, secretaries, commissioners, prosecutors and counselors. The cabildos are selected by the Mamos in special councils and decisions are made in assembly considering the advice and words of the Mamos" (Romero Infante and Guzman Barrios 2007, 55; my translation).

This dual power system was evident during my stay in Colombia, as on May 17, 2014, the Wintukua chose a new cabildo governor, Mr. José María Arroyo. The process of choosing him followed the traditional model. First, Mamos agreed on who should be the new governor. Seventy Mamos Wintukuas in multiple meetings and after several spiritual consultations, deliberated up to the point at which everyone agreed with the candidate. This process took several weeks. Then the candidate was presented to the general assembly. In the first phase, there was no voting, but a deliberative process that lasted until all seventy Mamos agreed. Then there was a general meeting, open to all.

Margarita Villafaña explains:

We live apart, in families, but weekly, or monthly, depending on the need, we meet to make decisions. In these assemblies in the villages, everyone has a voice, including women, youth and children. When we have to make major decisions that affect everyone, we hold a general meeting with all the people. (Interview, Santa Marta, June 1, 2014, my translation)

Thus, among the Wintukua, two basic principles are of central importance: the deliberative process among the leaders, in this case to choose a new cabildo governor, and the general public assembly of the Wintukua people, where the decision of the seventy Mamos is presented to the people. On this occasion, the attending Wintukuas decided whether to accept the candidate suggested by Mamos or not and they listened to the rendering of accounts of the outgoing governor, as well as to the proposals of the incoming team.

Moisés Villafaña explains:

First, each village holds assemblies to discuss. Then they communicate their decisions to the authorities. Then all the Mamos gather and finally the Mamos take their decision to the general assembly for discussion, where the final decision is made. (Interview, Santa Marta, June 1, 2014, my translation)

To my question "how many times does the general assembly meet?" the Wintukua representatives explained: "as often as necessary—whenever there is a decision to take or a project to be approved." They also explained that each investment and proposed intervention project must be approved by an internal deliberative process followed by a process of discussion and approval at a general assembly.

Hence, the political system of the Wintukua is characterized by deliberation and by public assembly. Assemblies are held frequently, always when there is need. Public meetings are open to all men, women, youth, and children and they are held at different levels: in the villages or special village meeting places, among Mamos, and at the national level, involving all. Wintukua democracy thus is deliberative and direct.

In the traditional Indian practice, and due to the fact that land titles given by the federal government to indigenous reservations are of a collective nature, an individual person cannot own land. It may be that a family considers land as belonging to this family out of habit, but in reality it is not theirs and can go back to the community at any time. At the same time, it is up to each family to take care of their ancestral land and each family has an ancestral land containing a sacred site for just this family—a site that connects family members with their ancestors. They can never sell this land. They are only allowed to sell the surplus produced on this land—the fruits of their labor. At the same time, a family cannot have more land than needed and the community is watching to achieve a balance between the families as a way to maintain equality among themselves. According to Margarita Villafaña, "a few years ago the Wintukua began a process of land redistribution, because they realized that the lands of some families, because it was high up in the mountains, did not yield enough to feed their families" (interview, Santa Marta, June 1, 2014; my translation).

Thus, the citizenship of the indigenous groups living in the Sierra Nevada de Santa Marta is active, full of responsibilities that extend beyond their own groups, because according to their worldview, they have a responsibility to the whole world. With this, their culture contrasts sharply with the white and mestizo culture that surrounds them; for the Wintukuas and their brothers, citizenship is not constituted by rights, but by responsibilities. In addition, for the Wintukua, the law does not grant rights—it imposes obligations.

The Law

The Wintukua law is not a written law. Ati Sarai explains: "The tree and the river is our law. The mountains and rivers are our code" (interview, Santa Marta, May 17, 2014; my translation). The *Jaba y Jate* magazine (2012), published by the Gonawindua Tayrona Indigenous Organization (OGT) and coordinated by the Mamo Kaggaba Arregocés Conchacala and the Kaggaba Cabildo governor Jose de los Santos Sauna lists forty-nine *Jabas* and *Jates*, some of them including other sites plus four to be recovered, all in the region of the Sierra Nevada de Santa Marta. According to Arregocés Conchacala,

The Sierra Nevada de Santa Marta is a sacred territory par excellence, con-
formed by a large number of sacred places. For the Kaggaba people, the Sierra is
Se Nenulang—the physical and spiritual universe with all its components—and
in it are the codes from the rest of the Earth. (Organización Indígena Gonawindua Tayrona 2010, 7; my translation)

It is worth noting that the world is represented in the stones, tumas, mountains, and lakes of the Sierra. According to Conchacala,

The Sierra Nevada de Santa Marta has its principles and fundamentals in the Se
or Law of Origin. This means that everything that exists materially has always
existed in spirit. With the embodiment of the world, everything was well ordered
and had clear functions. The order of the territory and of the life forms are written in codes of nature—in lagoons, in the stones, in the hills, in the birdsongs,
and the sound of the breeze. Our Mamos know and spiritually and materially
handle these codes which contain the guidelines for the proper education and
training, for the organization and maintenance of social welfare, for the balance
of the environment, the protection of nature and to all physical and spiritual existence. (Organización Indígena Gonawindua Tayrona 2010, 9; my translation)

The Sierra Nevada and sacred sites in her function together as a whole and
as a living organism. Nature is not, as in the "Western" thought, a mere substrate of life. For the Wintukua, Kaggaba, Kankuamo, and Wiwa, similar to
other natives of the Americas, nature *is* life. And it is a well-arranged life in
which every place has rules and specific functions. Each site contains a law.
That's the Wintukua, Kaggaba, Wiwa, and Kankuama law. A law manifested
in the earth. To read, understand, and interpret this law is the central work
of their Mamos and they are prepared for this task during most of their lives.
According to Wiwa authorities,

The mother is also a transmitter of knowledge; from her comes the law of origin. As a mother she passed her knowledge on to her son Siokokui through "a
book" from which he learned and from which the Wiwa life unfolded. . . . This
knowledge includes all the parameters for the organization of the social and
natural life, standards for words and behavior, as well as the handling and timing
of personal events, family, and community history. They are also forms of communication that allow us to return to the ancestors and talk with them, to read
and to hear their words. . . . And those same ancestors make us remember. And
they are telling us: Wake up! Continue with your story telling, your divinations,
your offerings. (Organization Yugumaiun Tairona Bunkuanarua Wiwa, cited in
Rocha Vivas 2010, 508; my translation)

Nature *is* the law. The problem is that many people are no longer able to
read the book that is nature and to understand its laws. So we need the Mamos

because they have kept this capability alive. Colombian anthropologist Cristina Echavarria explains:

> The Mamos are always saying that "the birds still do as mother told them," but we're already forgetting; we need to study the birds to remember and do like them. (Echavarría Usher 1993, 221; my translation)

According Wintukua thinking, which is very similar to the thinking of other groups living in the Sierra Nevada de Santa Marta, the social and political life is not separate from the spiritual life and nature. If something happens in the life of an individual, it affects the community and it has a spiritual and natural roots. For life to flow well, there must be balance between all these areas. Reestablishing a broken balance involves all levels affected by this imbalance. The clean-up process begins on the spiritual level, which in turn is anchored in nature because nature is the spirit and it contains the law. In this view, there is no room for punishment and the focus is not on punishing but cleaning up and reestablishing the lost balance. To return to the law, sacred sites are key and Mamos are the judges that guide and preside over this process.

The Mamos

Mamos are the spiritual leaders of the Wintukua. They are priests, guides, and counselors. They are leaders, but they are not representatives. They are counselors, but they wield no political power. To become a Mamo, a person has to be prepared from youth. The future Mamos have to go through times of seclusion and meditation. Their lives have to follow strict behavioral and dietary codes. They do not eat meat or salt. They must live exemplary lives. At the same time, Mamos are connected to the sacred sites of the Sierra. They serve as interpreters and conduits of these sites, as they interpret them for others. Each Mamo is responsible for a different site. According to Miguel Rocha Vivas,

> The *mamu-*, mama or mamo, are priests, doctors, and community leaders who have different specializations and titles, depending on their place of origin, community, descent, preparation, religious prestige, and so on. In that sense, the mamas are the bearers par excellence of original words, major words that when written in Latin characters have led to the kinds of texts that are called myths, stories, songs, and what we call traditional literature and wisdom, or *oralituras*, referencing their origin and preeminently oral transmission. (Rocha Vivas 2010, 503f; my translation)

Like the European classical and medieval republics, Wintukua citizenship is characterized not by rights, but first and foremost by duties and responsibilities. These responsibilities, for the Wintukua, reach well beyond their own community because according to their belief they are responsible for the whole world. That is because the Sierra Nevada contains the whole world. The Mamo Vicencio Torres Márquez, in his complaint letter to the president of the republic from July 7, 1968, expressed a conviction that I heard a lot during my research:

> This place is the heart of all human beings who exist everywhere in the world. (Sánchez Gutiérrez and Molina Echeverri 2010, 76; my translation)

In the same letter, this important Mamo explains:

> This is what our law, our religion, and our customs are: we have to protect and assist all these sites and fulfill our duties through our hidden and traditional science. That's our obligation. (Sánchez Gutiérrez and Molina Echeverri 2010, 70; my translation)

The Mamos are, in the words of Moises Villafaña, spiritual guides, counselors, astrologers, and sages. They do not command; they give advice. For internal issues, they also have the responsibility to judge civil and criminal cases not involving non-Indians. For the Wintukua, crime and other antisocial behavior is the result of a spiritual problem. It is part of the responsibility of Mamos to identify the root of this problem and address it.

Moisés Villafaña explains:

> For us, the conflict comes from a spiritual disease and we must heal this disease. If it is not repaired, it will continue to spread. For us, unlike the Western system, the emphasis is not on punishment, but on the repair, which may also involve community work or work for the victim. (Interview, Santa Marta, June 1, 2014; my translation)

The Sierra Nevada and the sacred sites it contains, in this way, work as a whole and as a living organism. Nature is not, as in the "Western" thought, a mere substrate of life. For the Wintukua, Kaggaba, Kankuamo, and Wiwa, similar to other first people of the Americas, nature *is* life. And it is a well-arranged life in which every place has rules and specific functions. Each site contains a law. That is the law of the Wintukua, Kaggaba, Wiwa, and Kankuama. To read, understand, and interpret this law is the central work of the Mamos and they are prepared for this during all their life. Furthermore, social and political life is not separate from the spiritual life and from nature. If something happens in the life of an individual, it affects the community and has spiritual and natural roots. For life to flow well, there must be balance between all these realms. Reestablishing a broken balance involves all levels affected by an imbalance. The healing process begins on the spiritual level, which in turn is anchored in nature because nature is spirit and it contains the law.

GUMLAO VILLAGES IN ZOMIA

James Scott (2009), in his discussion of statelessness in the Zomia region, which crosses India, Burma, China, Vietnam, Laos, Thailand, and Cambodia, dedicates some space to the Gumlao villages of Highland Burma. Scott finds that "Gumlao areas were anathema to the state. An early British account of the Kachin areas contrasted the ease of marching through the villages of a well-disposed hereditary chief with the difficulty of traversing 'a gumlao village which is practically a small republic, the headman, however well-meaning he may be, is quite unable to control the actions of any badly-disposed villager.' Gumlao social organization was state repelling in a number of ways. Its ideology discouraged, or killed, would-be hereditary chiefs with feudal pretensions. It was resistant to tribute or control by the neighboring Shan principalities. Finally, it presented a relatively intractable anarchy of egalitarian, Lilliputian republics that were hard to pacify, let alone govern" (Scott 2009, 215).

For Scott (2009), Gumlao villages have evaded statehood. Instead of confronting and fighting encroaching states and their leaders and apparatuses, they have instead fled them. Thus for Scott, "Flight, not rebellion, has been the basis of freedom in the hills; far more egalitarian settlements were founded by runaways than by revolutionaries" (Scott 2009, 218).

Gumlao villages, similar to other groups in the region such as the Hmong and the Lahu, have thus averted encroaching states by moving or dispersing. According to Scott, "Here, we are not dealing not merely with 'jellyfish' tribes but with 'jellyfish' lineages, villages, chiefdoms, and, at the limit, jellyfish households. Along with shifting agriculture, this polymorphism is admirably suited to the purpose of evading incorporation in state structures. Such hill societies rarely challenge the state itself, but neither do they allow the state an easy point of entry or leverage. When threatened, they retreat, disperse, disaggregate like quicksilver—as if their motto was indeed 'Divide that ye be not ruled'" (Scott 2009, 219).

The villages Scott (2009) describes are thus all high up in the mountains. They have retreated, step by step, from the expanding and encroaching states of the lowlands.

However, such people as the Kachin and their Gumlao villages have not only successfully evaded neighboring states, they have also avoided the build-up of internal hierarchies—sometimes with radical means. According to Scott, "The gumlao Kachin, as we have seen, have a history of enforcing egalitarian social relations by deposing or assassinating overreaching chiefs" (Scott 2009, 217).

Much of Scott's account relies on the earlier ethnographic work of Edmund Leach (1964), who has described the Gumlao Kachin in more detail. Leach relates the effort of the British colonizers to subdue the Kachins. He quotes an official British government document from 1929, relating the British difficulties:

> More than half a century ago, a spirit of republicanism manifested itself in the unadministered territory known as the Triangle and thence found its way to the west of the Mali Hka. Certain tribesmen, who found the yoke of the Duwa irksome and were impatient of control, declared themselves Kumlaos or rebels, threw off their hereditary connection with the Duwa, and settled themselves in solitary villages of their own. The British government steadily set its face against this movement and has declined to recognize Kumlaos." (Leach 1964, 199)

Leach himself describes the Gumlao in a tone of amazement: "In gumlao theory there are no chiefs. All lineages are of the same rank; no one brother is ritually superior to another" (Leach 1964, 203). He further characterizes Gumlao villages in contrast to the surrounding Gumsa villages. He finds that among the Gumlao,

> Villages of equal status form a *mung*; lineages are all of one rank; no tributary dues of any kind are due from villagers towards village headmen; the scale of compensation does not vary with the rank of the individual; In theory there is no rank difference between siblings. Gumlao lineages appear to fragment with great rapidity. Any particular named lineage is likely to be shallow and there is no precise hierarchy connecting these segments; the most stable gumlao communities appear to be those in which lineage is virtually neglected and loyalty to a particular place is emphasized instead; Judicial authority rests with a Council of the Elders, who are usually representatives of lineages. (Leach 1964, 204–7)

While Leach (1964) finds that the Gumlao villages will be politically instable as a result of their egalitarianism, Scott (2009) does not see this as a weakness, or even a consequence. To him, groups like the Gumlaos, the Hmongs, the Lahu, and many others he discusses have deliberatively chosen a path that has allowed them to avoid rule, both external and internal, from their own leaders. To achieve this goal, Scott highlights not only the importance of geographical mobility and evasion, but also the impact of not having a written language. For as Claude Levi-Strauss also understood, "Writing appears to be necessary for the centralized, stratified state to reproduce itself. Writing is a strange thing. . . . The one phenomenon which has invariably accompanied it is the formation of cities and empires: the integration into a hierarchy of castes and slaves. . . . It seems rather to favor the exploitation than the enlightenment of mankind" (Levi-Strauss 1968, 291, quoted in Scott 2009, 228). States, as such authors as Benedict Anderson (2006) have demonstrated, rely on censuses and create categories to count and account for the populations they seek to control. Accordingly, one way to avoid state capture is to not provide the information necessary for state apparatuses to process populations. Where there is no written language, no clear name, no consistent lineage, several overlapping languages and dialects, and no fixed physical location, states are unable to grip onto people. The history of the Sinti and Roma people provides a telling case.

Among the Kachin, fluidity has allowed them not be to counted and categorized. To most, they are simply known as the "hill people." However, as Scott (2009) shows, this fluidity is in part deliberate and strategic and related to a history of fleeing states and giving up those characteristics that "citizens" must have in order to enable rule. The mountains have become their place of refuge from state rule.

COMMUNAL DEMOCRACY IN BOLIVIA[1]

In 1993, Bolivian president-elect Sanchez de Lozada enacted the Law of Popular Participation (LLP). The LLP allowed for the incorporation of Bolivia's previously excluded, mostly rural and indigenous populations into political life. According to Mala Htun and Juan Pablo Ossa, "in the 1995 local elections, record numbers of Indians (around 470) were elected to municipal councils: they represented 29 percent of the total and 62 percent of councils in the highland regions" (Htun and Ossa 2013, 89). In 2005, Bolivia elected Evo Morales as its first indigenous president. In 2009, a new constitution was enacted after a three-year process of broad popular participation (*constituyente*) in its drafting. The ratification of the constitution was done by referendum and received 67 percent of the popular vote. In it, Bolivians gave themselves the right to communal landownership, political autonomy for indigenous groups, and they limited land ownership to 5,000 hectares. Municipalities now have the right to elect and participate in deliberative councils, and indigenous groups now have the right to self-rule (*autogobierno*). In general, democracy in Bolivia is now exercised through direct and participative democracy and referendums. Legislative initiative, revocation of the mandate, the assembly, the cabildo, and the previous consultation (*consulta previa*) make Bolivia one of the most participatory democracies in the world. The new constitution—and the new political forces in power—opened the door for an ongoing and gradual process of deepening Bolivian democracy, envisioned as a movement toward more direct involvement and more decentralization. By asserting the power of popular democracy, Bolivians also seek to rein in the economy. According to former Bolivian Minister of Education Felix Patzi,

We propose the third communal economic model economy where the means and materials of production are not privately owned, nor State property, but are collective property, i.e., they belong to the workers who are associated freely in communal form. (Patzi 2011, 10; my translation)

Patzi (2011) further explains that Bolivia is moving toward system of communal democracy or communal socialism in which power is constituted and controlled directly, at the local level, in local communities. In additional to this component of local direct democracy, exercised through village-wide assemblies, Bolivians still elect representatives to the national level, thus constituting a mixed direct and representative political system. According to Patzi,

In the communal democracy representatives at the national, departmental, and municipal levels are not elected by competition from political parties, associations or other forms of organization in favor of universal suffrage, but directly. In other words, it is collective deliberation, which defines how to choose their representatives. Particularly in urban areas prevails a system of rotation, as this is a social technology and completely banishes the emergence of a political elite as in the liberal representative democracy and totalitarian socialism. Actually, the rotation principle should be applied to the central, provincial government and municipal governments as well. It means that there would be no choice, but the position of National President shall be exercised by each department on a rotating basis, and within you choose the best man or woman for the exercise of such a public office. (Patzi 2011, 31; my translation)

The Aymara and Quechua, the two predominant indigenous groups of Bolivia, have a long tradition of self-government and of rotating legislative, executive, and judicial positions among themselves. In the new, plurinational Bolivia, this tradition has been anchored into the constitution, and the new constitution, itself the result of indigenous pressure and mobilization, has provided incentives for an expansion of local self-governance in the form of *juntas*. The city of El Alto provides a telling example of the degree to which local self-organization and self-governance has advanced in Bolivia. According to such authors as Pablo A. Uc González (2013), Gomez (2003), and Pablo Mamani (2006), during the 2003 uprisings, the city of El Alto counted on some 500–520 local *juntas* that effectively substituted the state. During the uprisings, according to Mamani, the people established a "mini-state within the State" (Mamani 2006, 286). Since then, the 2009 constitution has anchored the right to create local mini-states on Bolivian territory. Indigenous communities, who can dwell on traditional institutions of self-rule and collective ownership, are the central beneficiaries of this process. The new

Bolivian constitution thus recognizes customary law and allows indigenous communities to exercise their own system of justice, according to their own traditions. Central to this tradition is the collective ownership of land, the *ejido*. In indigenous communities, land titles are held by an association, who distributes them to individual families. The concentration of land and property in a few hands is thus avoided and any disputes over landownership are addressed by the collective. Each generation has a new chance to address the existing landholding structures and adjustments as well as redistributions of land are common—not just in Bolivia, but among all Native American tribal societies, north or south.

CONSTITUTIONAL REDESIGN IN BHUTAN[2]

Bhutan is a constitutional monarchy. In 2008, the country gave itself a new constitution, under the guidance of the king, Jigme Khesar Namgyel Wangchuk, and his father and predecessor, King Jigme Singye Wangchuk. In it, Bhutan proclaimed its intention to aim for "Gross National Happiness." The term was coined in 1972 by Jigme Singye Wangchuk, fourth king of the Wankchuk dynasty, who ended absolute monarchy and stepped down from the throne to instate his son in 2006. Research conducted in 2012 shows that

> Overall, in 2010, 8.3% of Bhutanese people are "deeply happy" according to GNH; 32.6% are "extensively happy"; 48.7% are "narrowly happy," and 10.4% are "unhappy." These four groups correspond to people who have achieved sufficiency in more than 77%, 66–76%, 50–65%, and less than half of the nine domains, respectively. (Ura and Galay 2012, 8)

Bhutan held its first elections in 2008, the same year the new constitution was ratified. According to Ura and Galay,

> In order to translate the *multidimensional concept* of GNH into core objectives . . . *four strategic areas* were initially defined. These areas, called the "four pillars of GNH," are: 1. Sustainable & equitable socio-economic development; 2. Environmental conservation; 3. The preservation and promotion of culture; and 4. Good governance. (Ura and Galay 2012, 9; emphasis mine)

According to the 2014 World Bank Report on Bhutan, "Bhutan's success in reducing absolute poverty is noteworthy, with the poverty rate falling from 23 percent in 2007 to 12–13 percent in 2012, improving the lot of the poorest segments of the population rather than merely that of those clustered around the poverty line" (World Bank 2014, 2).

The GNH assessment conducted in Bhutan in 2010 uses thirty-three indicators of nine domains, namely, psychological well-being, health, time use, education, cultural diversity and resilience, good governance, community vitality, ecological diversity and resilience, and living standards. Happiness was thus elevated to a paradigm that provides guidance for national policies. According to Ura and Galay, "Increasing happiness is a policy concern that involves civil servants, business leaders, and all citizens of Bhutan. The GNH Index can help them address it in practical ways. To increase happiness one needs to identify people who are not yet happy. Once this segment of the population is identified, one needs to know the domains in which they lack sufficiency. This two-step identification procedure provides the basis for analysis that is of direct relevance for policy" (Ura and Galay 2012, 53f).

In Article 5, No. 2, the constitution of Bhutan demands that the government shall

a. Protect, conserve and improve the pristine environment and safeguard the biodiversity of the country;
b. Prevent pollution and ecological degradation;
c. Secure ecologically balanced sustainable development while promoting justifiable economic and social development; and
d. Ensure a safe and healthy environment.

The same article states, under No. 3:

The Government shall ensure that, in order to conserve the country's natural resources and to prevent degradation of the ecosystem, a minimum of sixty percent of Bhutan's total land shall be maintained under forest cover for all time.

While Article 7 of this constitution lists twenty-three fundamental rights of each Bhutanese citizen, Article 8 of the same constitution lists the eleven duties of each citizen. Of those, the following are particularly noteworthy:

2. A Bhutanese citizen shall have the duty to preserve, protect and respect the environment, culture and heritage of the nation.
3. A Bhutanese citizen shall foster tolerance, mutual respect and spirit of brotherhood amongst all the people of Bhutan transcending religious, linguistic, regional or sectional diversities.
5. A person shall not tolerate or participate in acts of injury, torture or killing of another person, terrorism, abuse of women, children or any other person and shall take necessary steps to prevent such acts.
6. A person shall have the responsibility to provide help, to the greatest possible extent, to victims of accidents and in times of natural calamity.

7. A person shall have the responsibility to safeguard public property.
8. A person shall have the responsibility to pay taxes in accordance with the law.
9. Every person shall have the duty to uphold justice and to act against corruption.
10. Every person shall have the duty to act in aid of the law.

In Article 9, the Bhutanese constitution lays out the "Principles of State Policy." These include:

1. The State shall endeavour to apply the Principles of State Policy set out in this Article to ensure a good quality of life for the people of Bhutan in a progressive and prosperous country that is committed to peace and amity in the world.
2. The State shall strive to promote those conditions that will enable the pursuit of Gross National Happiness.
3. The State shall endeavour to create a civil society free of oppression, discrimination and violence, based on the rule of law, protection of human rights and dignity, and to ensure the fundamental rights and freedoms of the people.
7. The State shall endeavour to develop and execute policies to minimize inequalities of income, concentration of wealth, and promote equitable distribution of public facilities among individuals and people living in different parts of the Kingdom.
8. The State shall endeavour to ensure that all the Dzongkhags (municipalities) are treated with equity on the basis of different needs so that the allocation of national resources results in comparable socioeconomic development.
9. The State shall endeavour to achieve economic self-reliance and promote open and progressive economy.
10. The State shall encourage and foster private sector development through fair market competition and prevent commercial monopolies.
12. The State shall endeavour to ensure the right to work, vocational guidance and training and just and favourable conditions of work.
13. The State shall endeavour to ensure the right to rest and leisure, including reasonable limitation of working hours and periodic holidays with pay.

Bhutan's national assembly only meets when needed and the office of the prime minister is limited to two terms. In Article 22, the constitution declares that

1. Power and authority shall be decentralized and devolved to elected Local Governments to facilitate the direct participation of the people in the

development and management of their own social, economic and environmental well-being.

2. Bhutan shall have Local Governments in each of the twenty Dzongkhags
comprising the Dzongkhag Tshogdu, Gewog Tshogde and Thromde
Tshogde.

3. Local Governments shall ensure that local interests are taken into account
in the national sphere of governance by providing a forum for public consideration on issues affecting the local territory.

4. The objectives of Local Government shall be to:

   a. Provide democratic and accountable government for local communities;
   b. Ensure the provision of services to communities in a sustainable manner;
   c. Encourage the involvement of communities and community organizations in matters of local governance; and
   d. Discharge any other responsibilities as may be prescribed by law made
   by Parliament.

The importance of this approach toward happiness is not diminished by the
reality that Bhutan has been accused of mistreating their Nepalese minorities
(Pellegrini and Tasciotti 2014), as the importance of the institutions introduced in Bhutan are relevant for their capacity to achieve positive outcomes
for those who fall under their jurisdiction. It might well be, as I have suggested elsewhere (Reiter 2013), that strong and pronounced citizenship rights
are bought with exclusivity, that is, citizenship might be intrinsically connected to exclusion. However, the tradeoffs between rights and exclusion are
not the focus of this book and cannot be adequately be treated here.

THE ZAPATISTAS OF SOUTHERN MEXICO

The Zapatistas of southern Mexico are probably the most widely known and
debated example of indigenous resistance and the construction of genuine
alternatives to liberal democracy and capitalism in the Americas. Their story
is widely told and known (for example, by Bruno Baronnet, Mariana Mora
Bayo, and Richard Stahler-Sholk [2011], on whose very detailed accounts I
shall mostly rely for the sake of this case).

In the 1980s, different Mayan indigenous peoples living in the southern Mexican state of Chiapas, formed the Ejercito Zapatista de Liberacion
Nacional (EZLN; Zapatista Army of National Liberation) (Harvey 1998).
Famously, on January 1, 1994, the day that the North American Free Trade
Agreement (NAFTA) went into effect, this army declared war on the Mexican government. War, however, did not last long (twelve days), and was followed by the pursuit of another strategy: local political autonomy.

Instead of fighting the Mexican government on the battleground, the Zapatistas, as they became widely known, declared their homelands an autonomous territory. On that territory they broke away from the content and form of the Mexican State, giving themselves their own government structures and filling them with their own content. The autonomous reorganization of their territory and their lives led to a reorganization of almost all aspects of life—from families to work, landownership, education, the production of knowledge, and to the very definition what it meant to be a citizen, Mayan, Mexican, and Indian. Initially, thirty-eight local communities declared themselves autonomous from the Mexican State and later, in 2003, they formed five regional units known as "Caracoles." Each autonomous community decided for itself how to organize and proceeded as a collective. Each Caracol has a Junta de Buen Gobierno (a Council of Good Governance). According to Baronnet, Bayo, and Stahler-Sholk, "the members of the JBG [Junta de Buen Gobierno] serve on a rotation basis between 8 days and one month (dependent on the Caracol), where village assemblies select shortlists every three years" (Baronnet, Bayo, and Stahler-Sholk 2011, 25; my translation).

Each autonomous village has a general assembly as its ultimate and authoritative power. This general assembly not only decides on general legislative issues, but it also has judicial power and is actively involved in the provision and regulation of education and health. Given that the Mexican government does not allow for political autonomy to the extent practiced by the Zapatistas, the Zapatista communities are under constant pressure and threat as the government seeks ways to destabilize and discredit them (Stahler-Sholk 2014). As a result, those communities continue to live in a state of uprising and rebellion against the government and under constant strain from its low-intensity oppression.

During an event organized and promoted by the Zapatistas in October 2006 attended by 2,335 people from fifty countries, the Zapatistas laid out their vision in eight areas. The descriptions contain the essence of the Zapatista proposal and praxis:

1. *Health:* Before autonomy, health among indigenous people was very precarious. After 1994, the Zapatista communities selected and trained their own volunteer health promoters, who assist families with community-based, preventive health care. Services provided include midwifery, dental care, mental health, and laboratory technicians. The Zapatistas now count on nursing homes in several communities, municipal clinics, and a hospital in San José del Río, Caracol Realidad, offering surgical services. The Zapatistas are recovering the traditional knowledge of indigenous doctors, especially herbalists, midwives, and bone setters.

2. *Education:* Similar to health, education was very poor before 1994. State teachers only appeared for two or three days a week and did not take the culture, language, and needs of indigenous people into account. Since 1994, the Zapatistas have achieved significant progress in building their own system of autonomous education. Given the need to care for children and girls, communities selected their own education promoters, took their time to train them well, and created curricula more in tune with the reality of the history and culture of the people. The promoters are not paid, but their expenses, like those of the health promoters, are paid with the profits from the collective work done by the community. In each Caracol they have created new training centers, primary schools, secondary schools, and a technical secondary in the Caracol of Morelia. The content focuses on the thirteen Zapatista demands and is supported by the old men and women in areas of history, language, life and nature, and mathematics. Tests are held in public, with the presence of the parents and all the community, so that they can see how much their children have advanced. Finally, considering the child as a subject and not an object of education, another goal of the Zapatista promoters has been to create open spaces for children to express themselves in full freedom, using their language and their dress to imagine, create, and participate in the organization of school parties and collective work. Clearly the autonomous education plays a central role in maintaining the Zapatista movement. The Zapatista education system is aimed at creating new technical skills, along with training new promoters and authorities.

3. *Organization of communities:* Following the 1994 rebellion, the Zapatistas recovered lands and thus the ability to administer their own people. Parallel to the official positions, they have created their own. They differ in the way that the communities names and removes their administrators (recall). Autonomous authorities are working without pay. The most important positions are:

   i. The commissioners of ejido and communal lands are elected by local assemblies to attend to local agricultural problems and to seek peaceful solutions with the commissioners of the government when land disputes arise; the commissioners coordinate their work with the autonomous municipal councils and various committees—for example, education and health—and they act under the agreement to refuse the entry of land title programs of the government: Procede and Procecom;

   ii. The autonomous municipal agents are selected by the municipal assembly and have the function of administering justice and ensuring that the rivers are not contaminated, that no trees are cut near the banks, and that there is no planting of marijuana or trafficking of wood or drugs;

iii. The autonomous municipal judge is appointed by the municipal assembly and attends to the most serious problems that cannot be solved by the commissioners and agents; unlike the public prosecutor, the autonomous judge investigates without pay; penalties vary, but most commonly they consist of twenty-four hours in jail and several days of work on collective projects;

iv. The Zapatista communities also have health and education committees to monitor that the promoters and commissioners work well.

All these fields are based on a strong grassroots organization that can remove their autonomous authorities if they fail to meet their work.

4. *Collective work:* It would be very difficult to imagine the exercise of autonomy and education and health projects without collective works. First, the organization of a wide variety of collective works has been possible due to land recuperation since 1994. With this territorial base, communities are working on different projects in order to support the autonomous authorities and commissions. The travel and other expenses of local and regional officials, of representatives of the Good Government Juntas, as well as of the health and education promoters are all covered by the proceeds of collective works. This allows expenses to be covered and the people who conduct these tasks have the support of their communities. Collective works are also important to teach the sons and daughters to work and organize themselves and to demonstrate to the government that communities can move forward without government projects. In several autonomous municipalities, collective work has also allowed communities to suppress the coyotes or middlemen who buy cheap products and then sell them expensive. It should be noted that collective work is dedicated to the production of healthy food. Instead of using chemicals, the collectives use bio-insecticides and apply green manure.

5. *The struggle of women:* Zapatistas remember that before 1994 women were not taken into account. They could not leave their communities, and they suffered contempt and violence related to alcohol abuse. They were afraid to speak and did not have the right to participate in the offices of their communities and municipalities. These conditions have changed, although not 100 percent. In the Zapatista communities, most women are already involved in some capacity or another. Although some men continue to oppose this change, many women have lost their fear and participate as local officials, promoters, and autonomous authorities. Several of the women explained at the meeting that their participation still felt

difficult because of their lack of experience in public speaking, besides the problem of having to speak in "Castilla." However, they also mentioned major changes, having achieved more recognition of their rights to decide whom they marry and how many children to have. Now women are present in all the committees and all the Councils of Good Government. In the Caracol of La Realidad, six women and six men make up the current board, compared to one woman and four men that made the same board in 2003–2006. Women are also learning new skills in the operation of radio, photography, and video production.

6. *Autonomy:* The recovery and administration of land, the health and education programs, the collective works, and the participation of women are the basis on which the autonomous and rebellious Zapatista municipalities (Marez) have been constructed. On December 19, 1994, the EZLN announced the creation of thirty-eight Marez in different areas of Chiapas in order to govern according to their ways and needs, a demand that was included in the agreements of San Andrés in 1996. On this subject the Marez representatives noted that the principle of "lead obeying" (*mandar obedeciendo*) is manifested in practice by a high level of community control achieved through committees and local leaders, but especially through the assemblies of the communities that name and remove its authorities according to their ability and job performance. No authority of the Marez receives a salary. As mentioned, all commissions and authorities are supported by the collective work done by the community. Among the functions of the Marez are the following: monitoring group work and projects in health and education; apply justice and mediate conflicts that may not be solved by the commissioners and autonomous agents; operate the autonomous civil registration; evaluate proposals agreed at the general assemblies; and send proposals to them for approval.

7. *Good Governance (Buen Gobierno):* The five Good Governance Juntas (JBG) were created in August 2003 with several objectives, including that of attaining more equality in the distribution of the support received from the solidarity groups from Mexico and of the world among the autonomous communities and municipalities. Delegates of the JBGs reported that one of their tasks is precisely to monitor that all municipalities receive support. They are also in charge of establishing contact with solidarity groups and collectives. Like other autonomous authorities, the JBGs work without pay. The municipal assemblies elect people who have the capacity, but they retain the right to replace them if they do not comply with the mandate of the communities. The JBGs monitor that no transgenic seeds enter the territory and that no commercial projects of pharmaceutical companies enter the territory, taking advantage of local plants and indigenous knowledge. The JBGs also oversee the contractors

carrying out projects in their territories and they collect 10 percent of the value of their works. In the area of justice, the JBGs apply the Zapatista laws without receiving payment. Thus the JBG and Marez represent to the Zapatistas the recovery of the ability to freely govern themselves as indigenous peoples.

8. *Balance of the process of constructing autonomy:* The last issue was entrusted to the commanders of the Clandestine Revolutionary Indigenous Committee (CCRI). All these interventions highlight the advances that have already been achieved in the areas of education and health by the Marez and the JBGs. However, they also indicated that much remains to be done. The commander Moises spoke these developments as the fruit of the sacrifice by the men and women who have fallen in this struggle. For their part, commanders Miriam, Sandra, Delia, and Gabriela emphasized the fact that many women have lost their fear and are now involved, "rescuing the equality we deserve." (Reproduced in Baronnet, Bayo, and Stahler-Sholk 2011, 178–84; my translation [I have translated freely and cut out several sentences and paragraphs])

LESSONS LEARNED FROM THE NON-WESTERN WORLD

Palenqueros practice an active and participatory form of citizenship. Its emphasis is not on rights, entitlements, and privileges, but on responsibilities. Palenqueros do not have political autonomy anymore. They lost it after independence. As a consequence, their political traditions are now reduced to the civic and cultural realms, even though they take advantage of the political opportunities left to them by the current constitution. With their *kuagros, juntas*, and councils, they have created a system in which very few of the 4,000 Palenqueros currently living in San Basílio de Palenque do not participate in public life. It rather seems that all of them are actively involved in the political and civic affairs of the village in one way or another.

The central institution to achieve, maintain, and protect this sort of very active and involved sort of citizenship is the *kuagro*, a voluntary association of same-aged citizens, male and female. Through the *kuagro*, Palenqueros exercise and practice solidarity and communality. Because of it, a strong sense of belonging and shared interest is maintained and renewed. From the *kuagro*, other associations of civic and political character are formed so that literally every Palenquero is actively involved in village life.

Since the 1991 institution, land tenure in Palenque is collective and inalienable, that is, no outsider can buy land in Palenque. However, despite this innovative arrangement, Palenque does not offer many lessons in terms of economic organization, as they currently do not have the right to control this aspect of their collective lives.

On the political level, in contrast, the Palenque offers rich insights and valuable institutions for consideration. The *kuagro* seems the central institutional arrangement to create and protect solidarity, civic involvement, and strong participation. The *kuagro* also influences the other associative forms created among Palenqueros, the juntas and councils, which ensure and protect a plethora of deliberative spaces and forums. In this sense, Palenque fulfills criteria numbers 6 to 10 of the political criteria outlined earlier, namely:

1. For people to participate, they must have real and tangible power, that is, they must be able to influence outcomes and be able to see and experience the impact of their participation. The more power citizens have, the more democracy. The more and the more immediately they are able to experience their power, the better.
2. Deliberation is central to democracy. The more deliberation, the more democracy. The more forums and spaces for deliberation, the better. Deliberation is not only instrumental to democracy, it is also a core element of it.
3. Common or shared interest is a crucial condition for consensual collective decision making. How to foster common interest in different ways beyond nationalism and xenophobia is an empirical question.
4. The more consensual the collective decision-making process, the better.
5. Decentralization and devolution of administrative power to local levels is a necessary ingredient of the empowerment of ordinary citizens and democratic rule.
6. Direct interaction is a necessary ingredient of democracy as it provides the basis upon which deliberation, mutual trust, and a shared interest can and must be constructed.

The Wintukua speak their own language. They live together on their own reservation (even though they share it with the Wiwas and Kogis). They adhere to one shared cosmovision and religious cult, which finds expression in their Mamos. Living together, they face similar problems and external threats from the surrounding dominant white society, which looks upon them with suspicion and disdain, at times invading their lands (settlers and peasants). They also face the additional threat of guerillas, who have also invaded their lands at times, even though this threat has subsided now. Wintukuas are strongly involved in their community affairs. They participate actively and feel a very strong sense of obligation, thus carrying strong responsibilities toward the collective and beyond.

The Wintukua choose their executive leaders in open assemblies—their captains, commissioners, and governors. Lawmaking is reserved to open assemblies, which are held regularly and frequently at the local and at the national level. In lawmaking, there are no representatives as there are in the "civilized" world. Wintukua citizenship is active, direct, involved, and participatory. Its main trait is responsibility—a responsibility that extends far beyond their group. The people of the Sierra carry the world on their shoulders. Accordingly, their leaders live lives dedicated to service to the community. They undergo lifelong training and practice behavioral and dietary restrictions. They live exemplary lives. While they might remind us of Plato's guardians, they do not have actual political power. They only give advice. They are leaders by example, sages, and healers. They are not representatives.

Wintukua land is owned collectively and the community does not allow a concentration of riches in few hands. Instead of insisting on unearned rights, the Wintukua, like the Palenqueros, construct their rights through active engagement and shared responsibility.

The law among the Wintukua is not a written law. It is a law contained in nature. Nature provides the lessons and contains the guidelines for a well-ordered and harmonious life. If disturbed, the balance has to be reestablished and brought back in accordance with the law of nature. Any conflict or disturbance has spiritual and natural components, and the healing process necessarily involves spirits and nature. The process of healing and reestablishing guidance is guided by their priests and guides—the Mamos.

The Wintukua, just like the Kaggaba, Wiwa, and Kakuamo of the Sierra Nevada de Santa Marta, thus fulfill most of the democracy criteria listed earlier. They rely on deliberation and they have several forums for collective decision making. Their leaders do not vote, but deliberate until they reach agreement. They do delegate executive power to captains and other Cabildo officers, but their tenure is restricted.

There is a radically different conception of the law among them from the "Western," maybe Roman, tradition. The Wintukua law is not codified, written down, or customary. It is contained in nature and has a metaphysical aspect. Lawmaking in the strict sense does not exist among them. There is rather the task of "law interpretation," which falls back on their sages. Given that nature contains the law, there is no need or possibility to enact new laws.

Their leaders are also very different from "Western" leaders. They wield no real power and instead live by example. They do not earn money for their services, but they are sustained by the community. They are required to fast and they undergo lifelong training in spiritual matters.

In Zomia, hierarchy and rule come to people and groups in the form of states. Retreat and avoidance might be more successful strategies to avoid statehood, and with it hierarchy and rule, than fighting states by staging a revolution. New, post-revolutionary states will enact new hierarchies and forms of rule. It is of great relevance to this book to verify that many if not all of the egalitarian experiences and communities described here occur in some remote region, either beyond the core of a centralized state (as the Tolstoyan communities in Siberia), in remote areas that are out of reach of armies and bureaucracies (Palenque), or on the top of mountains (Zomia and the Wintukua).

Bolivia, under its new indigenous leadership, has enacted a new constitution, which puts upper limits to landownership. It has also recognized the customary practices of its native, indigenous peoples. Indigenous people, given their shared belief in the sacredness of the earth, own land collectively and distribute it to individual families according to their needs. They select local leaders and rely on local assemblies to make collective decisions. Legislative power is thus divided or split in Bolivia. While the national assembly is responsible for the national constitution, local indigenous communities enact their own laws and rules and thus have legislative authority. Local communities also have judicial and executive autonomy, which together makes them politically autonomous. This autonomy is limited, however, by the contours of the national framework. In practice, such a mixed system allows broad and active public participation on the local level, while also providing access to the national legal system in cases in which local authorities fail to address individual concerns. Alienation and apathy are thus actively counteracted, while the principle of equal rights for all is upheld. The limitations on landownership must be seen as a first, even if timid, step in the direction of safeguarding equal opportunities while still maintaining a market system based on private property.

The constitutional kingdom of Bhutan has anchored decentralization, participation at the local level, protection of the environment, as well as equality and the protection of human rights and dignity into its constitution. It has also elevated happiness to its main development goals—different from income. Furthermore, Bhutanese citizenship is not only characterized by the right to education, dignity, happiness, and the right to live in a clean environment, but it also comes with a list of duties and responsibilities. Public office holding has term limits and the members of the upper house, who represent the twenty municipalities and are elected in those, cannot have a party affiliation. With this, Bhutan has created a legal framework in which human dignity, equality, and environmental protection are all made legally binding.

As the previously discussed document demonstrates, political autonomy and self-administration are at the core of the Zapatista way. Indigenous communities organize in village assemblies that legitimate and oversee all collective activities. The involvement and participation of all community members is great and demands many sacrifices, as all collective tasks are performed without payment. The Zapatista way of organizing collectivities thus stands at the opposite end of the liberal emphasis on individual rights and the claiming of entitlements. Instead, the Marez communities construct their own rights and fight to uphold them against the constant threat from the Mexican State and other outside agents. They have taken control of their own education and health provision, they administer their own justice system, and the legislative functions are conducted by all in open and public assembly. Executive functions are limited and subject to recall.

NOTES

1. It is important to highlight that Bolivia "is moving toward" the institution of a different, more just society in which indigenous people play a more active role in national politics while also retaining local autonomy and securing the right to protect their own "usos y costumbres" (customs) in their own communities. This is not to say that justice has been achieved in Bolivia. Here, as in all my other cases, I am primarily interested in the political institutions that were put in place, bearing the potential to rein in elite rule and control asset concentration. Clearly, fully democratic political systems and markets, even with highly efficient institutional frameworks in place, will not come about instantly. In the meantime, my analysis focuses on the innovative institutions proposed and the reality of indigenous communal life.

2. Similar to the case of Bolivia, my analysis focused on the innovative institutions, in this case the constitution, of Bhutan. I am aware that not all aspects of what has been codified into law are reality. However, the legal framework provided by the 2008 Bhutan constitution highlights possibilities and points the way for action in Bhutan and elsewhere.

Chapter 8

Contemporary Western Cases

Not all is lost in the West, one is tempted to say. There are some promising attempts to address elitism and offer new or different political institutions to regulate collective life differently from the predominant representational and capitalist model. Some of these solutions are new, as the case of the participatory budgeting, first applied in Brazil, will show. Others count on millennial traditions, such as the Swiss system of direct democracy. The New England town hall democracy is old enough, considering the history of the United States. All three of these cases show that variety within the "Western model" is possible. I have added a fourth case here on the German, French, and Swiss book market, not because it provides another case of innovative, egalitarian political institution building, but rather because it demonstrates how smart institutions can achieve unexpected, sometimes even counterintuitive goals, for example, how the fixing of (book) prices is able to keep small bookstores alive.

PARTICIPATORY BUDGETING IN BRAZIL

According to Gianpaolo Baiocchi, "The idea of participatory governance of cities predates the PT [Workers' Party], and began with the variety of new urban social movements in the 1970s that brought new visions of urban democracy and participation to Brazilian politics" (Baiocchi 2005, 7). The first and most well-known implementation of PB occurred, however, in 1989, in the southern Brazilian city of Porto Alegre, under the newly elected mayor of the Workers' Party. From there it spread across Brazil and the globe, promoted by the World Bank and other international agencies promoting "good governance." Today, in Brazil alone, 140 cities practice some version of participatory budgeting. Worldwide, some 1,500 cities have implemented this policy (www.participatorybudgeting.org). According to the Participatory Budgeting Project, an American nonprofit organization whose mission it is to "empower people to decide together how to spend public money,"

Participatory budgeting (PB) is a different way to manage public money, and to engage people in government. It is a democratic process in which community members directly decide how to spend part of a public budget. It enables taxpayers to work with government to make the budget decisions that affect their lives. (www.participatorybudgeting.org)

The basic premise of participatory budgeting is to allow the citizens of a city to influence the yearly spending plan, which is normally passed by the city legislator. Particularly, the model that emerged in Porto Alegre was one that explicitly favored poor neighborhoods and directly involved neighborhood associations in the process of deciding next year's budget. The intent of this proposal was, according to most analysts, to empower the poor and to fight back against clientelism. Clientelism in this arena has produced a consistent bias of city spending toward the already privileged so that most Brazilian cities, similar to most Latin American cities, are extremely unequal and geographically divided into "modern" neighborhoods that count on expensive, "first world"–type equipment and infrastructure, and poor neighborhoods that lack the most basic infrastructure and urban equipment. It is thus not rare to see neighborhoods in Brazilian cities that closely resemble cities such as New York, Berlin, Boston, or other relatively rich cities of the Northern and Western hemisphere. Other neighborhoods, in turn, more resemble the streets of Mumbai or Dhaka, having led some observers to refer to Brazil as "Belindia"—Belgium and India in one.

The participatory budgeting of Porto Alegre remains the most studied. It is also where PB has the longest history and where it underwent different cycles, thus allowing for the richest insights into its promises, shortcomings, and achievements. In this southern Brazilian city of some 1.5 million inhabitants, some 15,000 people attended budget assemblies in 1995 (Abers 2000). According to the World Bank,

Participatory budgeting has resulted in improved facilities for the people of Porto Alegre. For instance, sewer and water connections went up from 75 percent of total households in 1988 to 98 percent in 1997. The number of participants in the participatory budgeting process in Porto Alegre reached 40,000 per year in less than a decade, indicating PB's ability to encourage increasing citizen involvement. The success of people's participation in determining the use of public welfare funds in the city of Porto Alegre has inspired many other municipalities to follow suit. So far, of the 5,571 municipalities in Brazil, more than 140 (about 2.5 percent) have adopted PB. (http://siteresources.worldbank .org/INTEMPOWERMENT/Resources/14657_Partic-Budg-Brazil-web.pdf)

The World Bank also finds that

> The share of PB in total budget allocations has increased considerably. In Porto Alegre, for instance, 17 percent of the total budget was allocated through PB in 1992; this share grew to 21 percent in 1999. In Belo Horizonte, half of the city's local investment resources, about US$64 million, was allocated after PB in 1999. An indicator of PB's success is the enhanced level of participation. The number of participants in Porto Alegre grew from less than 1,000 per year in 1990 to more than 16,000 in 1998, to about 40,000 in 1999. Participation is not just restricted to the middle class or the conventional supporters of the Workers Party. People from low-income groups also take an active part in the process. (http://siteresources.worldbank.org/INTEMPOWERMENT /Resources/14657_Partic-Budg-Brazil-web.pdf)

According to Brian Wampler, PB has the potential to "transform how the state functions and how citizens interact with the state, thus helping to deepen democracy, promote pluralism, and lay the foundations of social justice" (Wampler 2007, 3). Wampler also finds that, when successful, PB "delegates real authority to citizens and implements a range of public policies selected by PB participants" (Wampler 2007, 7). This has an effect on citizens, who can become more aware, more involved, and more knowledgeable about politics.

In Porto Alegre in 2004, when a new center-leftist administration took office after fourteen years of PT rule, PB underwent some important changes. On one hand, it consolidated and became further institutionalized and is still a part of the city's budgeting process. However, the new mayor, Jose Fogaça, cut back the amount of money that can be decided upon through PB. His administration is also much less invested and less involved in the PB process (Fox 2008). According to the report of Michael Fox, "'Before we got in front of the leaders and they had to listen to us. Now they hide, they don't come,' says João 'Chiquinho'" (Fox 2008).

The structure and procedure of PB in Porto Alegre is highly complex. In 1989, after the Brazilian Workers' Party (PT) had won the majority and moved into city hall, the secretary of municipal planning first organized meetings with neighborhood associations to inform them about their plan to implement PB. Meetings were held in the five regions of the city. A second round of meetings in sixteen regions followed. According to Rebecca Abers, "each region presented a long lists of demands" (Abers 2000, 72). Abers also found that "those areas where the Popular Councils (*Conselhos Populares*) were active sent the majority of participants" (Abers 2000, 72). The next step consisted of the election of ten budget delegates and to organize municipal meetings with ninety delegates. The delegates then elected a "consolidating commission" of one representative from each region. The outcome of this first attempt to establish PB in Porto Alegre was the creation of an "unrealistic wish list" (Abers 2000), which produced frustration and skepticism among most people when no concrete actions had been taken during 1990 to actually put the wish list into action. After this first failed attempt, the PT undertook administrative reform, which made the municipal administration more capable of action and also freed up revenue that could actually be allocated toward PB. The PT administration embraced strategic planning to set far-reaching goals and avoid being caught up in daily procedures. They agreed on five government priorities: 1) Urbanization; 2) Public transportation; 3) "Organization of the city"; 4) Health; and 5) Education. They also put more emphasis on how to develop investment priorities. To that end, the municipal government organized bi-yearly assemblies to inform the citizenry. Delegates and councilors were now representing regions. The result of this restricting was that the PB process now produced regional lists of priorities. In addition, PB now contained a quota system based on the level of popular mobilization, the strategic importance of the region for Porto Alegre, the population in needy areas, and the infrastructure deficiency. Sixty-five percent of revenues were allocated to the five top-rated regions. When a new administration, still from the PT, took office in 1992, participation in the process increased further, with an average of six thousand participants in the public meetings. In 1993, the administration created Thematic Forums for transportation and circulation, urban planning and the organization of the city, education and culture, health and social assistance, and economic development and tax reform. According to Abers, "Like the regional assemblies, the second round of thematic assemblies elected two members and two alternates to the Municipal Budget Council, giving that group forty-two voting members" (Abers 2000, 85).

The success of PB in Porto Alegre, according to Rebecca Abers, was due to broad popular participation, which was fully embraced by the top administrators, the fact that government was flexible enough to respond to changing citizen demands and deliver on those demands in a timely fashion, and finally an increased control of bureaucracy through information. Wage increases would mean reduced budgets for projects, so the population pressured not to increase the wages of the city personnel. Abers finds that the key to the PT success was transparency, redistribution, and efficiency, which produced a change of political culture from clientelism to active participation and a sense of control and ownership among the citizenry.

Abers also finds that poor people participated more in regional budget assemblies that dealt with concrete infrastructure improvements, whereas middle classes participated in thematic meetings focused on larger projects. She also finds that "the very poor and the middle classes were underrepresented" (Abers 2000, 126).

In an effort to explain why PB was able to mobilize poor citizens living in underserved neighborhoods, Abers finds the answer that PB "effectively reduced the costs and increased the perceived benefits of participation in several ways" (Abers 2000, 135).

However, after its bureaucratization in 2004, PB has lost much of its appeal and vitality in Porto Alegre and neighborhood associations have largely withdrawn from the process. With the withdrawal of the mayor and his secretaries and the cutting back of the decidable budget, PB has lost much of its importance and verve. An unresolved issue in this is the role of the city legislator (Camara de Vereadores, in Brazil), as the city legislator retains, in most cases, the authority to propose and pass the yearly budget after consulting and taking in the recommendations of the PB process. In theory, city legislators have an incentive not to go against the recommendations of the PB, but their adherence to the preferences agreed upon in the PB depend on a large enough involvement and the active participation and monitoring by ordinary citizens and their associations. The less involved citizens are, the less bound the city legislators will feel to actually follow the PB priorities.

DIRECT DEMOCRACY IN SWITZERLAND

While shrouded in myth, the Old Swiss Confederacy is said to have been established in 1291 as a defensive pact among the cantons of Schwyz, Uri, and Unterwalden. In 1231 and 1240, respectively, the Habsburg monarchy granted the valleys of Uri and Schwyz autonomy from regional power holders, the counts and dukes controlling this strategically important region connecting northern from southern Europe. In 1291, the valley of Unterwalden joined Uri and Schwyz, signing an agreement to protect their autonomy against the surrounding states and potentates. Lucerne joined the confederacy in 1332, Zurich in 1351, Zug in 1352, Berne and Glarus in 1353, Appenzell in 1411, and St. Gallen in 1412.

According to official Swiss historiography,

> In 1477 the confederates did quite disagree on the future of the confederacy: The rural communes Uri, Schwyz, Unterwalden, Zug and Glarus allied to the bishop of Constance, the cities of Berne, Lucerne and Zurich to the cities of Fribourg and Solothurn. The admission of Fribourg and of Solothurn to the confederacy became a breaking test for the confederacy: The rural communes feared dominance of the cities and did not want to enlarge the old Swiss confederacy. Finally in 1481 a suggestion of Niklaus of Flüe, a former peasant, commander of troops, politician and respected judge to Obwalden, that had withdrawn from public life and lived as a hermit, liberated the way to the admission of Fribourg and Solothurn. The treaty is called *"Stanser Verkommnis"* [agreement at Stans]. The

confederates (but without Berne) also made alliances to the three confederacies of Graubünden (Grisons) in southeastern Switzerland. Negotiations with the city of Constance (Germany, on the Rhine border) ended without result because Zurich feared competition. (http://history-switzerland.geschichteschweiz. ch/old-swiss-confederacy-1291.html)

In 1797, revolutionary France invaded Switzerland, breaking up old hierarchical and patrimonial structures and implementing a new constitution, decided upon by a constitutional assembly meeting in Aargau in 1798. The new constitution provided the basis for the modern system of direct democracy at the national level, as national referendums were anchored into the constitution. In fact, Swiss citizens voted for the new constitution in 1802 in their first nationwide referendum (Kobach 1993).

According to Kris Kobach,

In response to the perceived unfairness of the outcome, supporters of the Old Regime led Swiss soldiers in a rebellion that threatened to topple the government once and for all. Napoleon responded by reintroducing the French army and intervening personally as the self-proclaimed "Mediator" in the conflict. Under the Act of Mediation of 19 February 1803, he imposed a new Constitution, which restored the sovereignty of the cantons in a federal system, officially legitimized the new cantons and set the cantonal boundaries that have persisted to the present day. The framework replaced the Helvetic Republic with a new Confederation, in which 19 cantons were formally recognized. The Confederation did not include Neuchâtel, Valais, or Geneva, all of which were annexed to France. A streamlined and more powerful Federal Diet was created. Respecting traditional Swiss democracy, Napoleon presented forms of cantonal government more closely related to those of the old confederate system. However, the hereditary basis of suffrage that had existed in some cantons was replaced by a straight wealth qualification. The structure of the new system would offer clear advantages to the liberal allies of France. (Kobach 1993)

In 1848, Switzerland adopted a federalist system with a two-chamber parliament, the national council, and the council of states. It created a federal government ("Bundesrat") consisting of seven members elected by the parliament and a federal court of justice. However, considerable power was retained at the member state level—the cantons. The 1848 Constitution also created constitutional referendums at the federal level. It furthermore established the constitutional initiative for total revision and imposed both the constitutional initiative for total revision and the obligatory referendum (for constitutional amendments) upon the cantons that did not already possess the institutions. In 1869, mandatory referendums were introduced for all changes of the constitution and all laws. The 1869 reforms also protected the election of cantonal governments by local citizens, the abolition of lifelong office holding, and progressive taxation.

Today, Swiss cantons retain political autonomy to a large extent. The Swiss constitution regulates that anything not explicitly mentioned therein is left to the legislation of the cantons. Popular referendums are frequent and so are popular initiatives for changes in the constitution. However, for the purpose of this book, a closer look at those cantons still practicing direct democracy is of most interest.

While originally practiced in eight Swiss cantons, today only Glarus and Appenzell Innerrhoden continue to rely on general assemblies, or "Landsgemeinden" in German. Glarus is divided into three municipalities and counts a total of some forty thousand inhabitants. The Landsgemeinde Glarus maintains its own website. On it one can find a general description of direct democracy as practiced in the canton Glarus, Switzerland:

> The Landsgemeinde is the gathering of the electorates of Canton Glarus and it is the highest legislative body of the canton. Some elections take place here; first the Governor, the most senior official of the canton and his deputy are elected from the council of 5 senior executive officers already voted into office by ballot, followed by the judges and the public prosecutor. Above all the Landsgemeinde is responsible for passing the constitutional and the legislative laws, for the fixing of the tax rate and for making decisions on functional issues. Every electorate has the right to support a motion, to suggest an amendment, to reject or postpone a motion or send it back for review. This characteristic marks the difference between the Glarner Landsgemeinde and other Landsgemeinden and ballot elections, where the electorates can only vote for or against a motion and are unable to have any direct influence on the local politics. Every person with the right to vote can at any time put forward a motion to the Landsgemeinde without having to previously collect signatures. The Landsgemeinde takes place in the open air on the first Sunday in May on the Zaunplatz in Glarus. There are stands reserved for interested spectators. The Landsgemeinde is conducted by the Governor, the senior official of the canton who leans on his sword during the discussions. He starts the proceedings with a speech and then goes on to swear-in the electorates. The agenda together with a briefing is distributed to every household in which at least one electorate lives in the form of a brochure. The information in the briefing is based on the discussions which have taken place at the county council meetings. Furthermore the budget and the balance sheet of the canton are presented in the brochure. People have been provided with coloured voting cards which they must raise in the air to cast their vote. The Governor makes an estimate on the majority. If he is doubtful he can consult the other 4 members of the Government but his decision is definite and incontestable. (http://www.landsgemeinde.gl.ch/node/2)

Glarus organizes special trains so that inhabitants from farther away can join the public assembly. On the day of the assembly, all public transportation is free. To participate in the Landsgemeinde, one must be a Swiss citizen and have resided in the Canton for a minimum of three months.

In the 2015 Glarus Landsgemeinde, the Glarus citizens, after opening the assembly at 9:30 in the morning, had a list of eleven items to decide on. Each of them was previously available to them, made available on the Internet (http://www.landsgemeinde.gl.ch/sites/landsgemeinde.gl.ch/files/2015 /Memorial_2015.pdf). In this ninety-page document, each item that was to be discussed was described and explained in great detail. The pros and cons are explained in the document, as are the legal foundations and possible consequences of taking action. For each item, a rubric exists explaining why a change is necessary and who has advocated for a change and brought this item onto the agenda. Reports of special commissions who have studied the issue are included and thus made broadly available.

The Memorial for the 2015 Landsgemeinde includes such items as adjusting the 2016 tax base (to 53 percent), canceling previously enacted construction restrictions, making changes to the current tax law, handling violence at sports events more efficiently, adjusting the universal health care system, making changes to the law of social security, imposing more regulation on the Canton Bank, the "Glarner Kantonalbank," expanding coverage of canton-wide preschool and daycare centers, cutting back cantonal spending given the shortage of income and the reluctance to further raise taxes (seventy measures were approved by the canton government and these had to be approved by the Landsgemeinde), and expanding the usage of unpaved roads cutting through local forests. Each item is analyzed in terms of its (financial) consequences and likely benefits. On May 3, 2015, the Landsgemeinde decided each one, whereupon a Swiss cantonal bill became a law.

NEW ENGLAND TOWN HALL DEMOCRACY

In some towns of New England in the northeast of the United States, citizens to this day hold town hall meetings in which they decide in face-to-face interaction and debate what to do throughout the year, that is, how to spend the money the town has and what public works to prioritize. They give each other legally binding laws. According to Frank Bryan, the number one specialist on American town hall democracy, "Town meetings are usually held only once a year. Most town meetings in Vermont are held on the same day, the first Tuesday after the first Monday in March" (Bryan 2004, xiii). My account of New England town hall democracy is largely based on Bryan's research and his plentiful publications on this topic.

Town hall meetings are a reality in over 1,000 New England towns. In Vermont alone, more than 230 towns hold town hall meetings on a regular basis—at least once a year. According to Bryan, the average attendance at New England town hall meetings from 1970 to 1998 was 20.5 percent of registered voters. The variance, however, was large, ranging from an attendance of 72.3 percent of registered voters to 1 percent of registered voters.

Against the broadly accepted rule that citizens of higher social and economic status participate more in politics (Verba and Nie 1972), when it comes to direct democracy and town hall meetings, no such bias toward the affluent and better educated is detectable (Bryan 2004, 115). To the contrary, below average income–earning farmers and craftsmen dominate most town halls in New England. In fact, Bryan finds that "the higher the education level of a town's citizens, the more the income, and the greater the percentage of managers and professionals in the workforce, the smaller the percentage of registered voters at the town meeting" (Bryan 2004, 116).

While this phenomenon is not explained by Bryan, it appears that affluent citizens participate more in interest groups, seeking to obtain advantages and privileges for themselves and their offspring (for example, in school district meetings), whereas workers, farmers, and other "average" local people seem more invested in matters of the common good, which rely more on mutual obligations than on special benefits.

SIZE MATTERS

According to Susan Clark and Frank Bryan, "Town meetings work better, dramatically better, in towns with small populations. Towns like Waltham, Grafton, Sandgate, Belvidere, Roxbury and Wheelock (all with fewer than 600 voters on the checklist) average 30 percent attendance at town meeting, while towns like Middlebury, Bennington, Hartford, Waterbury and Swanton (all with more than 3,600 voters on the checklist) average about 5 percent" (Clark and Bryan 2005, 40).

These authors find that the decline in participation they have witnessed since the 1970s is mostly due to the increased size of towns. The larger the town, the less each participant counts and the less responsible each one feels. Implied in this logic is that here as in other cases, active participation is a matter of responsibility. When the number of participants rises, individual responsibility gets diluted. These same authors also find that the participation in town meetings has declined because their power has been curtailed, that is, the range of issues that can be decided in town meetings has been diminished over time.

In fact, analyzing data gathered from 1,435 town meetings, selected randomly from 1970 to 1998, Frank Bryan is able to show that the smaller the town, the higher the percentage of citizens participating in town meetings and the more likely they are to speak at the event. Bryan combines these two indicators into one, calling it "democraticness." Democraticness measures the percentage of registered voters attending a town meeting and actually saying something there, that is, it measures active participation or active citizenship. He finds that "for every increase of one rank of its population size, a town's town meeting will lose about nine-tenths (0.88) of a rank in 'democratic-ness'" (Bryan 2004, 18). To Bryan, size is the most important factor explaining participation in direct democratic procedures. He finds that

> In the description of the towns one condition overwhelms: their size. By nearly every standard a political scientist might employ, they are tiny. One-quarter of the meetings were held in towns that averaged fewer than 1,000 residents. Of the 1,435 meetings, 113 were held in towns that averaged fewer than 200. Only 2 percent of the meetings were held in towns of more than 5,000. (Bryan 2004, 20)

Indeed, Bryan found that "about 42 percent of the variance in attendance at the 1,435 town meetings is associated with the size of the town where the meeting is held" (Bryan 2004, 73). The relative power to influence collective decisions, another measure of size, explains some 58 percent of the variance. Among the large sample Bryan assembled, participation in town meetings dropped off at around one thousand registered voters. In some of the smaller towns, attendance was as high as 74 percent, whereas in the larger towns (3,500 registered voters and above), attendance dropped as low as 1 percent.

The same research also found that "in general town meetings with the smallest number of people in attendance have the largest percentage of participators and the best distribution of participation among those present" (Bryan 2004, 157).

Another important factor detected by this research is that mobility impacts participation negatively. The more people move and the less time they have actually lived in a place, the less likely they are to participate in town halls. This finding is of course not surprising, as the very meaning of "community" requires that one is actually present and knows one's community before one participates. Stability is thus positively correlated to town hall democracy. Surprisingly, so is socioeconomic diversity (Bryan 2004, 186). Bryan and his team did not find a systematic exclusion of women in the 1,435 town hall meetings they researched. Female participation was lower than male participation (around 46 percent of participants were female in their sample) and they were less active, that is, they spoke less and for shorter periods of time. Bryan found, however, that when daycares were an option, female participation increased to 49.5 percent (Bryan 2004, 208). Female participation also increased over time from 1970 to 1998.

While Bryan does not give a precise upper limit for meaningful direct democracy based on direct personal interaction, his numbers closely resemble those proposed by Robin Dunbar, who has asserted that the human brain is only able to maintain 150 stable relationships, thus forming the upper limit of stable, cohesive groups (Dunbar 1992). Dunbar in fact argues that "when a group's size exceeds this limit, it becomes unstable and begins to fragment. This then places an upper limit on the size of groups which any given species can maintain as cohesive social units through time" (Dunbar 1992, 469).

Rules

Town meetings follow an established procedure and rules. A board of select-men sets the agenda, in Vermont called "the warning." In Vermont, the warning must be published at least thirty days before the meeting. Agenda articles can be either open for discussion or closed for vote. Meetings start in the morning and can take all day. To initiate debate, a formula is uttered, often "what is your pleasure?"

In regular meetings, items that have not been previously been placed on the agenda cannot be voted on and thus cannot become law. Voting happens by voice, hand, or by secret ballot. Oftentimes a meeting is opened with a prayer. Town officers are selected, nominated, or voted on and hold office for one year until they are either confirmed or replaced. Bryan explains that "most elections for a town officers must (by law) be resolved by ballot vote. If no contest develops, a motion is made that the clerk be instructed to 'cast one ballot' for the lone nominee. When this motion has been approved (it almost always is) the election is official. Budgets do not require a ballot by law, but often a ballot is requested from the floor. If some people at the meeting request a ballot, then one must be held on any issue before the meeting" (Bryan 2004, 17).

The moderator of last year's meeting calls the meeting to order and the first order of business always is the confirmation or change of the moderator.

The Meaning of Citizenship

According to Bryan, Vermont towns administer citizenship because "Vermont citizens' right to vote in statewide elections is validated when their names appear on the town's 'grand list'" (Bryan 2004, 10). Town citizenship thus enacts broader state citizenship. Towns also send representatives to larger legislative bodies. In Vermont, smaller towns share a representative in the state legislature. Beyond this local enactment of statewide citizenship, it is the local practice of direct democracy that gives meaning to the word citizenship. Those who participate know what it means to be a citizen by experience and by practice. Instead of insisting on having certain rights and treating them as entitlements, they construct their rights and duties in mutual agreement and face-to-face interaction. Charles Kuralt has described his impressions of a Vermont town meeting in the following way:

This one day in Vermont, the town carpenter lays aside his tools, the town doctor sees no patients, the shopkeeper closes his shop, mothers tell their children they'll have to warm up their own dinner. This one day, people in Vermont look not to their own welfare but to that of their town. It doesn't matter that it's been snowing since four o'clock this morning. They'll be in the meeting house. This is town meeting day. Every March for 175 years, the men and women of Strafford, Vermont, have trudged up this hill on one day which is their holiday for democracy. They walk past a sign that says: THE OLD WHITE MEETING HOUSE—BUILT IN 1799 AND CONSECRATED AS A PLACE OF PUBLIC WORSHIP FOR ALL DENOMINATIONS WITH NO PREFERENCE FOR ONE ABOVE ANOTHER. Since 1801, it has also been in continuous use as a town hall.

Here, every citizen may have his say on every question. One question is: Will the town stop paying for outside health services? The speaker is a farmer and elected selectman, David K. Brown. And farmer Brown says yes.

DAVID K. BROWN: This individual was trying or thinking about committing suicide. Se we called the Orange County Mental Health. This was, I believe, on a Friday night. They said they'd see him on Tuesday afternoon [*mild laughter*], and if we had any problems, take him to Hanover and put him in the emergency room. Now I don't know as we should pay five hundred and eighty-two dollars and fifty cents for that kind of advice.

They talked about that for half an hour, asking themselves if this money would be well or poorly spent.

This is not representative democracy. This is pure democracy, in which every citizen's voice is heard.

JAMES CONDICT: We will vote on this before we go to Article four. All those in favor signify by saying "Aye."

PEOPLE: Aye.

CONDICT: All opposed.

PEOPLE: Nay.

CONDICT: I'm going to ask for a standing vote. All those in favor stand, please.

It's an old Yankee expression which originated in the town meeting and has entered the language of free men: Stand up and be counted. And when the judgment is made, and announced by James Condict, maker of rail fences and moderator of this meeting, the town will abide by the judgment.

CONDICT: There are a hundred votes cast—sixty-one in favor and thirty-nine against. And it then becomes deleted from the town budget.

This is the way the founders of this country imagined it to be—that citizens would meet in their own communities to decide directly most of the questions affecting their lives and fortunes. Vermont's small towns have kept it this way.

Will or will not Strafford, Vermont, turn off its streetlights to save money?

CONDICT: All those in favor—
MAN [shouting]: —Paper ballot!—
CONDICT: —signify by saying—
MAN [shouting] —Paper ballot!—
WOMEN: What?
MAN: That's my right, any member's right at a meeting—to call for a paper ballot.
CONDICT: Is that seconded?
WOMAN: I'll second it.
CONDICT: It's seconded.
MAN: It doesn't have to be seconded.
CONDICT: Prepare to cast your ballots on this amendment.

If any citizen demands a secret ballot, a secret ballot it must be. Everybody who votes in Vermont has taken an old oath—to always vote his conscience, without fear or favor of any person. This is something old, something essential. You tear off a little piece of paper and on it you write "yes" or "no." Strafford votes to keep the streetlights shining. (Charles Kuralt 1985, 288–91, quoted in Bryan 2004, 22)

While this account is from 1985, it conveys the promise of town hall democracy. The same town was visited in 2000 and, even though some of the high spirits were lost, the annual meeting was still held.

LESSONS LEARNED FROM WESTERN POLITICAL INSTITUTIONS

Participatory budgeting bears the potential to induce more active citizen participation. The involvement of ordinary citizens critically depends on their ability to see the tangible results of their participation. Only if there is something important at stake will citizens sacrifice their evenings and attend different meetings. The more bureaucratized this process becomes, the less it provides for forums of debate and discussion and the more it becomes a matter of voting. The more voting is involved, the less PB becomes an alternative to politics and instead becomes "politics as usual." When that happens, PB becomes an instrument to improve governance, not democracy. Its dependence on the goodwill of the mayor and the city legislators makes the whole process weak and easy to distort or end. Power, again, is not easily or willingly shifted away from those who have a mandate to rule.

The lessons from Switzerland are clear: direct democracy is possible today. For it to work, a larger unit, such as a nation-state, must be broken up into federal units and political power must be guaranteed and protected at the local level. Modern infrastructure, such as public transportation, can and should be put to use, making direct participation possible by easing the cost of attendance.

Whenever real, that is, significant and consequential decisions affecting a community are made, citizens have a strong incentive to participate and, as the Swiss case shows, they will do so. The Internet can play a role in this process, not as a substitute for direct and face-to-face interaction of citizens, but as a tool to broadly disseminate the decisions reached in popular assembly.

The Swiss case also allows for the gazing of some of the limitations of the kind of direct democracy practiced in Glarus and Appenzell Innerrhoden. Given the large number of citizens (40,000 for Glarus and 15,500 for Appenzell Innerrhoden), Landsgemeinschaften come together not to debate, but to vote, as meaningful debate among such a large number of citizens is impossible. The complexity of the national legal system affecting and overlapping with the local legal system makes for a highly complex and bureaucratized procedure in which ordinary citizens face ardent tasks of informing themselves and working through many pages of "legalese" in order to grasp the meaning and significance of the proposed measure. Clearly, local self-rule requires that the issues at hand be presented in a clear and straightforward manner. The more they become entangled with national politics and legal frameworks, the more muddled these local issues become. Overly convoluted and complicated legal codes, typical of many European countries, thus stand in the way of local self-rule and must be seen as a way to distance and encapsulate elitist state power, requiring specially trained interpreters and translators (that is, lawyers). By creating such complicated legal systems, states seek to protect themselves against the influence of ordinary citizens.

Participation in town meetings in New England is steadily declining according to the specialist in this field, Frank Bryan. He attributes this decline to the gradual loss of power and local autonomy and to the growth of cities, complicating face-to-face interaction. If people have nothing of substance to decide on, they are reluctant to participate. In fact, the most emblematic state for American town hall democracy, Vermont, has shifted more power away from town halls than most others, maybe because Vermont counted on more to begin with. Both Frank Bryan (2004) and Jane Mansbridge (1980) find that the gradual decline in town meetings they witnessed and measured is attributable to the gradual decline of power these forums wield.

The most important finding of Bryan's extensive research on this matter is that the size of the town is by far the most significant factor predicting active participate in town hall meetings. When towns consist of more than 1,000 registered voters, attendance and active participation in the yearly town hall meetings drops off. Small towns of a few hundred voters, who have a relatively stable population, count on participation rates of over 70 percent.

A SPECIAL CASE: FIXING PRICES AND PROTECTING EQUAL OPPORTUNITY

Several countries in Europe—Germany, Austria, Switzerland, and France—have found an innovative way to protect small bookstores. In those countries, book prices are fixed. Books cannot be sold at a discount. In fact, the price of every book is printed on the book cover and selling it below that price is illegal. While "fixing prices" sounds unfair and is in most instances an illiberal practice benefitting not the consumer but the producer, fixing book prices has not only kept competition alive, but also invigorated it. In fact, fixing the prices of books, combined with a very efficient and quick book distribution system, has had very positive outcomes for all the agents involved in these markets: consumers, bookstores, authors, and distributors.

This is thus a case of how smart institutions can regulate markets in such a way that more than one goal, the traditional goal under free market conditions, that is, maximizing profit for the producers, can be achieved and sustained. The maybe surprising outcome of the institutional arrangements around bookselling in those countries is that small stores can effectively compete with big retail stores—and because of that they can survive. The survival of small (book)stores in turn must be seen as not only instrumental to a more vibrant and dense market, making it convenient for anybody in these countries to buy books, but also a desirable outcome in itself, which has positive spillover effects or externalities on its immediate environment, as a dense network of small (book)stores contributes to more livable cities and urban environments.

Maybe counterintuitively, fixing book prices has not ended competition, but invigorated it. Instead of competing for cheaper prices, bookstores compete for better service, nicer and more welcoming environments, and expertise. A "good bookstore" in any of the countries applying this rule is not a bookstore in which books are the cheapest, but one in which the staff is most knowledgeable about the kind of books they hold and the kind of advice the bookstore staff can give. Bookstores in any of these countries can be small oases in the middle of the hustle and bustle of hectic city life. Many offer places to sit down and drink a coffee, while perusing through the assortments and catalogues. Most work with staff that actually knows a lot of the books they sell. You can walk into a good bookstore in those countries saying something like: "I just read this or that book—and I liked it. Which one should I read next?" Given extremely quick book distribution systems, bookstores can specialize on one theme for which they can have great expertise, while at the same time being able to sell any book not on the shelves by tomorrow.

Fixing Prices for the Common Good in Germany

To demonstrate exactly how this systems works, I will focus on Germany as an ideal case. In Germany since 1887, books have a fixed price and no one can sell books at a discount. In 1878, Adolf Kröner, then the new head of the "Börsenverein des Deutschen Buchandels e.V.," the association of independent German booksellers who represented (and still represents) the interests of publishing houses, book distributors, and bookstores (Hiller and Füssel 2006), pressed for the fixing of book prices. The rationale was to protect the availability and access of books and through them the availability and access to knowledge. The book was thus conceived not just as a product for sale, but also as a product of cultural value that deserved protection, as it serves the common good. Triggered by the availability of cheap books sold by nonprofessional, that is, not trained and certified book salespeople, the first movement toward fixing the prices of books emerged in 1845, when regular bookstores started losing ground against all those selling books cheaper and treating books not as culturally valuable goods, but as simple merchandise.

When Kröner took office, he pressed for reform by pointing out to all the involved companies that if book prices were not protected, their own future would be at risk. On September 25, 1887, the association of German bookstores and distributors thus passed the first reform protecting book prices. The reform came to known as the "Kröner Reform." The reform included sanctions for violations and put the association in charge of enforcing the new rules (Möbes 2007).

The background to this reform is the German tradition of professional associations, which grew out of professional guilds. Professional guilds constituted themselves in the emerging free cities of medieval Europe and became very strong and influential associations in European, particularly German, city life (Weber 1968). Professional guilds of different crafts not only regulated, but also controlled and enforced the standards not just of the products they produced, but also of the people working in the field. To this day, without the proper training (typically three years) and the passing of a final examination administered by the guild, no one is allowed to exercise a profession. German booksellers, similar to all other crafts and service professionals, must undergo a minimum of three years of training and must pass the final examination in order to become licensed to exercise their profession.

In Germany, the reform of 1887 was integrated into the 1891 law regulating bookselling and later into the 1909 general law regulating the German book market. It remained unchanged until 1945 (Möbes 2007). In 1958, the new German law regulating competitiveness allowed for book price regulation as long as it was legally anchored, and in 1966, this legal anchoring was achieved, thus exempting books from the general rule that demanded open competition. In 1975, a new regulation was enacted, shifting over the responsibility of ensuring book price fixing away from the professional association to the "Bundeskartellamt," the executive federal agency responsible for ensuring and enforcing market competition and avoiding the formation of cartels and monopolies. A German law firm was designated to oversee and enforce this law. In 1990, with German unification, this West German rule was extended to East Germany.

On January 1, 1993, when Germany joined the European Union treaty establishing a common economic region, Germany, Austria, and Switzerland were forbidden to coordinate their prices for books across national borders, which they had done up until then. However, each country was allowed to set and control the prices for books within their own borders. In 2000, the European Commission declared the national fixing of book prices as not constituting a threat to general competitiveness—an opinion confirmed in 2002 by the new law, the "Buchpreisbindungsgesetz." This law, amended slightly in 2006, allows for book prices to be fixed at the national level, but demands transparency and public display of those prices. Paragraph one of the law provides its rationale:

> The law serves the protection of the book as a cultural good. The fixing of prices for the consumer secures a broad listing of available books. The law also secures access to books by a broad public in that it protects the existence of a large number of sale points and stores. (§1, BuchPrG; my translation)

The other element to the survival of a large number of bookstores in Germany is the very efficient book distribution system. Companies like "Libri," based in Bad Hersfeld, Germany, ensure a swift overnight delivery of almost any book available on the German book market. Anything ordered before 4:00 p.m. on one day will be available for pick up the next morning at your local bookstore. Libri, according to their website (http://home.libri.de/), delivers to over 4,500 bookstores in Germany and the neighboring countries. Six hundred thousand titles are in stock in Bad Hersfeld, located in central Germany, and ready for immediate delivery. Five million titles are available on demand.

The Results: More Books, More Stores, More Competition

Along with a very efficient and fast distribution system, this allows any small bookstore to compete with any big store. Any book ordered in even the smallest German bookstore before 4:00 p.m. will be ready for pick up the next morning. This means that in Germany, fixing book prices, together with a quick and efficient distribution system, allows small bookstores to compete with big bookstores. It's a fair competition. To be sure, there is still competition because stores that do not provide good service or stores that do not look welcoming and inviting will not be able to compete with pretty stores that offer good services and professional and friendly staff. But there is a real and fair opportunity for small bookstores to survive despite the new threat they all face from Amazon.com today. The result is that there are 2,062 towns and cities in Germany (settlements with more than 5,000 inhabitants) and there are about 6,600 bookstores—one for every 12,424 inhabitants. Each town or city, no matter how small, has at least one.

Compare this to the United States, where the book market is "free." There are about 10,800 bookstores—one for every 29,000 inhabitants. The density of coverage in Germany is more than double. Worse is that in the United States, there are large cities without a single bookstore. Consider the story of Laredo, Texas, where in 2010 the only bookstore of this city of 250,000 inhabitants closed. Small bookstores simply cannot compete with big business if and as long as the only criterion for this competition is the price. Big retailers can take advantage of buying in great bulk, thus obtaining better prices. And they can pressure producers to produce cheaper and cheaper products to the detriment of the quality of these products, as we can easily witness in the food market.

Where there is a Wal-Mart, small shops are closing. Competing with Wal-Mart is not a serious competition—not for a small store. Real competition requires that small stores can offer their products at the same price as large companies. Then there would be competition—a competition that would favor customers, as competition would be about other things: quality of the product, quality of service, proximity, cleanliness, etc. Fixed prices could also ensure a decent living for producers or healthy conditions for animals in the food industry, where most animals are treated with hormones and drugs so they can be grown cheaply and quickly today. With the vanishing of small stores, we lose urban diversity and density of services, and we now have to drive to big stores that are farther away, spending more time in cars, losing more time in traffic, and polluting the environment. We all lose.

If big companies like Wal-Mart were to be charged for these negative spillovers or "externalities" and as a result had to increase the prices of their products, and if small stores that are environmentally friendly and spare local people long car trips while also contributing to dense and vibrant urban environments were to be rewarded for these positive spillovers or "externalities," then there would be fair competition and we would all win (Felber 2010). There are at this point plenty of empirical examples in which instead of maximizing profit for a few large companies, the collective benefit has been elevated into the measure of success, making this a real, not just a theoretical, possibility (https://www.ecogood.org/; http://www.communityeconomies .org/Home).

LESSONS FROM PRICE FIXING

The special case of fixed book prices in Germany does not fit into the general comparison of the other cases described earlier. It lacks the communal dimension of all the other examples and I have excluded this case from the qualitative comparison to follow, as it would score 0 on all but one of the criteria I assess. While not a good case for comparison, the fixing of book prices allows for one important insight, namely that highly regulated markets *can* protect small business, competitiveness, and equal market opportunities, contrary to free and open markets that tend toward monopoly and crisis.

The capitalist free market is not the best way to ensure and protect competitiveness. For a market to function well and sustainably, it has to have rules that protect the competitiveness and guarantee that small producers can compete with large producers. Capitalism will favor large-scale producers and destroy the small producer. Always. Capitalism is going to sell you cheaper and cheaper products, which will necessarily lead to more and more unhealthy products. Nobody wins with this, just a few very large producers. In capitalist systems today, we do not have policies that favor the consumer but policies that favor the largest producers. With this, the promise of the invisible hand benefitting consumers is broken.

Part III

ANALYSIS AND SYNTHESIS

Chapter 9

Learning and Comparing

The empirical cases described earlier provide a rich pool of institutional solutions to the common problem of elite rule and elite (economic) dominance. Each one offers such solutions. Without comparing them, it becomes clear that citizens have many options to organize their political life, and once they have done so, to control their markets in order to avoid abuse, excess, exploitation, and the build-up of unfair advantages. Even without systematic comparison, the previous chapter should make it evident that there are indeed many possible alternatives to the Western political and economic recipes. In fact, it seems that the Western recipes have not cured us, but made us sick. Much more promising political solutions can be found in the non-Western world, where the "Western disease"—"Wetiko" to some North American Native Americans (Forbes 2008)—has not destroyed alternative political and economic institutions.

This book could thus end here and provide those interested in alternatives to Western, liberal, representational democracy and capitalist markets empirical examples for how to organize differently. However, the question remains: What can we learn from all the cases described here *taken together*? Multivariate regression or even factor analysis will not help for that purpose. This is so because I am interested in determining the different factors and conditions—and their potential interplay—in bringing about one outcome, egalitarianism, or at best two, political and economic egalitarianism. Charles Ragin (2014) explains that multivariate statistical analysis is only able to assess the weight of each causal factor independently, but unable to account for different factors coming together to produce one outcome. However, most outcomes cannot be attributed to just one factor in isolation, an "independent" variable. According to Ragin, "That social causation is often both multiple and conjunctural is consistent with commonsense notions about how the world works" (Ragin 2014, 25).

What to do? Luckily, a new way of comparing qualitative cases emerged in the 1980s called Qualitative Comparative Analysis (QCA). It was first systematically proposed in 1987 by the American sociologist Charles Ragin. Ragin adapted set theory to this effort, arguing that set theory allows for the retention of rich, qualitative cases and their systematic comparison by searching for potential overlap among those elements that characterize or constitute each of them.

Ragin has also created a software package that allows for the systematic processing of those constituting elements that make up a case—and for their systematic comparison (available for free download at http://www.u.arizona.edu/~cragin/fsQCA/).

What this software can achieve is to compute the different factors, identified by the researcher, contributing to a given outcome. It can also weigh them and thus produce information on their relative importance. Furthermore, beyond weighing single factors, Ragin's approach can consider different combinations of potentially relevant causal factors and assess their combined strength in producing a given outcomes, egalitarianism here. Finally, this approach can calculate the relevance of the absence of a condition in producing an outcome.

Equipped with this possibility and after describing the twenty-two cases I have been able to find information on, I will thus proceed in comparing them systematically in order to detect common and hence *necessary* factors. I should highlight that the more cases we have for this sort of analysis, the more reliable this analysis will be. Twenty-two cases is, I think, a good start, but the call is out to collect and analyze more cases from different times and places, all representing different solutions to the universal problem of (in)egalitarianism. While some factors identified here might not be transferable and others might require a very specific historical context and social forces to bring them about, as well as very specific conditions to make them effective, I nevertheless think that identifying those factors that have enabled direct democracy and equitable markets at different times and different places and under different circumstances is of great value. It allows us to see what is possible under what conditions. As such, a systematic comparison of relevant causal factors across all the cases promises to identify the necessary conditions for egalitarianism. In keeping with the aim of this book, identifying the necessary conditions of egalitarianism is only half the story, as it will take concrete action and political pressure to enact those laws, regulations, and institutions identified here as necessary. In other words, the identified conditions are not sufficient to bring about egalitarianism. They demonstrate what has been done, and hence, what can be done.

The end result of this analysis is an institutional toolbox of sorts. Equipped with the distilled wisdom of 2,500 years of political institutions, specifically crafted to hold inequality and elite rule at bay, we can then offer policy advice by focusing on one particularly effective political institution or by thinking about a mix of two or three. As I already stated, the motivation in writing this book is to move beyond understanding problems and instead thinking about promising solutions.

FUZZY SET QUALITATIVE COMPARATIVE ANALYSIS

Qualitative comparative analysis as a subset of comparative analysis is located in between more in-depth historical comparative analysis, which, by its very nature, is less systematic and quantitative comparison, which is very systematic and rigorous, but has to pay for that rigor with an inability to maintain rich and complex historical and institutional information. Stripped down to variables, social reality loses much of its appeal as well as its validity. Numbers, after all, only *represent* reality and this representation is very limited. Qualitative comparative analysis (QCA), as initially proposed by Charles Ragin (1987) in the 1980s and later further developed by him and others, promises to retain the rich historical and institutional information contained in a case. It proceeds by comparing complex cases, by sorting out and mapping the relevant factors involved in producing a certain outcome. By doing so, QCA is able to capture how different causally relevant factors work together in producing one outcome. It then proposes to search for overlap in the occurrence of causally relevant factors, thus seeking to detect necessary and sufficient conditions associated with a certain outcome, direct democracy and equitable markets here.

By proceeding in this way, QCA is best operationalized through truth tables and Fuzzy Set Analysis (Ragin 2000, 2008a). The comparative analysis conducted here explicitly follows this research design. My theoretical treatment of political representation, coupled with the search for empirical examples of anti-elitism, has led me to cases of (partial) direct democracy and market regulations aimed at protecting equality, equal opportunity, and fairness. The cases I analyze present one or both of these outcomes to some extent. I did not include any negative cases, as I am only interested in the causal mechanisms and paths leading to political and/or economic equity among those cases I have been able to collect.

Proceeding in this way is unorthodox in several ways. Instead of theory testing, I use theory as a means to discover reality and I use reality to refine theory. I select on the outcome and do not include any negative cases, as my interest is not to formulate high-level abstractions and laws about

egalitarianism, but rather to identify the relative importance of different causally relevant factors and their interactions in concrete cases. I do not believe
that such laws exist in the social world to begin with, and if they do, they
are not "governing" (Little 1998, 237), that is, there is nothing we can learn
from them about the "why" and "how" they work and under what conditions. Concretely, Ragin's approach allows for an analysis of necessity and
sufficiency, but the sufficiency analysis requires cases that do not present the
outcome. However, for the outcome of democratic equity, I have no negative
cases and I can thus not establish sufficient conditions. This is so because I
spent much time and effort, including field research, on societies and groups
practicing promising alternatives to representative democracy. I did not spend
time studying cases from which I did not hope to learn something new and
positive in terms of their democratic practice. The comparative analysis for
the outcome of democracy thus focuses only on necessary conditions.

As democracy was the primary focus of my research, I did come across
cases in which equitable markets were achieved, partially achieved, or not
achieved at all. This more mixed picture allows me to also conduct an analysis of sufficient conditions in addition to the necessary ones.

My cases do not constitute a sample of a larger universe. They *are* the
universe and "sampling" is not the procedure I used to select them. I selected
them instead because they allow me to see and analyze different causal
mechanisms and how they interact in producing a certain outcome. The cases
I selected are "rich" in their causal complexity and thus constitute ideal cases
to analyze.

I also clearly compare apples to oranges, or maybe broadly different cases,
another faux pas among quantitatively trained researchers. Indeed, the cases
described earlier are very divergent, but that is, in my mind, precisely their
strength, as they offer a broad spectrum of possible factors and conditions—
and their combination—for producing a certain outcome. One caveat I see is
that some factors present in one case might be contained in another complex
case and logically imply it. Hence, upper limits to asset holding can be perceived as a subset of communal ownership of all assets under certain circumstances. I have decided to still list them separately here, as I am interested in
determining the importance and influence of each single factor and condition.

Another caveat is that the factors I have identified as potentially relevant
for producing the outcome of direct democracy, equitable markets, or both
(called here "Freedomism") are of different nature. There are internal factors,
such as sharing interest, a religion, or a culture, and there are external factors,
such as living in isolation. Furthermore, there are factors that explain the
emergence of a commune or community, such as war and crisis. All these are
driven by different questions: Under what conditions can direct democracy
emerge? How can it endure? What are the internal and external factors that

contribute to the emergence and endurance of direct democracy and/or equitable markets? While this heterogeneity poses challenges for my analysis, I will seek to control this problem by analyzing different relevant factors and related outcomes separately.

Overall, Fuzzy Set Qualitative Comparative Analysis allows for the sorting out of these different factors. It also allows for the combination of all the different factors identified. Charles Ragin explains that "relevant objects can have varying degrees of membership in the set" (Ragin 2000, 3). To him, "Fuzzy sets are especially valuable in the back-and-forth between theory and data analysis precisely because they are heavily infused with theoretical and substantive knowledge" (Ragin 2000, 7). Fuzzy Set logic and research, instead of seeking for correlations, seeks to identify communalities in terms of shared causes or factors present in a given and fixed outcome. If the outcome, as in this case, is direct democracy, then the question for Fuzzy Set Analysis becomes: What are the necessary and the sufficient factors that are or must be present for this outcome to result? In Ragin's words,

> In a comparative case study of commonalities, by contrast, causation is typically understood conjuncturally, in terms of combinations of conditions. The goal of this type of analysis is to identify the causal conditions shared by these cases. Causal conditions do not compete with each other, as they do in correlational research; they combine. How they combine is something that the researcher tries to piece together using his or her in-depth knowledge of the cases. (Ragin 2000, 33)

Hence, instead of searching for single variables and their relationship to a given outcome, Fuzzy Set Analysis seeks to identify the accumulative effect of the relative presence or absence of different factors in order to explain an outcome. According to Schneider and Wagemann, "A condition can be considered sufficient if, whenever it is present across cases, the outcome is also present in these cases. In other words, there should not be a single case that shows the condition but not the outcome" (Schneider and Wagemann 2012, 57). The logic symbol for this relationship is $X \rightarrow Y$. On the other hand, necessity is defined by the same authors in the following way: "Condition X is necessary if, whenever the outcome Y is present, the condition is also present. In other words, Y cannot be achieved without X" (Schneider and Wagemann 2012, 69). The symbol for this relationship is $X \leftarrow Y$. In other words, Fuzzy Set Analysis seeks to identify those factors or conditions that must be present for a given outcome to occur. Among those, it seeks to distinguish necessary and sufficient conditions.

The tables shown here are constructed according to the logic of Fuzzy Sets, in which 1 indicated full membership and 0 nonmembership. I have

Table 9.1 Outcome Direct Democracy (DD): Data Matrix Fuzzy Sets

Cases// Conditions	Strict separation of political from economic power: X1:SEP	Term limits of executive: X2:LIM	Accountability of executive: X3:ACC	Federalismand decentralization: X4:FED	Shared interest: X5:INTER
1 Athens	1 (Cleisthenes reforms; lot)	1	1	1 (assumed)	1
2 Medieval city	0.25 (guilds)	0 (no info)	0.25	0	1 (Stadtluft macht frei)
3 Paris Commune	1 (citizen councils)	0 (no info)	1 (through public councils)	1 (neighborhood councils)	1 (freedom)
4 German Räte	1 (councils)	1 (imperative mandate)	1 (recall)	1 (local, regional, and national councils)	1
5 Anarchist Spain	1 (councils)	1 (imperative mandate)	1 (recall)	1 (local, regional, and national councils)	1
6 Tolstoyans	1 (general assembly)	0.75 (assumed, through regular assemblies)	0.75 (through regular assemblies)	0.25 (weak network between communes)	1
7 Kibbutzim	1 (general assembly)	1 (rotation of office holding)	1 (through regular public assemblies)	1 (strong network between kibbutzim)	1
8 Amish	1 (religious leadership with no economic power)	0.25 (change of leadership possible, but not likely)	0 (assumed: religious obedience)	1 (strong intercommunity networks)	1
9 Hutterites	1 (no private property; religious leadership)	0.25 (change of leadership possible, but not likely)	0 (assumed: religious obedience)	1 (strong intercommunity networks)	1
10 Twin Oaks	1 (assemblies)	1 (rotation)	1 (through regular assembly)	0	1
11 Wintukua	0.75 (juntas)	0.25 (limited through assemblies)	1 ("prestacion de cuentas")	1	1
12 Bolivia	0.75 (juntas)	0.25 (limited by regular assemblies)	0.25 (through regular assemblies and juntas)	1 (mixed constitutional design and network of indigenous groups)	1
13 Zapatistas	1 (juntas)	0.25 (limited through regular assemblies)	1 (through regular assemblies and juntas)	1 (caracoles)	1
14 Swiss	0.25 (assemblies)	0.75 (regulated through once-a-year assemblies)	0.75 (through once-a-year assemblies)	1 (local decision making in cantons)	1
15 Vermont	0.25 (assemblies)	0.75 (regulated through once-a-year assemblies)	0.75 (through once-a-year assemblies)	1 (local decision making in towns)	0.75 (limited by mobility)

Shared culture or religion: X6:CULT	Physical proximity: X7:PROX	Less than 200 participants: X8:U200	Absence of external threats: X9:PEACE	Internal homogeneity: X10:HOM	Outcome Y:Direct democracyDD
1	1	0.25 (assumed)	0.25	0.75 (metics)	1
1 (exclusion of nonbelievers)	1	0.25	0 (militias)	1	0.75
1 (urban French)	1 (neighborhood councils)	1 (assumed, in neighborhood councils)	0	0.75	1
1	1 (in local councils)	0.25 (only in some local councils)	0	0.75 (workers and soldiers with different backgrounds)	1
1	1 (in local councils)	0.25 (only in some local councils)	0	0.75 (workers with different backgrounds)	1
1	1	1	0	1	1
1	1	0.75 (in most cases)	0.25	0.75 (Jews with different national backgrounds)	1
1	1	1	1	1	0.75
1	1	1	1	1	0.75
0.75 (differently motivated members)	1	1	1	0.75 (different backgrounds)	1
1	1	0.75 (in most local assemblies)	0.75 (achieved through retreat)	1	1
1	1	0.75 (in most local communities)	1	1	0.75 (mixed system: direct and representational)
1	1	1	0.25	1	1
1	1	0	1	0.75	0.75 (limited to once-a-year assembly)
0.25 (limited by mobility)	1	0.75 (in most cases)	1	0.25 (limited by mobility)	0.75 (limited to once-a-year assembly)

Table 9.2 Outcome Direct Democracy, Simplified Data Matrix Fuzzy Sets

Cases // Conditions	X1:SEP	X2:LIM	X3:ACC	X4:FED	X5:INTER	X6:CULT	X7:PROX	X8:U200	X9:PEACE	X10:HOM	Outcome Y:DD
1 Athens	1	1	1	1	1	1	1	0.25	0.25	0.75	1
2 Medieval city	0.25	0	0.25	0	1	1	1	0.25	0	1	0.75
3 Paris Commune	1	0	1	1	1	1	1	1	0	0.75	1
4 German Räte	1	1	1	1	1	1	1	0.25	0	0.75	1
5 Anarchist Spain	1	1	1	1	1	1	1	0.25	0	0.75	1
6 Tolstoyans	1	0.75	0.75	0.25	1	1	1	1	0	1	1
7 Kibbutzim	1	1	1	1	1	1	1	0.75	0.25	0.75	1
8 Amish	1	0.25	0	1	1	1	1	1	1	1	0.75
9 Hutterites	1	0.25	0	1	1	1	1	1	1	1	0.75
10 Twin Oaks	1	1	1	0	1	0.75	1	1	1	0.75	1
11 Wintukua	0.75	0.25	1	1	1	1	1	0.75	0.75	0.75	1
12 Bolivia	0.75	0.25	0.25	1	1	1	1	0.75	1	1	1
13 Zapatistas	1	0.25	1	1	1	1	1	1	0.25	1	0.75
14 Swiss	0.25	0.75	0.75	1	1	1	1	0	1	0.75	0.75
15 Vermont	0.25	0.75	0.75	1	0.75	0.25	1	0.75	1	0.25	0.75

also scored 0 where the condition in question does not apply or where I was unable to find information on this condition. The midpoint or point of indifference between membership and nonmembership is 0.5, which indicates either a halfway membership or a mixed membership. Where I lacked specific information but had good grounds to assume a value, I added "assumed" to the description I provided for each calibration. I did not provide descriptions for those calibrations that were obvious.

THE CONDITIONS AND THEIR CALIBRATION

Guided by theory, the empirical cases contained political institutions that seem causally relevant for the outcome of either direct democracy or equitable markets. These are, in the economic realm,

1. Communal ownership of assets;
2. Upper limits to asset ownership; or
3. Redistribution schemes.

In the political realm, I have identified:

4. Short term limits on the executive power;
5. Accountability of the executive after his or her terms ends;
6. Federalism or confederation;
7. Strict separation of the economic from the political realm in order to avoid the spilling over of economic power into political power;
8. Shared interest;
9. Shared culture or religion;
10. Physical proximity, that is, living in a community that allows for face-to-face interaction;
11. Less than 200 participants in general assemblies;
12. Absence of external threats;
13. Internal homogeneity.

Those thirteen conditions are either fully or partially present in all my cases and I have calibrated them accordingly, either as 1 (fully present or in), 0 (nonpresent or out), 0.25 (mostly nonpresent or almost out), and 0.75 (almost fully present or mostly in). I opted against finer calibration (0.2, 0.4, 0.6, 0.8) to increase the reliability of this method, as it becomes more difficult to make and justify more fine-tuned calibrations. All cases relied on either general assembly, councils, or *juntas* to reach collective decisions. Given that making collective decisions in open public assembly or councils *is* direct democracy, I have not included this condition in the list of causally relevant

Table 9.3   Outcome Equitable Markets, Data Matrix Fuzzy Sets

Cases// Conditions	Communal asset ownership: X1:COM	Upper limits to asset ownership: X2:UL	Redistribution of assets (taxes): X3:RED	Outcome equitable markets Y:EM
1 Athens	0	0	0.25 (taxes)	0.25 (assumed)
2 Rome	0.25 (Ager Publicus)	0.25 (different laws)	0.25 (taxes)	0
3 Medieval city	0.25 (commons)	0	0.25 (taxes)	0.25 (guilds vs. patricians)
4 Tolstoyans	1 (no private property)	1 (no private property)	0	1 (equal share of fruits of labor)
5 Kibbutzim	1 (no private property)	1 (no private property)	0	1 (equal share of fruits of labor)
6 Amish	0.25 (commons)	1 (Ordnung; poverty)	0	0.75 (assumed)
7 Hutterites	1 (no private property)	1 (no private property)	0	1 (equal share of fruits of labor)
8 Twin Oaks	1 (no private property)	1 (no private property)	0	1 (equal share of fruits of labor)
9 Palenque	1 (collective land title)	1 (collective land title)	0	0.75 (family-owned land within the collective)
10 Wintukua	1 (collective land title)	1 (collective land title)	0	0.75 (family-owned land within the collective)
11 Bolivia	1 (collective land title)	1 (collective land title)	0.75 (taxes)	0.75 (family-owned land within the collective)
12 Zapatistas	1 (collective land title)	1 (collective land title)	0	0.75 (family-owned land within the collective)
13 Swiss	0	0	0.75 (taxes)	0.25 (unregulated private property)
14 Vermont	0	0	0.75 (taxes)	0.25 (unregulated private property)

factors. Relying on a general assembly, councils, or *juntas* can thus be treated as an outcome, but the question remains: How can we get there? The thirteen conditions I identified all seem causally related to this outcome.

Calibrating conditions was relatively unproblematic, as all thirteen conditions can easily be identified from the information I obtained on each case. I have conflated scope and depth in my calibration of conditions, so that a

Table 9.4   Equitable Markets, Simplified Data Matrix Fuzzy Sets

	Cases// Conditions	Communal asset ownership: X1:COM	Upper limits to asset ownership: X2:UL	Redistribution of assets (taxes): X3:RED	Outcome equitable marketsY:EM
1	Athens	0	0	0.25	0.25
2	Rome	0.25	0.25	0.25	0
3	Medieval city	0.25	0	0.25	0.25
4	Tolstoyans	1	1	0	1
5	Kibbutzim	1	1	0	1
6	Amish	0.25	1	0	0.75
7	Hutterites	1	1	0	1
8	Twin Oaks	1	1	0	1
9	Palenque	1	1	0	0.75
10	Wintukua	1	1	0	0.75
11	Bolivia	1	1	0.75	0.75
12	Zapatistas	1	1	0	0.75
13	Swiss	0	0	0.75	0.25
14	Vermont	0	0	0.75	0.25

weak number (0.25) for internal population homogeneity expresses both relative internal heterogeneity of a community and, if the case contains more than one community, more heterogeneous than homogeneous communities. The same is true for all conditions.

I operationalized communal ownership of assets through the relative presence or absence of commons, private property, and collective land titles. I operationalized upper limits to asset ownership by focusing on the relative presence or absence of laws limiting property or measures taken to disown factory owners or rich landowners. Cases that did not allow for private property were automatically included in this condition. I operationalized redistributive schemes through the relative presence or absence of taxes on income, wealth, and inheritance.

In the political realm, I operationalized strong democracy as direct democracy without representatives. I assessed strict separation of political from economic power by the relative presence or absence of specific laws, as in Athens, but also through the existence and strength of institutions counterweighing the political power of the rich. General assemblies, councils, and *juntas*, as well as guilds and *comitias* and the Concilium Plebis all work to secure political power to the average citizen.

To calibrate term limits of the executive I scored any measure limiting power holding to one year or less as 1 and measured to limit the terms of executive political leaders less than five years 0.75. For accountability of the executive, I looked for mechanisms that force the outgoing office holder to face scrutiny, either publicly (as with the Wintukua) or legally (as in Rome). For federalism or confederation, I looked for the absence/presence of federal structures. I assessed strict separation of the economic from the political realm through the absence/presence of institutions protecting the political power of ordinary citizens. General assemblies, councils, or *juntas* achieve this goal, as does the type of reform conducted by Cleisthenes in Athens, as he forced rich and poor to forge civic bonds and make decisions together. Shared interest turns out to be a very fundamental condition, present in almost all cases, particularly in smaller intentional communities, where people joined out of conviction. Whenever I detected such a motivation, I calibrated it with 1. Shared culture or religion is strongly related to shared interest and can be perceived as a means to achieve it. It can also be perceived as a subset of shared interest. I calibrated this condition by the relative absence or presence of shared cultural backgrounds and shared religious practices. Some have argued that physical proximity is a condition for direct democracy and I thus included this item. Proximity scores high in almost all my cases, with the exception of Rome. I also scored it high in those cases that relied on federalism or confederation, like the anarchist cases, as local communes still had physical proximity. Such systems consisted of multiple local communities. To assess the importance of upper limits to collective, face-to-face decision making, as the work of Boix (2015) and Bryan (2004) suggest, I included the condition of having no more than two hundred participants. Given the state and power theories introduced earlier, I also included the absence/presence of external threats. My final condition is internal homogeneity, which refers to cultural, ethnic, and national backgrounds of the participants.

Where assets were held in common or where upper limits regulated asset holding, as in all intentional communities and among indigenous groups, I calibrated redistribution 0, as it is mutually exclusive with those two conditions. Once all assets are held in common or asset concentration is controlled, redistribution is no longer necessary.

A potentially complicating dimension is time, as reality changes and the analysis has to make a decision about what moment to consider for calibration. If a condition is only present for a relatively short period of time, but is very strong and pronounced while present, what score should it get? The solution to this problem comes from my interest in identifying those factors or conditions that *can* bring about direct democracy and/or equitable markets. In other words, I am interested in determining what a condition such as internal homogeneity can achieve when and as long as it is present or absent. I have thus not adjusted values in some sort of effort to score median or medium values over time. I focused instead on those times when a factor was either strongly present or absent so that the outcomes represent an ideal rather than a real situation. I am, after all, interested in identifying causal mechanisms and their potentials.

Calibrating the outcomes was more complicated than calibrating conditions. On the time dimension, I sought coherence, that is, if a condition was strongly present during a given time period, I scored the outcome for that same time. Given my interest in finding alternatives to political representation, I rated "direct democracy" higher, the more elements of direct decision making by ordinary citizens was possible. On that account, I calibrated Athens, most intentional communities, and most indigenous communities as "all in" (1). I calibrated mixed systems, such as the one in Bolivia, which combined direct democratic mechanisms at the local level with representative mechanisms at the national level 0.75 (mostly in), as I am interested in determining the potential of such mixed systems.

Equitable markets were the most difficult to define, operationalize, and hence, calibrate. Fairness and preserving equal opportunities over generations were the two main dimensions derived from the literature, and I used those as my two main criteria for calibration. My cases contain only three institutional measures that are specific to this outcome: communal ownership of all assets, as in the kibbutzim, the Tolstoyans, and most indigenous groups, all of which I calibrated 1 (all in). I treated communal ownership of assets as a subset of upper limits to asset holding, as both limit the amount of assets one person or family can hold or accumulate, but regulates this outcome in different ways. Thus all communal ownership of assets implied upper limits of ownership, but not the other way around, as Bolivia, for example, has established upper limits of land ownership nationwide, but not communal ownership, which only exists among indigenous groups. Redistribution schemes represent a more traditional way of ensuring fairness and equal opportunity, for example, through welfare measures and progressive taxes, and I calibrated cases such as Switzerland and Vermont as 1, while most indigenous groups score rather low on this condition. Athens provides a case in which, instead of instituting upper limits to asset holding or communal ownership, the main way to secure fairness and equal opportunity was through a strict separation of political from economic power and a replacing of traditional associations and bonds with civic ones.

Given the scant information on Bhutan, Gumlao, and the Owenite communes, I decided not to include them in the comparative analysis for the outcome direct democracy. I also excluded my special case on book prices and the Brazilian experience with participatory budgeting from the systematic comparison, as both examples are only partial in their reach, not structuring a whole society and imposing rules on a polity. Furthermore, my interest in political institutions also led me to exclude cases in which the outcome was not the direct result of the conditions listed, but caused externally. In Palenque de San Basílio, while the conditions for direct democracy are there, the Colombian government does not allow Palenque to practice its own autonomy, thus undermining the conditions and distorting the outcome. Finally, I excluded the case of Rome, as there is no broad agreement among scholars if the Roman Republic was indeed a direct democracy or not.

For the outcome "equitable markets" I excluded all the anarchist cases from my analysis, as the outcome "equitable markets" was not the result of institutions put in place to achieve this goal; it rather resulted from the expulsion of capitalists and the takeover of workplaces by workers. While such a takeover was able to achieve equality and fairness at the workplace, my focus is on the institutions put in place that avoid the formation of elites—old and new. None of the anarchist cases lasted long enough to allow for an assessment of the long-term protection of equal opportunities and fairness.

FUZZY SET QUALITATIVE COMPARATIVE ANALYSIS

Analysis of Necessary Conditions, Outcome Direct Democracy (Software Results)

Outcome variable: DD

Conditions tested:

	Consistency	Coverage
inter	**1.000000**	0.915254
prox	**1.000000**	0.900000
cult	**0.944444**	0.910714
hom	0.851852	0.920000

The following results are obtained by running the software for those conditions that have a theoretical potential to be necessary for the outcome of direct democracy. In the analysis of necessary conditions shown below using the Fuzzy Set data for direct democracy (DD) as the outcome, I find that shared interest (inter) and physical proximity (prox) are necessary conditions (consistency of 1) and culture is "almost always necessary" (consistency of 0.94). Using a cut-off of 0.9 for consistency, homogeneity fails to meet the threshold to be considered almost always necessary. Because there are no cases that are NOT DD, an analysis of sufficiency is not possible.

Analysis of Necessary Conditions, Outcome Equitable Markets (EM) (Software Results)

In the necessary analysis for the outcome equitable markets (EM), the absence of redistribution (red) is "almost always" necessary for the presence of the outcome EM (based on consistency of 0.94). None of the other conditions when absent or present are necessary for EM (results below).

Analysis of Necessary Conditions

Outcome variable: EM
Conditions tested:[1]

	Consistency	Coverage
com	0.857143	0.857143
~com	0.200000	0.333333
ul	0.885714	0.837838
~ul	0.114286	0.210526
red	0.200000	0.583333
~red	**0.942857**	0.750000

In the necessary analysis for the **absence of EM**, NONE of the conditions or absence of the conditions are necessary for the lack of the outcome EM (consistencies all fall below the 0.9 threshold).

Analysis of Necessary Conditions

Outcome variable: ~EM
Conditions tested:

	Consistency	Coverage
com	0.333333	0.200000
~com	0.761905	0.761905
ul	0.285714	0.162162
~ul	0.714286	0.789474
red	0.476190	0.833333
~red	0.761905	0.363636

Truth Tables and Analysis, Sufficiency for the Outcome Equitable Markets (EM)

File   Edit   Sort

com	ul	red	number	~em	raw consist. ▽	PRI consist.	SYM consis
0	0	1	2	1	1.000000	1.000000	1.000000
0	0	0	3	1	1.000000	1.000000	1.000000
0	1	0	1	0	0.500000	0.333333	0.333333
1	1	1	1	0	0.500000	0.333333	0.333333
1	1	0	7	0	0.193548	0.038462	0.043478

Results

Truth Table Analysis
　Model: EM = f(com, ul, red)
　Rows: 5
　Algorithm: Quine-McCluskey
　True: 1

Complex Solution

　frequency cut-off: 1.000000
　consistency cut-off: 0.870968

	raw coverage	unique coverage	consistency
com*ul*~red	0.771429	0.771429	0.870968

　solution coverage: 0.771429
　solution consistency: 0.870968

Truth Table Analysis

　Model: EM = f(com, ul, red)
　Rows: 5
　Algorithm: Quine-McCluskey
　True: 1-L

Parsimonious Solution

　frequency cut-off: 1.000000
　consistency cut-off: 0.870968

	raw coverage	unique coverage	consistency
com*~red	0.800000	0.800000	0.875000

　solution coverage: 0.800000
　solution consistency: 0.875000

Truth Table Analysis

Model: EM = f(red, ul, com)
Rows: 1
Algorithm: Quine-McCluskey
True: 1
0 Matrix: 0L

Intermediate Solution

frequency cut-off: 1.000000
consistency cut-off: 0.870968
Assumptions:
~red (absent)
ul (present)
com (present)

	raw coverage	unique coverage	consistency
	----------	----------	----------
~red*ul*com	0.771429	0.771429	0.870968

solution coverage: 0.771429
solution consistency: 0.870968

Analysis of Sufficient Conditions, Outcome Equitable Markets (EM) (Software Results)

In the sufficiency analysis using the Fuzzy Set Data to evaluate the presence of the outcome EM, the intermediate solution is the same as the complex solution and they reveal only a single "recipe" suggesting that the presence of communal ownership of assets (com) *and* presence of upper limits to asset holding (ul) *and* the absence of redistribution (red) are together sufficient for the outcome of equitable markets (EM). Consistency is 0.87 and coverage is 0.77.

GENERAL FINDINGS AND CONCLUSIONS

To allow for an overview of the findings achieved through systematic comparison of my empirical cases, I will bring them together here, grouped by outcome:

1. Outcome direct democracy, necessary conditions: Shared interest and physical proximity are necessary conditions and culture is "almost always necessary" for the outcome of direct democracy. Homogeneity fails to meet the threshold to be considered almost always necessary.
2. Outcome equitable markets, necessary conditions: The absence of redistribution is "almost always" necessary for the presence of the outcome. None of the other conditions when absent or present are necessary for the outcome of equitable markets.
3. Outcome equitable markets, sufficient conditions: There is only a single "recipe" suggesting that the presence of communal ownership of assets and presence of upper limits to asset holding and the absence of redistribution are together sufficient for the outcome of equitable markets.

IMPLICATIONS AND CONCLUSIONS

Democracy cannot survive without shared interest and physical proximity. Face-to-face interaction is not only essential for real democracy, it is also necessary. A shared culture can achieve such shared interest, but it is not necessary for achieving it. There are cases, such as Vermont, in which shared interest has been achieved despite cultural and population heterogeneity. After all, a shared interest can be constructed across cultural and ethnic cleavages. While the study of Vermont conducted by Frank Bryan (2004) highlights that there are upper limits to direct democracy and Charles Boix (2015) put that upper limit at 200 participants, the empirical data indicate that direct democracy can be achieved beyond this limit. In fact, there are plenty of empirical examples of direct democracies able to function beyond the 200 threshold.

While the absence of external threats emerged as a condition derived from theory, it appears that empirically, direct democracies have survived even when they faced outside threats. This raises important questions about statehood and the exercise of power, as theoretically, direct democracies dilute or even dissolve centralized states and thus weaken their defensive capabilities. At the same time, however, we know of historical cases in which the citizens of direct democracies took responsibility of their own defense through militias or the formation of citizen armies (as in Athens, the European medieval city states, and most recently the Kurds). This finding suggests the need for a deeper inquiry about the relationship between state power and "people power," for lack of a better term.

Strict separation of political from economic power, limits to the terms of the executive, and accountability of the executive, while important on their own terms, are not necessary for the outcome of direct democracy. This finding is in tune with the emphasis on the legislative branch given by Jean-Jacques Rousseau, Cornelius Castoriadis, Hanna Pitkin, Jane Mansbridge, Jürgen Habermas, and others, all discussed earlier. For a democracy to be real, citizens have to make their own laws—or at least have to have a say in the making of them. Lawmaking cannot be delegated. This is what the theory indicates and what the data also support. This finding also strengthens my assessment that the central problem of our current democracies is the excessive focus on representation and on voting. Voting is not related to democracy. The data thus support my locating of the problem of contemporary democracies with elected representatives. Elected lawmakers stand in the way of true democracy.

Federalism seems an important condition for real democracy to work, or better "confederation," as Murray Bookchin has defined it. If local communities make decisions about their laws and budget allocations for themselves, then confederation must be the way for different local communities to cooperate and coordinate their actions. However, federalism did not emerge as a necessary condition for direct democracy in the data analysis. This is so, one can assume, because in some cases in which local direct democracy was a successful practice (as among the Tolstoyans, the Twin Oakers, and the medieval city-states), there was no need or even possibility for local communities to cooperate and coordinate their actions simply because there were no others to cooperate with or because local democracies did not want to cooperate. However, confederation still emerges as the next logical step in scaling up direct democracy.

For markets to work properly and provide opportunities and fairness to new generations, redistribution is not enough. The data indicates this clearly. Fairness and equal opportunity over generations can only be achieved through either communal asset holding or the establishment of upper limits to income and wealth. The institutions we would need to put in place to achieve this goal would come very close to what has been labeled by such authors as Jacob Hacker, John Rawls, James Meade, and Anthony Atkinson as "pre-distribution" or "property-owning democracy." In theory, these are systems in which all members of a community are given the same tools to succeed on competitive markets *before* they compete. There will still be winners and losers in such a system and incentives to strive and succeed, thus avoiding the known disincentives and moral hazards created by state-dominated markets.

The morale of my analysis is that if we want fair markets, we have to regulate them in such a way that all of us have a fair chance to win and lose every new generation. Systems that favor the few over the many and then allow those few to dispense some of their extra earnings in the form of charity are profoundly unfair. Redistribution cannot bring about fair markets and equal opportunities.

What my analysis adds to these recipes is that beyond ensuring equal starting positions, resource limitations imposed by nature and the incentive structures imposed by relational markets make upper limits to income and asset holding a necessity. Given the fragility of our ecosystem and the dynamics of relational markets, we have to think beyond growth as a strategy to achieve welfare for all. We cannot afford to count on the repeated crises caused by unregulated capitalism for average people to have a fair chance on competitive markets. Our next severe crisis might be our last.

Interestingly, the market distortions resulting from asset concentration and inequality demand similar remedies as those real democracies demand. To be sure, for democracy to work, a community must be constructed is such a way as to avoid the consolidation of political power and assets in a few individuals and families. It must also be guarded against the handing down of political power and wealth, as the formation of elitism in the form of an aristocracy will result. Those wielding power and controlling wealth will seek ways to hold on to it and pass it on to their children and family members. The people must find ways to avoid this tendency and they must erect institutional barriers against it if they want their democracies to remain real, deep, and lasting. My analysis shows that very similar measures must be taken for the sake of keeping markets open and fair to all.

While my empirical analysis examined real direct democracy and fair markets separately, it becomes clear that they are indeed related. Just as the theory indicates, it is through fixing our democracies that we can and must fix our economies. This relationship is not symmetrical, however, as we cannot hope to fix our markets and through it also fix our democracies. Politics trumps economics in that it is through politics and by devising political institutions and regulations that we can rein in our different markets and ensure fairness and equal opportunity on them.

My findings about the centrality of shared interest, physical proximity, and face-to-face interaction thus also apply to markets. Markets work best if they are embedded in local communities and constituted through trust-building, repeated, face-to-face interactions.

THE STEPS WE NEED TO TAKE

Instead of debating minimum wages, we need to start debating maximum earnings and institutions able to avoid the formation of intergenerational dynasties. The proper place to have these debates is the community or municipality, as it is only here that a discussion about "how much should any single member of our community be allowed to accumulate" makes sense and can be legitimate.

Active community membership and an active exercise of citizenship at the local level promise to provide the canvas upon which political decisions can and must be made. Finding ways to avoid that one member of the community occupies half of the land, owns most of the houses, and controls most of the assets of a community is a political decision par excellence. Thus the key to rein in economic excesses and inequalities consists of invigorating local communities and shifting more political decision-making power to local communities, particularly legislative power.

At times, it seems necessary to exercise a break with the past and start anew if social, political, and economic hierarchies have become too entrenched. However, even such a new start is prone to lead to the formation of new hierarchies that again tend to threaten democracy, equal opportunity, and fairness. Democrats thus have to be constantly in "reform mode" and willing to devise new ways to protect what is the core of democracy rule: self-rule, fairness, and equal opportunity.

These are some of the main findings of this book. There are more specific lessons to be learned from the twenty-two empirical cases assembled here. Participation breeds more participation, as long as there are tangible outcomes of this participation that are clear, visible, and more or less immediate, as the case of participatory budgeting shows. Shared interest can result from different sources, as we have seen—religious, secular, visionary, or ideological—but it must be there and provide the bonds that unite the people, creating the sort of friendship that Aristotle mentions and Jane Mansbridge also highlights. It seems clear that diversity does not stand in the way of maintaining such a culture, nor does secularism, as the cases of the kibbutz, but also Palenque, Vermont, and Switzerland, demonstrate. This means that maintaining such a culture that binds can be achieved in contemporary, post-traditional societies. The most obvious and direct way to foster such a culture is through direct democracy itself, that is, the strong commitment to self-rule and to the democratic values of respect, tolerance, listening to others, openness to discuss one's opinions and willingness to revise them, and a strong commitment to anti-authoritarianism, fairness, and equal opportunity. This also includes opposition to any other sort of rule that is not based on deliberation, but on power, privilege, tradition, charisma, or threat.

Where the participants have no real power, they will not participate. If they cannot make decisions that affect their lives, they tend to stay at home and let others do the job for them. Having the power to make real decisions that affect lives creates responsibility and a sense of duty without which direct rule is impossible, as we have seen here. All cases share a focus on responsibilities and duties over rights and entitlements, from Athens, to the medieval European city-states, to the Zapatistas. Rights, it turns out, must first be constructed collectively and they must be upheld, defended, and enforced by the community. They cannot simply be called in and requested. If they are, then they are no longer "rights" but entitlements. Constructing rights together creates a strong obligation to participate and contribute to the collective in what becomes a quid pro quo relationship: the more work and effort each individual puts into the collective, the more rights the community can offer to each individual. Strong communities thus offer the strongest rights and protections for the collective *and* for individuals. At the same time, citizens without responsibilities will act irresponsibly, and extreme voices will distort the democratic process and its outcome. After all, speaking up loudly is cheap when it bears no consequence. The flipside of this insight is that people who have to face the consequences of their actions will act more responsibly. Liberal democracy, which relies on political representation, thus discourages political responsibility among its citizens; it favors the extreme voices and it condemns ordinary citizens into political passivity. As Alexis de Tocqueville (1988 [1835]) already diagnosed in the 1830s, liberal democracy fosters individualism and materialism. This tendency can only be counterbalanced, according to Tocqueville, with strong associations and a very vibrant civic culture.

Instead of advocating for a strong civic culture able to counterbalance the destructive tendencies of liberal democracy, I think it is time to rethink and reform liberal democracy itself. This reform must start and be anchored in the constitution of political community.

For citizenship to be meaningful, it must be powerful, and it must be invested not just with rights, but with duties and with responsibilities. Only if people are actively involved in the process of government will they learn and know how to govern themselves (Neblo 2017). Some of the examples highlighted here clearly demonstrate that actively involved citizens take more responsible decisions.

The core mechanism of legitimate, democratic decision making at the local level is deliberation, as both shared interest and physical proximity provide the conditions for face-to-face deliberation. Real democracy demands taking power away from legislators and for citizens to become their own legislators, or at a minimum to take on much stronger roles in the legislative process. We could think of such institutions as jury duty and devise "legislative duty" as a way toward fully deciding, locally in popular assembly, what the binding law should be. This is not as far-fetched as it may seem. It is a reality in many towns of Vermont and Switzerland every year. The same way, budgets, as we have seen in the case of Porto Alegre, *can* be decided by communities.

The cases analyzed here also allude to some very concrete measures able to hold professional politicians and representatives accountable. Professional politicians, as long as we have them, *can* be held responsible by limiting their term to one year and one round per lifetime, as the Romans did, thus avoiding all the current efforts toward seeking reelection. Politicians can also be held accountable by forcing them to be accountable to the public after they finish their term, as the Romans did and the Wintukua still do today. Of course, we cannot expect professional politicians to enact such restrictions on their own. Citizens must assert popular pressure and insist on sovereignty and democracy to impose rules and regulations onto politicians and elected officials, most likely against their will.

On the economic front, if we want to protect equal opportunity and democracy, we have to find ways to bar the creation of empires—individual, family, and corporate—and we have to devise laws that reintroduce accumulated assets back into generally accessible markets. While I was not able to include inheritance tax in the systematic analysis, the evidence presented clearly points to this policy as a central tool to achieve this. The only alternative to avoiding the accumulation of personal, family, and corporate riches beyond any reason is to bet on crisis, war, and disaster as "natural" equalizers and providers of new opportunities. This is our current path: in the absence of upper limits to asset holding and earnings, only a massive earthquake can make housing in Los Angeles affordable again to the median earner.

As long as we have strong, centralized states, progressive tax regimes, high taxes on capital gains, and high inheritance taxes are central tools to avoid the accumulation and reproduction of economic and political privilege and the formation of (money) aristocracies. Privilege and elite rule always were, and continue to be, the main enemies of democracy. Maybe ironically, as my special case has shown, some "anti-market" measures, such as price fixing, are able to protect competition and equal opportunities.

Ensuring good quality education and health care to all citizens has already been achieved in some (mostly northern European) countries. If education, good health, and a fair chance to succeed in markets are ensured, people will have less need for equipping their children with unfair advantages. The need to do so is, after all, also born out of scarcity and uncertainty. Once uncertainty in these fields is reduced, there will be less need to engage in this hedging behavior. If I know that my children will have access to good quality education and health care and will be given access to startup funds to enter markets on equal and fair terms, then I don't have to worry about their future well-being and I don't need to equip them with the kind of startup funds and education that set them apart from everybody else.

Providing startup funds for all upon graduation or targeted specifically to those who suffer today from historical exclusion is the only way to ensure agency. If we believe in (regulated) markets and freedom, fairness, equal opportunity, and entrepreneurship, then Amartya Sen's approach to capabilities must resonate with us and lead us to embrace equipping the youth with the means to succeed.

The Bolivian constitution of 2009 limits landownership to 5,000 hectares. Many tribal and indigenous societies have effectively institutionalized similar upper limits of income and asset holding. While utopian, the policy propositions advanced here are not radical in the true sense. They are reasonable and necessary if a sustainable and harmonious future is our goal. To rely on unfettered capitalism as the only organizing principle of all our markets is not only radical, it is also unreasonable and irresponsible toward those who have no true chance of ever winning in this game of ants against giants. It is also irresponsible toward our next generations and the future of our planet. To leave lawmaking in the hands of a few elected elites is equally irresponsible and the hope that they will do what is in our best interest is naïve.

THE COURAGE TO DO WHAT IT TAKES

My policy suggestions are far removed from the liberal "invisible hand." Instead of an invisible hand, we need a smart hand that deals cards in such a way that the odds stay the same for all players in every new round. In other words, we need smart institutions able to protect equal opportunity, fairness, and freedom. Smart institutions are those that achieve several goals at once, while not producing unintended outcomes and spillovers. The smartest institutions and the ones this book is most concerned with are those that protect community, fair markets, *and* individual agency at the same time. Such institutions exist. We do not have to choose between (liberal) individualism and community. Instead, properly institutionalized communalism *is* the way to protect individual agency. The twenty-two cases discussed earlier contain many very promising institutional designs we should consider today. Most strongly, imposing upper limits on earnings and landholding can keep an incentive structure in place that provides enough motivation for individuals to strive and seek to excel, while at the same time also affording others to do the same.

Taken together, the strategies outlined here promise to reinvigorate politics *and* markets and return both to their original promise: average people having a real say in the laws and rules that govern them and average people having a fair and equal chance in the different markets in which they engage. None of the proposals advanced here produces the kinds of undesirable hazards and disincentives the currently applied policies carry. They are also not radical in any way, at least if democracy, self-rule, and equal opportunity are accepted as mainstream and broadly shared values. In the political realm, the move toward direct democracy would not have to be immediate or exclusive. An invigoration of local authority—not at the state but at the municipal level—could be an easy start, already under way in many countries. More challenging would be to curb the system of political representation of the legislative branches. Here empirical research should guide our steps, but designs focusing on "legal duty," similar to "jury duty," do not seem too far from the already known and proven.

Considering the current crisis scenario of politics and economics as well as the ecological problems looming ahead, there really is no alternative to moving toward the policies suggested here. The only alternative is a slow move toward disaster. With this in mind, revolution is neither a necessary nor a desirable strategy to enact these policies. Instead a critical public must form and press for the gradual expansion of participatory local politics that then, also gradually, can replace or cut back the representative system we currently have. This is the most difficult step, but once participation is expanded, the superfluity of elected lawmakers should become more and more obvious.

First signs of this process are already visible in those municipalities that have created participatory budgeting forums, all of which stand in tension with their legislative chambers and effectively already avoid them in those places where participation works the best. Self-reliant neighborhood movements are spreading in the United States. Solidarity economics are also expanding everywhere, and so are local self-help groups, farmers markets, and other similar attempts to escape the devastating mandate of financialized and hypercompetitive markets.

Given the current hegemony of political representation as the only way to exercise government and capitalism as the only way to organize markets, the proposals advanced here may still appear radical to some. If aiming for justice, fairness, and equal opportunity is deemed radical, then so be it. To me, it rather seems that accepting and reproducing a system that has no serious vision or utopia for a sustainable future, a system that is producing more and more poverty and exclusion on one side and more and more concentration of wealth and political power on the other, a system that is finally unable to answer the basic question of "where will this lead us" is much more radical. We should all be alarmed by the fact that our current system can only survive with massive media efforts to brainwash ordinary people, while at the same time distracting them with mindless consumption and keeping them artificially going with the help of psychotherapeutic drugs.

Citizens act irresponsibly because they have no democratic responsibilities toward the collective (Neblo 2017). We as citizens need to take matters into our own hands if we want to live in a democracy. We need to reach collective decisions, find compromise, and experience the consequences of our actions. Hoping for an invisible hand or for some wise ruler to make those decisions for us will not do. Most of us seem to know this instinctively. This knowledge, however, mostly finds expression only in negativity. We abstain. We say "no," we march, we protest, and we express our discontent to the state and the government. In doing so, we continue to refer to the state and the government, further invigorating their power and omnipresence.

An American Congress that can only count on the support of less than 20 percent of its people has no legitimacy whatsoever. It is time to substitute the legislator with participatory budgeting schemes and to take political power away from legislators in general and shift it toward local communities. It is time to become proactive and take on active citizen roles. This book points at the possibilities we have. There is plenty we can do. The time has come to step out of the matrix and work toward real democracy and real markets.

NOTES

1. ~ stands for absence.
2. * stands for the logical "and."
3. + stands for the logical "or."

Appendix

In the sufficiency analysis looking at the **absence of EM**, we find that the absence of ul *and* absence of com are sufficient for the absence of the outcome EM. Consistency is 0.83 and coverage is 0.71. Again the complex and intermediate solutions are the same.

TRUTH TABLE

Edit Truth Table						— ▢ ✕	

File Edit Sort

com	ul	red	number	~em	raw consist. ▽	PRI consist.	SYM consis
0	0	1	2	1	1.000000	1.000000	1.000000
0	0	0	3	1	1.000000	1.000000	1.000000
0	1	0	1	0	0.500000	0.333333	0.333333
1	1	1	1	0	0.500000	0.333333	0.333333
1	1	0	7	0	0.193548	0.038462	0.043478

TRUTH TABLE ANALYSIS

Model: ~EM = f(com, ul, red)
Rows: 5
Algorithm: Quine-McCluskey
True: 1

COMPLEX SOLUTION

frequency cut-off: 1.000000
consistency cut-off: 1.000000

	raw coverage	unique coverage	consistency
~com*~ul	0.714286	0.714286	0.833333

solution coverage: 0.714286
solution consistency: 0.833333

TRUTH TABLE ANALYSIS

Model: ~EM = f(com, ul, red)
Rows: 5
Algorithm: Quine-McCluskey
True: 1-L

PARSIMONIOUS SOLUTION

frequency cut-off: 1.000000
consistency cut-off: 1.000000

	raw coverage	unique coverage	consistency
~ul	0.714286	0.714286	0.789474

solution coverage: 0.714286
solution consistency: 0.789474

TRUTH TABLE ANALYSIS

Model: ~EM = f(red, ul, com)
Rows: 2
Algorithm: Quine-McCluskey
True: 1
0 Matrix: 0L

INTERMEDIATE SOLUTION

frequency cut-off: 1.000000
consistency cut-off: 1.000000
Assumptions:

red (present)
~ul (absent)
~com (absent)

	raw coverage	unique coverage	consistency
~ul*~com	0.714286	0.714286	0.833333

solution coverage: 0.714286
solution consistency: 0.833333

Bibliography

Abers, Rebecca. 2000. *Inventing Local Democracy*. Boulder, CO: Lynne Rienner.

Ackerman, Bruce, and Anne Alstott. 1999. *The Stake-Holder Society*. New Haven, CT: Yale University Press.

Adcock, Frank E. 1969. *Roman Political Ideas and Practice*. Ann Arbor: University of Michigan Press.

Aimer, P., and R. Miller. 2002. "Partisanship and Principle: Voters and the New Zealand Electoral Referendum of 1993." *European Journal of Political Research* 41, no. 6: 795–810.

Alba, Víctor. 2001. *Los Colectivizadores*. Barcelona: Laertes.

Albo, Greg, Sam Gindin, and Leo Panitch. 2010. *In and Out of Crisis*. Oakland, CA: PM Press.

Alcoff, Linda. 1991. "The Problem of Speaking for Others." *Cultural Critique*, Winter: 5–32.

Alexander, Michelle. 2012. *The New Jim Crow*. New York: The New Press.

Alonso, Sonia, John Keane, and Wolfgang Merkel, eds. 2011. *The Future of Representative Democracy*. Cambridge: Cambridge University Press.

Amin, Ash, ed. 2009. *The Social Economy*. London: Zed Books.

Anderson, Benedict. 2006. *Imagined Communities*. New York: Verso.

Arnold, Volker. 1985. *Rätebewegung und Rätetheorien in der Novemberrevolution*. Hamburg: JUNIUS Verlag.

Apter, David E. "Notes for a Theory of Nondemocratic Representation." In J. R. Pennock and J.W. Chapman (eds.), *Representation (Nomos X)*, 278–317. New York: Atherton Press, 1968.

———. 1987. *Rethinking Development: Modemization, Dependency, and Post-Modern Politics*. Beverly Hills, CA: Sage.

Arendt, Hannah. 1965. *On Revolution*. New York: Penguin.

———. 1973. *The Origins of Totalitarianism*. New York: Harcourt, Brace, Jovanovich.

Aristotle. 1892. *The Constitution of Athens*. Translated by E. Poste. London: MacMillan and Co.

————. 1992. *Politics*. New York: Cambridge University Press.

————. 2001. *The Constitution of Athens*. Translated by Sir Frederic G. Kenyon. Boston: Adamant

————. 2009. *The Nicomachean Ethics*. Chicago: University of Chicago Press.

Arrázola, Roberto. 1970. *Palenque, primer pueblo libre de América. Historia de las sublevaciones de los esclavos de Cartagena*. Cartagena: Ediciones Hernández.

Arx, Nicolas von. 2002. *Aehnlich aber anders. Die Volksabstimmung in Kalifornien und in der Schweiz*. Basel: Helbing und Lichtenhahn.

Asante-Muhammed, Dedrick, Chuck Collins, Josh Hoxie, and Emanuel Nieves. 2016. "The Ever Growing Gap." Report, Institute for Policy Studies, Washington, DC. http://cfed.org/policy/federal/The_Ever_Growing_Gap-CFED_IPS-Final.pdf, last downloaded on 8/10/2016.

Atkinson, Anthony. 2015. *Inequality: What Can Be Done?* Cambridge: Harvard University Press.

Auer, Andreas, and Michael Buetzer, eds. 2001. *Direct Democracy: The Eastern and Central European Experience*. Aldershot: Ashgate.

Avritzer, Leonardo. 2009. *Participatory Institutions in Democratic Brazil*. Baltimore: Johns Hopkins University Press.

Axelrod, Robert. 2006. *The Evolution of Cooperation*. New York: Basic Books.

Bahro, Rudolf. 1978. *The Alternative in Eastern Europe*. New York: Verso.

Baiocchi, Gianpaolo. 2005. *Militants and Citizens: The Politics of Participatory Democracy in Porto Alegre*. Stanford: Stanford University Press.

Bakunin, Michail. 1977. *Sozial-politischer Briefwechsel*. Berlin: Karin Kramer Verlag.

————. 2011 [1873]. *Staatlichkeit und Anarchie*. Berlin: Karin Kramer Verlag.

Baratz, Dagania. 1945. *The Story of Palestine's First Collective Settlement*. Tel Aviv: Zionist Organization.

Barber, Benjamin, 1984. *Strong Democracy*. Los Angeles: University of California Press.

Baronnet, Bruno, Mariana Mora Bayo, and Richard Stahler-Sholk. 2011. *Luchas Muy Otras*. Mexico: UAM Press. http://zapatismoyautonomia.wordpress.com.

Bayle, Constantino. 1952. *Los Cabildos Seculares en la América Española*. Madrid: Sapientia.

Beitz, Charles. 1989. *Political Equality*. Princeton, NJ: Princeton University Press.

Bendix, Reinhard. 1969. *Nation-Building and Citizenship*. New York: Anchor Books.

Benhabib, Seyla, ed. 1996. *Democracy and Difference*. Princeton, NJ: Princeton University Press.

Berger, Peter, and Thomas Luckmann. 1966. *The Social Construction of Reality*. New York: Penguin Books.

Berlin, Isaiah. 1998. *The Proper Study of Mankind*. New York: Farrar, Straus and Giroux.

Beyer, Hans, and Ernst Engelberg. 1998 [1957]. *Von der Novemberrevolution zur Räterepublik in München*. Berlin: Herzog.

Blasi, Joseph Raphael. 1978. *The Communal Future: The Kibbutz and the Utopian Dilemma*. Norwood, PA: Norwood Editions.

Bloch, Ernst. 1986. *The Principle of Hope*. New York: Blackwell.

Bohman, John. 1998. "Survey Article: The Coming of Age of Deliberative Democracy." *Journal of Political Philosophy* 6, no. 4: 400–25.

Boix, Carles. 2015. *Political Order and Inequality*. New York: Cambridge.

Bookchin, Murray. 1994. *To Remember Spain*. San Francisco: AK Press.

———. 1996. *The Third Revolution*. Vol. 1. London: Cassell.

———. 1998. *The Third Revolution*. Vol. 2. London: Cassell.

———. 2004. *The Third Revolution*. Vol. 3. London: Continuum.

———. 2015. *The Next Revolution*. New York: Verso.

Boseley, Sarah, Mona Chalabi, and Mark Rice-Oxley. 2013. "Antidepressant Use on the Rise in Rich Countries, OECD Finds." *The Guardian*, November 20. http://www.theguardian.com/society/2013/nov/20/antidepressant-use-rise-world-oecd.

Bouchard, Merle, ed. 2013. *Innovation and the Social Economy: The Quebec Experience*. Toronto: University of Toronto Press.

Bourdieu, Pierre. 1984. *Distinction*. Cambridge, MA: Harvard University Press.

Bowler, Shaun, and Todd Donovan. 1998. *Demanding Choices: Opinion, Voting, and Direct Democracy*. Ann Arbor: University of Michigan Press.

———. 2002. "Democracy, Institutions, and Attitudes about Citizens Influence on Government." *British Journal of Political Science* 32: 371–90.

Bowles, Samuel, and Herbert Gintis. 1998. *Recasting Egalitarianism*. The Real Utopia Project, edited by Eric Olin Wright. New York: Verso.

Brady, Henry, and David Collier. 2010. *Rethinking Social Inquiry*. New York: Rowman & Littlefield.

Brown, Mark. 2006. "Survey Article: Citizen Panels and the Concept of Representation." *Journal of Political Philosophy* 14: 203–25.

Brunt, P. A. 1971. *Social Conflicts in the Roman Republic*. New York: W. W. Norton.

Bryan, Frank. 2004. *Real Democracy. The New England Town Meeting and How It Works*. Chicago: University of Chicago Press.

Budge, Ian. 1996. *The New Challenge of Direct Democracy*. Cambridge: Polity Press.

Burke, Edmund. 1790 [1968]. *Reflections on the Revolution in France*. London: Penguin Books.

Buvinic, Mayra, Jaqueline Mazza, and Ruthanne Deutsch. 2004. *Social Inclusion and Economic Development in Latin America*. Washington/Baltimore: IDB/Johns Hopkins University Press.

Carpenter, D. A. 1996. *The Reign of Henry III*. London: The Hambledon Press.

Casanova, Julián. 2006. *Anarquismo y Revolución en la Sociedad Rural Aragonesa, 1936–1938*. Barcelona: Crítica.

Castoriadis, Cornelius. 1985. "First Institution of Society and Second-Order Institutions." In *Figures of the Unthinkable*. Open Manuscript.

———. 1990. "What Democracy?" In *Figures of the Unthinkable*. Open Manuscript.

———. 1991. "Aeschylean Anthropogony and Sophoclean Self-Creation of Man." In *Figures of the Unthinkable*. Open Manuscript.

———. 2001. "The Retreat from Autonomy: Post-Modernism as Generalised Conformism." *Democracy and Nature* 7, no. 1: 17–26.

Christiano, Thomas. 1996. *The Rule of the Many*. Boulder, CO: Westview Press.

Christin, Thomas, Simon Hug, and Pascal Sciarini. 2002. "Interests and Information in Referendum Voting: An Analysis of Swiss Voters." *European Journal of Political Research* 41, no. 6: 759–76.

Clark, Susan, and Frank Bryan. 2005. *All Those in Favor: Rediscovering the Secrets of Town Meeting and Community*. Minneapolis: Raven Mark.

Clarke, Harold, Allan Kornberg, and Marianne C. Stewart. 2004. "Referendum Voting as Political Choice: The Case of Quebec." *British Journal of Political Science* 34: 345–55.

Clayton, Joseph. 1908. *Robert Owen: Pioneer of Social Reforms.* London: A. C. Fifield.

Clastres, Pierre. 1989. *Society against the State.* New York: Zone Books.

Cohen, Jean, and Andrew Arato. 1994. *Civil Society and Political Theory.* Cambridge: MIT Press.

Cohen, Joshua, and Joel Rogers. 1995. *Associations and Democracy.* The Real Utopia Project, edited by Erik Olin Wright. London: Verso.

Cohen, Joshua, and Charles Sabel. 1997. "Directly-Deliberative Polyarchy." *European Law Journal* 3, no. 4: 313–42.

Collins, Chuck, and Josh Hoxie. 2015. *Billionaire Bonanza: The Forbes 400 and the Rest of Us.* Boston: Institute for Policy Studies.

Constant, Benjamin. 2003. *Principles of Government Applicable to All Governments.* Indianapolis: Liberty Fund.

Credit Suisse. 2015. *Global Wealth Report.* https://publications.credit-suisse.com /tasks/render/file/?fileID=F2425415-DCA7-80B8-EAD989AF9341D47E.

Cronin, Thomas. 1989. *Direct Democracy: The Politics of Initiative, Referendum, and Recall.* Cambridge: Cambridge University Press.

Dahl, Robert A. 1989. *Democracy and Its Critics.* New Haven, CT: Yale University.

Daly, Herman, and John Cobb. 1989. *For the Common Good.* Boston: Beacon Press.

Denver, D. 2002. "Voting in the 1997 Scottish and Welsh Devolution Referendums: Information, Interests, and Opinions." *European Journal of Political Research* 41, no. 6: 827–44.

Dinerstein, Ana Cecelia. 2014. *The Politics of Autonomy in Latin America: The Art of Organizing Hope.* Basingstoke, UK: Palgrave MacMillan.

Doherty, Brian. 2008. *Radicals for Capitalism.* New York: Public Affairs.

Dore, Ronald. 2000. *Stock Market Capitalism: Welfare Capitalism.* Oxford: Oxford University Press.

Dovi, Suzanne. 2007. *The Good Representative.* New York: Wiley Blackwell.

Dowbor, Ladislau. 2012. *Economic Democracy.* Creative Commons: Ladislau Dowbor. http://dowbor.org.

Downs, Anthony. 1957. *An Economic Theory of Democracy.* New York: Harper.

Dryzek, John. 1996. "Political Inclusion and the Dynamics of Democratization." *American Political Science Review* 90 (September): 475–87.

Dryzek, John, and Simon Niemeyer. 2008. "Discursive Representation." *American Political Science Review* 102, no. 4: 481–93.

Duffy, Bella. 2011 [1892]. *The Tuscan Republics.* New York: G. P. Putnam's Sons.

Dunbar, R. I. 1992. "Neocortex Size as a Constraint on Group Size in Primates." *Journal of Human Evolution* 22, no. 6: 469–93.

Echavarría Usher, Cristina. 1993. *Cuentos y cantos de las aves tairona, mitología ornitológica wiwa.* Medellín: Corporación Murundúa y Colciencias.

Economist. 2004. "Something to Be Proud Of," February 12.

Edgerton, William, ed. 1993. *Memories of Peasant Tolstoyans in Soviet Russia.* Bloomington: Indiana University Press.

Edwards, Steward. 1971. *The Paris Commune, 1871*. New York: Quadrangle Books.

Ellis, John, and G. R. Stanton. 1968. "Factional Conflict and Solon's Reforms." *Phoenix* 22, no. 2 (1968): 95–110.

Ellis, Richard. 2002. *Democratic Delusions: The Initiative Process in America*. Lawrence: University of Kansas Press.

Elster, John. 1998. *Deliberative Democracy*. New York: Cambridge University Press.

Enzensberger, Hans Magnus. 1977. *Der kurze Sommer der Anarchie*. Frankfurt: Suhrkamp.

Escobar, Arturo. 2011. *Encountering Development*. Princeton, NJ: Princeton University Press.

Fagotto, Elena, and Archon Fung. 2006. "Empowered Participation in Urban Governance: The Minneapolis Neighborhood Revitalization Program." *International Journal of Urban and Regional Research* 30, no. 3: 638–55.

Felber, Christian. 2010. *Die Gemeinwohl-Ökonomie*. Wien: Deuticke.

Feld, Lars, and Gebhard Kirchgaessner. 2001a. "Does Direct Democracy Reduce Public Debt? Evidence from Swiss Municipalities." *Public Choice* 109: 347–70.

———. 2001b. "The Political Economy of Direct Legislation: Direct Democracy and Local Decision-Making." *Economic Policy*, October: 331–67.

Feld, Lars, and Marcel Savioz. 1997. "Direct Democracy Matters for Economic Performance: An Empirical Investigation." *Kyklos* 50: 507–67.

Fiorina, Morris. 1999. "Extreme Voices: The Dark Side of Civic Engagement." In *Civic Engagement in American Democracy*, edited by Theda Skocpol and Morris Fiorina, 395–425. Washington, DC: Brookings Institution Press.

Fishkin, John. 1995. *The Voice of the People: Public Opinion and Democracy*. New Haven, CT: Yale University Press.

Forbes, Jack. 2008. *Columbus and Other Cannibals*. New York: Seven Stories Press.

Fox, Michael. 2008. *NACLA Report*. May 19. http://nacla.org/news/porto-alegre %E2%80%99s-participatory-budgeting-crossroads.

Frank, Robert. 1999. *Luxury Fever*. Princeton, NJ: Princeton University Press.

———. 2011. *The Darwin Economy*. Princeton, NJ: Princeton University Press.

Fraser, Nancy. 1989. *Unruly Practices: Power, Discourse, and Gender in Contemporary Social Theory*. Minneapolis: University of Minnesota Press.

———. 1997. *Justice Interruptus*. New York: Routledge.

———. 1998. "Heterosexism, Misrecognition and Capitalism: A Response to Judith Butler." *New Left Review* 228 (March/April): 140–49.

Freire, A., and M. A. Baum. 2003. "Referenda Voting in Portugal, 1998: The Effects of Party Sympathies, Social Structure, and Pressure Groups." *European Journal of Political Research* 42, no. 1: 135–61.

Freitag, Markus, and Adrian Vatter. 2000. "Direkte Demokratie, Konkordanz und Wirtschaftsleistung: Ein Vergleich der Schweizer Kantone." *Schweiz. Zeitschrift fuer Volkswirtschaft und Statistik* 136, no. 4: 579–606.

Frey, Bruno, and Alois Stutzer. 2002. *Happiness and Economics: How the Economy and Institutions Affect Human Well-Being*. Princeton, NJ: Princeton University Press.

Friedemann, Nina S., and Richard Cross. 1979. *Ma Ngombe. Guerreros y ganaderos en Palenque*. Bogota: Carlos Valencia Editores. http://www.lablaa.org/blaavirtual /antropologia/magnom/indice.htm.

Fung, Archon. 2006. *Empowered Participation: Reinventing Urban Democracy.* Princeton, NJ: Princeton University Press.

Furtado, Celso. 2002. *Em busca de novo modelo. Reflexões sobe a crise contemporânea.* Rio de Janeiro: Paz e Terra.

Gallagher, Michael, and Pier Vincenzo Uleri, eds. 1996. *The Referendum Experience in Europe.* London: MacMillan.

Garnett, R. G. 1972. *Co-Operation and the Owenite Socialist Communities in Britain, 1825–45.* Manchester: Manchester University Press.

George, Alexander, and Andrew Bennett. 2005. *Case Studies and Theory Development in the Social Sciences.* Cambridge: MIT Press.

George, Henry. 2006 [1880]. *Progress and Poverty.* Edited and abridged by Bob Drake. New York: Robert Schalkenbach Foundation.

Gerring, John. 2012. *Social Science Methodology.* New York: Cambridge University Press.

Gibson-Graham, J. K. 1996. *The End of Capitalism as We Knew It.* Minneapolis: University of Minnesota Press.

———. 2006. A *Postcapitalist Politics.* Minneapolis: University of Minnesota Press.

Gómez, Luis. 2003. *El Alto de pie.* Bolivia: Textos Rebeldes.

Gould, Roger. 1995. *Insurgent Identities: Class, Community and Protest in Paris from 1848 to the Commune.* Chicago: University of Chicago Press.

Gruner, Erich, and Hanspeter Hertig. 1983. *Der Stimmbuerger and die "neue" Politik.* Bern: Haupt.

Guinier, Lani, 1994. *The Tyranny of the Majority: Fundamental Fairness in Representative Democracy.* New York: Free Press.

Gutmann, Amy, and Dennis Thompson. 2004. *Why Deliberative Democracy?* Princeton, NJ: Princeton University Press.

Habermann, Frederike. 2009. *Halbsinseln gegen den Strom.* Frankfurt: Helmer Verlag.

Habermas, Jürgen. 1995. *The Theory of Communicative Action.* New York: Beacon Press.

———. 1998. *Between Facts and Norms.* Cambridge: MIT Press.

Hacker, Jacob. 2011. "The Institutional Foundation of Middle-Class Democracy." *Progressive Governance* (Oslo): 33–37. http://www.policy-network.net/pno_detail.asp x?ID=3998&title=The+institutional+foundations+of+middle-class+democracy.

Hansen, Mogens Herman. 1999. *The Athenian Democracy in the Age of Demosthenes.* Nebraska: University of Oklahoma Press.

Hardin, Russell. 2004. "Representing Ignorance." *Social Philosophy and Policy* 21: 76–99.

Hardt, Michael, and Antonio Negri. 2001. *Empire.* Cambridge, MA: Harvard University Press.

Harrington, James. 2006 [1656]. *The Commonwealth of Oceana.* http://www .gutenberg.org/ebooks/2801.

Harrison, John. 2009. *Robert Owen and the Owenites in Britain and America.* New York: Routledge.

Harvey, David. 2011. *The Enigma of Capital.* New York: Oxford University Press.

———. 2014. *Seventeen Contradictions and the End of Capitalism*. New York: Oxford University Press.

Harvey, Neil. 1998. *The Chiapas Rebellion*. Durham, NC: Duke University Press.

Hattersley, Roy. 1987. *Chose Freedom*. London: Michael Joseph.

Henderson, Hazel. 2011. "Real Economies and the Illusions of Abstraction." *CADMUS* 1, no. 3 (October): 60–65.

Held, David. 1987. *Models of Democracy*. Cambridge: Polity Press.

Hero, Rodney, and Caroline Tolbert. 2004. "Minority Voices and Citizen Attitudes about Government Responsiveness in the American States: Do Social and Institutional Context Matter?" *British Journal for Political Science* 34: 109–21.

Higley, John, and Ian McAllister. 2002. "Elite Division and Voter Confusion: Australia's Republic Referendum in 1999." *European Journal for Political Research* 41, no. 6: 845–63.

Hiller, Helmut, and Stephan Füssel. 2006. *Wörterbuch des Buches*. Frankfurt/Main: V. Klostermann.

Hirsch, Fred. 1976. *Social Limits to Growth*. Cambridge, MA: Harvard University Press.

Holzschuh, Franziska. 2016. *Herbsrucker Zeitung*, August 10.

Hostetler, John. 1993. *Amish Society*. Baltimore: Johns Hopkins University Press.

Hostetler, John, and Gertrude Enders Huntington. 1996. *The Hutterites in North America*. Stanford: Stanford University Press.

Holloway, John. 2010. *Change the World without Taking Power*. London: Pluto Press.

Htun, Mala, and Juan Pablo Ossa. 2013. "Political Inclusion of Marginalized Groups: Gender Parity and Indigenous Reservations in Bolivia." *Politics, Groups, and Identities* 1, no. 1 (March): 4–25.

Hug, Simon. 2002. *Voices of Europe: Citizens, Referendums, and European Integration*. Lanham, MD: Rowman & Littlefield.

Hug, Simon, and Pascal Sciarini. 2000. "Referendums on European Integration: Do Institutions Matter in the Voter's Decision?" *Comparative Political Studies* 33: 3–36.

Huntington, Samuel. 1991. *The Third Wave*. Nebraska: University of Oklahoma Press.

Jones, Nicholas. 1999. *The Associations of Classical Athens*. New York: Oxford University Press.

Kaufman, Alexander, ed. 2006. *Capabilities Equality*. New York: Routledge.

Kinkade, Athleen. 1973. *A Walden Two Experiment*. New York: William Morrow & Company.

Kirchgaessner, Gebhard, Lars Feld, and Marcel Savioz. 1999. *Die direkte Demokratie: Modern, erfolgreich, entwicklungs und exportfaehig*. Basel: Helbing und Lichtenhahn.

Klein, Naomi. 2008. *The Shock Doctrine: The Rise of Disaster Capitalism*. New York: Picador.

———. 2014. *This Changes Everything: Capitalism vs. the Climate*. New York: Simon and Schuster.

Knoll, Andalusia, and Silvia Rivera Cusicanqui. 2007. "Anarchism and Indigenous Resistance in Bolivia: Interview with Silvia Rivera Cusiqanqui." *World War 4 Report*, October 1. http://ww4report.com/node/4501. Last accessed 2/22/2015.

Kobach, Kris. 1993. *The Referendum: Direct Democracy in Switzerland*. Aldershot: Dartmouth University Press.

Kraybill, Donald. 2001. *The Riddle of Amish Culture*. Baltimore: Johns Hopkins University Press.

Kretzmann, J., and J. McKnight. 1993. *Building Communities from the Inside Out*. Evanston: ABCD Institute, Northwestern University.

Kriesi, Hanspeter. 2008. *Direct Democratic Choice: The Swiss Experience*. Lanham, MD: Lexington Books.

Kropotkin, Peter Harry. 2014 [1902]. *Mutual Aid: A Factor of Evolution*. Seattle: CeateSpace.

Kuhn, Gabriel, ed. 2012. *All Power to the Councils*. Oakland: PM Press.

Laclau, Ernesto, and Chantal Mouffe. 1985. *Hegemony and Socialist Strategy*. New York: Verso.

Laloux, Frederic. 2014. *Reinventing Organizations*. Millis: Nelson Parker.

Lascher, Edward, Michael Hagen, and Steven Rochlin. 1996. "Gun behind the Door? Ballor Initiatives, State Policies and Public Opinion." *The Journal of Politics* 58, no. 3: 760–75.

Layard, Richard. 2005. *Happiness*. New York: Penguin.

Leach, E. R. 1964. *Political Systems of Highland Burma*. London: C. Bell and Sons.

Lee, Dorothy. 1987. *Freedom and Culture*. Long Grove: Waveland Press.

Le Glay, Marcel. 2009. *A History of Rome*. West Sussex: Blackwell.

Leveque, Pierre, and Pierre Vidal-Naquet. 1996. *Cleisthenes the Athenian*. New York: Humanity Books.

Levin, Henry, C. R. Belfield, P. Muening, and C. E. Rouse. 2007. *The Costs and Benefits of an Excellent Education for America's Children—Overview*. New York: Teachers College, Columbia University.

Levitas, Ruth. 2013. *Utopia as Method*. New York: Palgrave MacMillan.

Linder, Wolf. 1994. *Swiss Democracy: Possible Solutions to Conflict in Multicultural Societies*. New York: St. Martin's Press.

Little, Daniel. 1998. *Microfoundations, Method, and Causation*. New Brunswick: Transaction Publishers.

Living Standards in the UK: PSE UK First Summary Report. March 2013. http://www.poverty.ac.uk/system/files/attachments/The_Impoverishment_of_the_UK_PSE_UK_first_results_summary_report_March_28.pdf.

Locke, John. 1986 [1689]. *The Second Treatise on Civil Government*. Amherst, NY: Prometheus Books.

Lublin, David. 1999. *The Paradox of Representation: Racial Gerrymandering and Minority Interests in Congress*. Princeton, NJ: Princeton University Press.

Lucas, Erhard. 1970. *Märzrevolution 1920. Der bewaffnete Arbeiteraufstand im Ruhrgebiet*. Frankfurt: Verlag Roter Stern.

———. 1974. *Märzrevolution 1920. Band 1*. Frankfurt: Verlag Roter Stern.

Luxemburg, Rosa. 1918. "Nationalversammlung oder Raeteregierung." *Rote Fahne*, no. 32, December 17.

Madison, James, Alexander Hamilton, and John Jay. 1787–1788 [1987]. *The Federalist Papers*. Edited by Isaac Kramnick. Harmondsworth: Penguin.

Magleby, David. 1984. *Direct Legislation: Voting on Ballot Propositions in the United States*. Baltimore: Johns Hopkins University Press.

Mahoney, James, and Dietrich Rueschemeyer, eds. 2003. *Comparative Historical Analysis in the Social Sciences*. New York: Cambridge University Press.

Mamani, Pablo. 2006. "Territory and Structures of Collective Action: Neighborhood Micro-Governments." *Ephemera* 6, no. 3: 276–86.

Mamdani, Mahmood. 1996. *Citizen and Subject*. Princeton, NJ: Princeton University Press.

Manin, Bernard. 1987. "On Legitimacy and Political Deliberation." *Political Theory*, no. 15 (August): 338–68.

———. 1997. *The Principles of Representative Government*. Cambridge: Cambridge University Press.

Mansbridge, Jane. 1980. *Beyond Adversary Democracy*. Chicago: Chicago University Press.

———. 2003. "Rethinking Representation." *American Political Science Review* 97, no. 4: 515–28.

———. 2004. "Representation Revisited: Introduction to the Case against Electoral Accountability." *Democracy and Society* 2, no. 1: 12–13.

———. 2009. "A Selection Model of Representation." *Journal of Political Philosophy* 17, no. 4: 369–98.

Manville, Philip Brook. 1997. *The Origins of Citizenship in Ancient Athens*. Princeton, NJ: Princeton University Press.

Martin, James Joseph. 1970. *Men Against the State*. Colorado Springs: Ralph Myles Publishers.

Marx, Karl. 2000 [1865]. *Value, Price, and Profit*. Amsterdam and New York: JAI/Elsevier Science.

Matsusaka, John. 2004. *For the Many of the Few: The Initiative, Public Policy, and American Democracy*. Chicago: University of Chicago Press.

Mauss, Marcel. 2000. *The Gift*. New York: W. W. Norton.

Meade, James Edward. 1965. *Efficiency, Equality, and the Ownership of Property*. Cambridge, MA: Harvard University Press.

Melman, Seymour. 2001. *After Capitalism*. New York: Knopf.

Mendelsohn, Matthew, and Fred Cutler. 2000. "The Effects of Referendums on Democratic Citizens: Information, Politization, Efficacy, and Tolerance." *British Journal of Political Science* 30, no. 4: 685–97.

Merriman, John. 2014. *Massacre: The Life and Death of the Paris Commune*. New York: Basic Books.

Mezzadra, Sandro. 2007. "Living in Transition: Toward a Heterolingual Theory of the Multitude." *EIPCP Multilingual Webjournal*. http://eipcp.net/transversal/1107/mezzadra/en.

Milgram, Stanley. 2009 [1974]. *Obedience to Authority*. New York: Harper and Row.

Mill, John Stuart. 2004. *Considerations on Representative Government*. Whitefish: Kessinger Publishing.

Millar, Fergus. 1998. *The Crowd in Rome in the Late Republic*. Ann Arbor: University of Michigan Press.

Miller, Fred. 1997. *Nature, Justice, and Rights in Aristotle's Politics*. Oxford: Clarendon.

Mintz, Frank. 2006. *Autogestión y Anarcosindicalismo en la España revolucionaria*. Madrid: Traficantes de Suenos.

Moeckli, Silvano. 1994. *Direkte Demokratie: Ein internationaler Vergleich*. Bern: Haupt.

Möbes, Nancy. 2007. *Die Preisbindung für Bücher im deutschen Sprachraum unter den Bedingungen des Europäischen Gemeinschaftsrechts*. Diplomarbeit. Hochschule für Technik, Wirtschaft und Kultur Leipzig (FH). Fachbereich Medien. Studiengang Verlagsherstellung.

Moore, John Preston. 1954. *The Cabildo in Peru under the Habsburgs*. Durham, NC: Duke University Press.

Morgan, Lewis H. 1877. *Ancient Society*. London: MacMillan.

Muni, S. D. 2014. "Bhutan's Defential Democracy." *Journal of Democracy* 25, no. 2: 158–63.

Nadeau, Richard, Pierre Martin, and Andre Blais. 1999. "Attitude toward Risk-Taking and Individual Choice in the Quebec Referendum on Sovereignty." *British Journal of Political Science* 29: 523–39.

Nef, Jorge, and Bernd Reiter. 2009. *The Democratic Challenge. Democratization and De-Democratization in Global Perspective*. New York: Palgrave MacMillan.

Neidhart, Leonhard. 1970. *Plebiszit und pluralitaere Demokratie: Eine Analyse der Funktion des schweizerischen Gesetzesreferendums*. Bern: Francke.

Nelson, Eric. 2004. *The Greek Tradition in Republican Thought*. New York: Cambridge University Press.

Nylen, William, and Lawrence Dodd. 2003. *Participatory Democracy versus Elitist Democracy: Lessons from Brazil*. New York: Palgrave Macmillan.

Ober, Josiah. 1989. *Mass and Elite in Democratic Athens*. Princeton, NJ: Princeton University Press.

Offer, Avner. 2006. *The Challenge of Affluence*. Oxford: Oxford University Press.

O'Neill, Martin, and Thad Williamson, eds. 2014. *Property-Owning Democracy: Rawls and Beyond*. Malden: Wiley Blackwell.

Organización Indígena Gonawindua Tayrona. 2010. *Jaba y Jate: Espacios Sagrados del Territorio Ancestral de Santa Marta*. Santa Marta: Duvan Silvera.

Ostrom, Elenor. 2015. *Governing the Commons*. New York: Canto Classics.

Ostwald, Martin. 1986. *From Popular Sovereignty to the Sovereignty of Law: Law, Society, and Politics in Fifth-Century Athens*. Berkeley: University of California Press.

———. 1996. "Shares and Rights: 'Citizenship' Greek Style and American Style." In *Demokratia*, edited by Josiah Ober and Charles Hendrick, 49–61. Princeton, NJ: Princeton University Press.

Owen, Robert. 1816. *A New View of Society*. http://la.utexas.edu/users/hcleaver/368/368OwenNewViewtable.pdf.

Oxfam. 2015. "Wealth: Having It All and Wanting More." *Oxfam Issue Briefing*. www.oxfam.org.

Pagès, Pelai. 2013. *El sueno igualitario entre los campesinos de Huesca [1936–1938]*. Huesca: Sariñena.

Palgi Michal, and Shulamit Reinharz, eds. 2014. *100 Years of Kibbutz Life*. New Brunswick: Transaction Publishers.

Pannekoek, Anton. 2003. *Workers' Councils*. Edinburgh: AK Press.

Papadopoulos, Yannis. 2001. "How Does Direct Democracy Matter? The Impact of Referendum Votes in Parkinson, John. 2001. 'Who Knows Best? The Creation of the Citizen-Initiated Referendum in New Zealand.'" *Government and Opposition* 36, no. 3: 403–21.

Pateman, Carole, 1970. *Participation and Democratic Theory*. Cambridge: Cambridge University Press.

Patzi, Felix. 2011. *Tercer Sistema: Modelo comunal: Propuesta alternative para salir del capitalismo y del socialismo*. La Paz, Bolivia: All Press.

Pellegrini, Lorenzo, and Luca Tasciotti. 2014. "Bhutan: Between Happiness and Horror." *Capitalism Nature Socialism* 25, no. 3: 103–9.

Pennock, J. Roland, and John Chapman, eds. 1968. *Representation*. New York: Atherton Press.

Peredo, D. de. 1972. *Noticia historial de la Provincia de Cartagena en las Indias, ano de 1772. Anuario Colombiano de Historia Social de la Cultura*. Bogota: Universidad Nacional de Colombia.

Piketty, Thomas. 2014. *Capital in the Twenty-First Century*. Cambridge, MA: Harvard University Press. http://resistir.info/livros/piketty_capital_in_the_21_century_2014.pdf.

Pitkin, Hanna Fenichel. 1967. *The Concept of Representation*. Berkeley: University of California.

———. 2004. "Representation and Democracy: Uneasy Alliance." *Scandinavian Political Studies* 27, no. 3: 335–42.

Plato. 348 BCE. *Laws*. Translated by Benjamin Jowett. http://www.gutenberg.org/ebooks/1750.

Plotke, David. 1997. "Representation Is Democracy." *Constellations* 4: 19–34.

———. 1998. *Democratie directe*. Paris: Economica.

Pocock, J. G. A. 1981. "Virtues, Rights, and Manners: A Model for Historians of Political Thought." *Political Theory* 9, no. 3: 353–68.

———. 2007. "The Ideal of Citizenship since Classical Times." In *Theorizing Citizenship*, edited by Ronald Beiner, 29–52. Albany: SUNY Press.

Polanyi, Karl. 1977. *Livelihood of Man*. New York: Academic Press.

Przworksi, Adam, Susan C. Stokes, and Bernard Manin, eds. 1999. *Democracy, Accountability, and Representation*. Cambridge: Cambridge University Press.

Przeworski, Adam, and Henry Teune. 1982. *The Logic of Comparative Social Inquiry*. New York: Krieger.

Psacharopoulos, George. 2007. *The Costs of School Failure: A Feasibility Study*. Brussels, Belgium: European Network on Economics of Education (EENEE).

Ragin, Charles. 1987. *The Comparative Method*. Berkeley: University of California Press.

———. 2000. *Fuzzy Set Social Science*. Chicago: University of Chicago Press.

———. 2008a. *Redesigning Social Inquiry: Fuzzy Sets and Beyond*. Chicago: University of Chicago Press.

——. 2008b. *User's Guide to Fuzzy-Set/Qualitative Comparative Analysis*. www .fsqca.com.

——. 2014. *The Comparative Method*, second edition. Berkeley: University of California Press.

Rawls, John. 1999. *A Theory of Justice*. Cambridge, MA: Harvard University Press.

——. 2001. *Justice as Fairness: A Restatement*. Cambridge: Harvard University Press.

Rehfeld, Andrew. 2005. *The Concept of Constituency: Political Representation, Democratic Legitimacy and Institutional Design*. Cambridge: Cambridge University Press.

——. 2006. "Towards a General Theory of Political Representation." *The Journal of Politics* 68: 1–21.

Reiter, Bernd. 2007. "Defendendo Privilégio: Os Limites da Participação Popular em Salvador, Bahia." *Antropolitica* 1, no. 22: 199–218

——. 2008. "The Limits of Popular Participation in Salvador, Brazil." *Journal of Developing Societies* 24, no. 3: 337–54.

——. 2013. *The Dialectics of Citizenship: Exploring Privilege, Exclusion, and Racialization*. East Lansing: Michigan State University Press.

——. 2015. "Palenque de San Basílio: Citizenship and Republican Traditions of a Maroon Village in Colombia." *Journal of Civil Society* 11, no. 4: 333–47.

——. 2017. "Alternatives to Representative Democracy and Capitalist Market Organization: The Wintukua, Guardians of the Earth." *Anarchist Studies* 25, no. 1: 68–93.

Ricardo, David. 1817: *On the Principles of Political Economy and Taxation*. https:// www.marxists.org/reference/subject/economics/ricardo/tax/ch01.htm.

Richardson, Henry, 2002. "Representative Government." In *Democratic Autonomy*, 193–202. Oxford: Oxford University Press.

Rihil, T. E. 1995. "Democracy Denied: Why Ephialtes Attacked the Areopagus." *Journal of Hellenic Studies* 115: 87–98.

Rocha Vivas, Miguel. 2010. *Antes el Amanecer: Antología de las Literaturas Indígenas de los Andes y la Sierra Nevada de Santa Marta*. Bogota: Ministerio de Cultura.

Romero Infante, Jaime Alberto, and Joaquin Alberto Guzman Barrios. 2007. "Administracion ambiental del pueblo Wintukua, un ejemplo de colaboracion Universidad El Bosque—Resguardo Indigena." *Cuadernos Latinoamericanos de Administración* 2, no. 4: 50–64.

Rosenstone, Steven, and John Hansen. 1993. *Mobilization, Participation, and Democracy in America*. New York: MacMillan.

Rosner, Menahem. 2000. "Future Trends of the Kibbutz: An Assessment of Recent Changes." University of Haifa. The Institute for Study and Research of the Kibbutz. Publication No. 83. http://research.haifa.ac.il/~kibbutz/pdf/trends.PDF.

Rosner, Menahem, and Shlomo Getz. 1994. "Toward a Theory of Changes in the Kibbutz." *Journal of Rural Cooperation* 12: 41–62.

Rousseau, Jean-Jacques. 2003 [1762]. *The Social Contract*. Translated by Judith Masters and Roger Masters. New York: St. Martin's Press.

Roy, William. 1997. *Socializing Capital*. Princeton, NJ: Princeton University Press.

Runciman, David. 2007. "The Paradox of Political Representation." *Journal of Political Philosophy* 15: 93–114.

———. 2010. "Hobbes's Theory of Representation: Anti-Democratic or Protodemoratic." In *Political Representation*, edited by Ian Shapiro, Susan C. Stokes, Elisabeth Jean Wood, and Alexander Kirshner, 15–34. Cambridge: Cambridge University Press.

Russell, Raymond, Robert Hanneman, and Shlomo Getz. 2000. "Processes of Deinstitutionalization and Reinstitutionalization among Israeli Kibbutzim, 1990–1998." Paper presented at the Annual Meeting of the American Sociological Association, Washington, DC, August 12–16. http://research.haifa.ac.il/~kibbutz/pdf/rusty2000.PDF.

Ryden, David K. 1996. *Representation in Crisis: The Constitution, Interest Groups, and Political Parties*. Albany: SUNY Press.

Ryerson, Ricard Alan. 1978. *The Revolution Is Now Begun: The Radical Committees of Philadelphia, 1765–1776*. Philadelphia: University of Pennsylvania Press.

Sabato, Larry, Bruce Larson, and Howard Ernst, eds. 2001. *Dangerous Democracy? The Battle over Ballot Initiatives in America*. Lanham, MD: Rowman & Littlefield.

Sabl, Andrew. 2002. *Ruling Passions: Political Offices and Democratic Ethics*. Princeton, NJ: Princeton University Press.

Sánchez Gutiérrez, Enrique, and Hernán Molina Echeverri. 2010. *Documentos para la historia del movimiento indígena colombiano contemporáneo*. Bogotá: Ministerio de Cultura.

Sandel, Michael. 1998. *Democracy's Discontent*. Cambridge, MA: Harvard University Press.

Santos, Boaventura de Sousa. 2014. *Epistemologies of the South: Justice Against Epistemicide*. Boulder, CO: Paradigm Publishers.

Saward, Michael, ed. 2000. *Democratic Innovation: Deliberation, Representation and Association*. London: Routledge.

———. 2008. "Representation and Democracy: Revisions and Possibilities." *Sociology Compass* 2: 1000–13.

———. 2009. "Authorisation and Authenticity: Representation and the Unelected." *Journal of Political Philosophy* 17: 1–22.

Schattschneider, E. E. 1960. *The Semisovereign People*. New York: Holt, Rinehart, and Winston.

Scheer, Ursula. 2013. *Frankfurter Allgemeine Zeitung*. http://www.faz.net/aktuell/wirtschaft/wirtschaftspolitik/politiker-in-aufsichtsraeten-gefaehrliche-aemter-ueberhaeufung-12026508.html.

Schmitter, Philippe. 2000. "Representation." In *How to Democratize the European Union and Why Bother?*, 53–74. Lanham, MD: Rowman & Littlefield.

Schneider, Carsten, and Claudius Wagemann. 2012. *Set-Theoretic Approaches for the Social Sciences*. New York: Cambridge University Press.

Schneider, Dieter, and Rudolf Kuda. 1969. *Arbeiterraete in der Novemberrevolution: Ideen, Wirkungen, Dokumente*. Frankfurt: Suhrkamp.

Schumpeter, Joseph. 1976. *Capitalism, Socialism, and Democracy*. London: Allen and Unwin.

Schwartz, Nancy. 1988. *The Blue Guitar: Political Representation and Community.* Chicago: University of Chicago Press.

Sciarini, Pascal. 1994. *Le système politique suisse face à la Communauté européenne et au GATT: Le cas-test de la politique agricole.* Geneva: Georg.

Sciarini, Pascal, and Lionel Marquis. 2000. "Opinion publique et politique exterieure." *Revue suisse de science politique* 6, no. 3: 71–83.

Scott, James. 2009. *The Art of Not Being Governed.* New Haven, CT: Yale University Press.

Sealey, Raphael. 1964. "Ephialtes." *Classical Philology* 59, no. 1 (January): 11–22.

Sen, Amartya. 1999. *Development as Freedom.* New York: Oxford University Press.

———. 2009. *The Idea of Justice.* Cambridge, MA: Harvard University Press.

Service, Elman. 1975. *Origins of the State and Civilization.* New York: W. W. Norton.

Shapiro, Ian, Susan C. Stokes, Elisabeth Jean Wood, and Alexander S. Kirshner, eds. 2010. *Political Representation.* Cambridge: Cambridge University Press.

Shatz, Marshall, ed. 1971. *The Essential Works of Anarchism.* New York: Bantam Books.

Shotter, David. 1994. *The Fall of the Roman Republic.* London: Routledge.

Simon, Herbert. 1990. *Reason in Human Affairs.* Stanford: Stanford University Press.

Sinnott, Richard. 2002. "Cleavages, Parties, and Referendums: Relationship between Representative and Direct Democracy in the Republic of Ireland." *European Journal of Political Research* 41, no. 6: 811–26.

Sitrin, Marina, and Dario Azzelini. 2014. *They Can't Represent Us.* New York: Verso.

Smith, Adam. 1976 [1776]. *The Wealth of Nations.* New York: Bantam Classics.

Smith, Mark. 2001. "The Contingent Effects of Ballot Initiatives and Candidate Races on Turnout." *American Journal of Political Science* 45, no. 3: 700–6.

Smith, Mark, and Caroline Tobert. 2004. *Educated by Initiative: The Effects of Direct Democracy on Citizens and Political Organizations in the American States.* Ann Arbor: University of Michigan Press.

Snyder, Richard, and Gabriel Torres, eds. 1998. *The Future of the Ejido in Rural Mexico.* San Diego: University of California Press.

Spiro, Medford. 1063. *The Kibbutz: Venture in Utopia.* New York: Schocken Books.

Stahler-Sholk, Richard. 2014. "Mexico: Autonomy, Collective Identity, and the Zapatista Social Movement." In *Rethinking Latin American Social Movements,* edited by Richard Stahler-Sholk, Harry Vanden, and Marc Becker, 187–207. Lanham, MD: Rowman & Littlefield.

———. 2015. "Resistencia, Identidad, y Autonomia: La Transformacion de espacios en las comunidades Zapatistas." *Revista Pueblos y Fronteiras* 10, no. 19: 197–226.

Strolovitch, Dara Z. 2007. *Affirmative Advocacy: Race, Class, and Gender in Interest Group Politics.* Chicago: Chicago University Press.

Stutzer, Alois, and Bruno Frey. 2000. "Staerkere Volksrechte—Zufriendendere Buerger: eine mikrooekonomische Untersuchung fuer die Schweiz." *Schweiz. Zeitschrift fuer Politikwissenschaft* 6, no. 3: 1–30.

Svensson, Palle. 2002. "Five Danish Referendums on the European Community and European Union: A Critical Assessment of the Franklin Thesis." *European Journal of Political Research* 41, no. 6: 733–50.

Tapia, Francisco Javier. 1965. *Cabildo Abierto Colonial*. Madrid: Ediciones Cultura Hispánica.

TATORT. 2013. *Democratic Autonomy in North Kurdistan*. Hamburg: New Compass Press.

Termes, Josep. 2011. *Historia del Anarquismo en España (1870–1980)*. Barcelona: RBA.

Thucydides. 1954. *History of the Peloponnesian War*. New York: Penguin Classics.

Tilly, Charles. 2007. *Democracy*. New York: Cambridge University Press.

Tocqueville, Alexis de. 1988 [1835]. *Democracy in America*. New York: Harper.

Toennies, Ferdinand. 1988. *Community and Society*. New York: Transaction Publishers.

Tolbert, Caroline, Ramona McNeal, and Daniel Smith. 2003. "Enhancing Civic Engagement: The Effect of Direct Democracy on Political Participation and Knowledge." *State Politics and Policy Quarterly* 3, no. 1: 23–41.

Torre, Alejandro R. Díez. 2009. *Trabajan para la Eternidad: Colectividades de trabajo y ayuda mutual durante la Guerre Civil en Aragón*. Madrid y Zaragoza: Malatesta.

Trail, J. S. 1975. "The Political Organization of Attica." *Hesperia Supplements* 14: i–iii, v–xi, xiii–xviii, 1–135, 139–69.

Trechsel, Alexander. 2000. *Feuerwerk Volksrechte: Die Volksabstimmung in den schweizerischen Kantonen 1970–1996*. Basel: Helbing und Lichthahn.

Truman, David, 1951. *The Governmental Process*. New York: Knopf.

Turnbull, Colin. 1968. *The Forest People*. New York: Touchstone.

Ura, Karma, and Karma Galay, eds. 2012. *Gross National Happiness and Development*. Proceedings of the First International Seminar on Operationalization of Gross National Happiness. Thimphu, Bhutan: The Centre for Bhutan Studies. http://www.fringer.org/wp-content/writings/gnh1999.pdf.

Urbinati, Nadia. 2000. "Representation as Advocacy: A Study of Democratic Deliberation." *Political Theory* 28: 258–786.

Urbinati, Nadia, and Mark Warren. 2008. "The Concept of Representation in Contemporary Democratic Theory." *Annual Review of Political Science* 11: 387–412.

Urma, Karma, Sabina Alkire, Tshoki Zangmo, Karma Wangdi. 2012. *An Extensive Analysis of GNH Index*. Centre for Bhutan Studies. http://www.grossnationalhappiness.com/wp-content/uploads/2012/10/An%20Extensive%20Analysis%20of%20GNH%20Index.pdf.

Vanderbroeck, Paul. 1987. *Popular Leadership and Collective Behavior in the Late Roman Republic (ca. 80–50 b.c.)*. Amsterdam: J. C. Gieben.

Vatter, Adrian. 2002. *Kantonale Demokratien im Vergleich. Enstehungsgruende, Interaktionen und Wirkungen politischer Institutionen in den Schweizer Kantonen*. Opladen: Leske and Budrich.

Veblen, Thorstein. 2009. *The Theory of the Leisure Class*. New York: Oxford University Press.

Verba, Sidney, and Norman Nie. 1972. *Participation in America*. New York: Harper and Row.

Victor, Peter, and Gideon Rosenbluth. 2007. "Managing without Growth." *Ecological Economics* 61: 492–504.

Vieira, Monica, and David Runciman. 2008. *Representation*. Cambridge: Polity Press.

Waley, Daniel, and Trevor Dean. 2010. *The Italian City-Republics*. Harlow, UK: Pearson Education Ltd.

Wampler, Brian. 2007. *Participatory Budgeting in Brazil*. University Park: Pennsylvania State University Press.

Warren, Mark. 2001. *Democracy and Association*. Princeton, NJ: Princeton University Press.

———. 2008. "Citizen Representatives." In *Designing Deliberative Democracy: The British Columbia Citizens' Assembly*, edited by Mark Warren and Hilary Pearse, 50–69. Cambridge: Cambridge University Press.

Warren, Mark, and Dario Castiglione. 2004. "The Transformation of Democratic Representation." *Democracy and Society* 2, no. 1: 5, 20–22.

Weber, Max. 1968. *Economy and Society*. Berkeley: University of California Press.

Wells, H. G. 1906. *The Future in America: A Search After Realities*. London: Chapman & Hall.

Wilkinson, Richard, and Kate Picket. 2010. *The Spirit Level*. New York: Bloomsbury Press.

Williams, Melissa. 2000. "The Uneasy Alliance of Group Representation and Deliberative Democracy." In *Citizenship in Diverse Societies*, edited by W. Kymlicka and Wayne Norman, 124–53. Oxford: Oxford University Press.

Williamson, Abby, and Archon Fung. 2004. "Public Deliberation: Where We Are and Where Can We Go?" *National Civic Review*, Winter: 3–15.

Wilson, William. 1967. *The Angel and the Serpent: The Story of New Harmony*. Bloomington: Indiana University Press.

Wolff, Edward N. 2014. *Household Wealth Trends In The United States, 1962–2013: What Happened Over The Great Recession?* Cambridge, MA: National Bureau of Economic Research.

Wolff, Richard. 2012. *Democracy at Work*. Chicago: Haymarket Books.

World Bank. 2014. *Bhutan Development Update: April 2014*. http://documents. worldbank.org/curated/en/2014/04/19455214/bhutan-development-update.

Wright, Eric Olin. 2010. *Envisioning Real Utopias*. New York: Verso.

Young, Iris Marion. 1996. *Justice and the Politics of Difference*. Princeton, NJ: Princeton University Press.

———. 1999. "Justice, Inclusion, and Deliberative Democracy." In *Deliberative Politics*, edited by Stephen Macedo, 151–58. Oxford: Oxford University Press.

———. 2000. *Inclusion and Democracy*. New York: Oxford University Press

Yunus, Mohammed. 2003. *Banker to the Poor*. New York: Public Affairs.

Zablocki, Benjamin. 1980. *Alienation and Charisma: A Study of Contemporary American Communes*. New York: Free Press.

Zaller, John. 1992. *The Nature and Origins of Mass Opinion*. Cambridge: Cambridge University Press.

Zenker, E. V. 1984. *Der Anarchismus*. Berlin: Rixdorfer Verlagsanstalt.

Index